ADAM
Loves
EVE

ADAM *Loves* EVE

THE BIBLE'S GUIDE FOR MEN SEEKING A BETTER MARRIAGE

FIRST FRUITS OF ZION WITH
GRANT LUTON AND RUSS RESNIK

FIRST FRUITS OF
ZION

First Fruits of Zion is a 501(c)(3) registered nonprofit educational organization.

Printed in the United States of America

ISBN: 978-1-941534-26-7

Quantity discounts are available on bulk purchases of this book for educational, fundraising, or event purposes. Special versions or book excerpts to fit specific needs are available from First Fruits of Zion.
For more information, contact www.ffoz.org/contact.

First Fruits of Zion

Israel / United States / Canada

PO Box 649, Marshfield, Missouri 65706–0649 USA
Phone (417) 468–2741, www.ffoz.org

Comments and questions: www.ffoz.org/contact

Be a disciple of Aaron, loving peace, pursuing peace, loving people by bringing them closer to the Torah. The entire house of Israel, both the men and the women, mourned over Aaron's death because he pursued peace and instilled love between husbands and their wives.

(*Avot* 1; Rashi on Numbers 20:29)

CONTENTS

A SPECIAL BLESSING FOR WOMEN AND WIVES

This book is for men only.

Women really should not read any further than this page. Wives should not look inside this book to see what it is going to say. Don't worry, there's no sinister misogyny or chauvinism hiding inside, just a lot of straight talk meant for men and not for women. Do yourself a favor and put this book down, and may the LORD smile upon you, his beautiful daughter, and bless you with a peaceful home.

Here is a personal blessing meant for you and for every wife who respects these boundaries and refrains from reading this book:

> May God bless you for your discretion by granting you a happy marriage and an abundant spiritual life through the merit and virtue of his holy Son, and may he give you gladness all the days of your life.

"The Accolade" by William Blair Leighton

FOREWORD

GRANT LUTON

> Marriage is an adventure, like going to war.
> —G.K. Chesterton

Marriage is the grand theme of the Bible. Genesis opens with the marriage of the first man and woman, and Revelation closes with the marriage of Messiah and his bride. The giving of the Torah on Sinai is traditionally viewed as a wedding between God and his people, and Jesus performed his first miracle at a wedding banquet.

Marriage is the uniting of two opposites—a man and a woman—to create something new. Something unique. A relationship wherein two people each relinquish self for the sake of fulfilling the other. It is two individual souls fused together in love yet maintaining their individual identities. Two opposite beings considering the other as better than themselves. Two becoming one by giving, not taking.

What? This doesn't sound like your marriage? You say it's too good to be true? Too idealistic? Marriage was intended to be ideal—almost too good to be true. But you can have this kind of marriage with the woman you're married to right now—if you stop waiting for her to change and start doing the work that only you can do. Your marriage is what you, the husband, make it.

Chesterton was correct when he said that marriage is like going to war. All marriage involves warfare. You may, however, have been fighting the wrong enemy. Your battle is not *with* your wife; your battle is for your wife. If you are up for the fight, this book will equip you with the necessary strategies and tactics to win the battle and become a hero in the eyes of your bride. If you are up for the fight.

In this battle you must build fortifications. The question is, are your fortifications *around* you and your wife, or are they *between* you and your wife? If you war against the correct enemy and build walls in the proper way, your marriage can be an epic success.

More than a century ago, Edmund Layton created a painting called *The Accolade*. It depicts a knight clad in chain mail kneeling before his queen. She is a beautiful and regal young woman bearing a crown on her head and a sword in her hand. She rests the blade of the sword on the knight's shoulder, its edge mere inches from his neck as she beknights him into her service.

To me no painting so beautifully depicts the delicate balance of a perfect marriage. I have shared this image with many acquaintances and solicited their opinions. Without exception, each woman who sees *The Accolade* wants to be like the queen, and each man wants to be like the knight. Every wife wants to be adored by her husband just as the queen is obviously adored by the knight. And every husband wants to be respected by his wife as the knight is respected and honored by the queen. Does this picture reflect the mutual love and adoration between you and your wife?

No? Well, there is more to this painting than its romantic imagery. *The Accolade* also depicts grave danger.

The queen and the knight are in somewhat of a Mexican standoff. The powerful knight, trained in weaponry and warfare, could, if he chose, snap the queen in two like a stick. She, on the other hand, holds a razor-sharp sword against his neck. Now, perhaps you say, this painting is starting to look like your marriage. Do you and your wife each fear the threat posed by the other? Do you fear vulnerability?

Vulnerability. That is the sticking point where honor and danger coincide. If you wish to have a blissful marriage, you must make yourself vulnerable. There is no exception to this rule. But do not mistake vulnerability for weakness. The image of a knight kneeling in submission before his queen is an image of power under control, and power under control is the essence of a real man.

This book is not for little boys or wimps. It is for men who want to be worthy of a wife's respect. It will challenge you to be hard on yourself but easy on her. It will provide a path of discipline that will make you uncomfortable. In fact, this may be the most difficult and unpleasant book you will ever read. But would you rather have a difficult and unpleasant marriage? The problem in your marriage is you. Change you, and you change your marriage. If you will accomplish that, then this book will be the most valuable book you will ever read.

Ego can make an otherwise sensible man into a fool. During my twenty years of leading a congregation, I have often heard a husband drone on about the troubles in his marriage caused by his wife's many flaws. What I *see*, on the other hand, is a man complaining about a mirror that reveals an ugly reflection. Your wife is your mirror, and only a fool blames a mirror for what it reveals. If you see that your hat is crooked, don't adjust the mirror. Adjust your hat. And if you don't like your wife's attitude, adjust your own. This book, if you do what it says, will help you make the necessary adjustments to your life so that you will like what you see in your mirror.

In some ways this book will do the dirty work your wife does not want to do. It will be a mirror, and probably a painful one, that will reflect the kind of husband you are. But it will also provide for you a secondary image: an image of the man you can be and the husband your wife needs you to be—the man you may have given up on becoming.

Men, you were born for battle. So know your enemy, and recognize his strategies. A clever general knows how to turn his enemy's troops against their own men. Historical and biblical examples exist of confused and disoriented armies fighting against themselves. In modern warfare this is called friendly fire. Friendly or not, the results are the same: death and disaster.

This book will teach you strategies and tactics that will garner victory in your battle for your marriage. It will equip you to drag your enemy out of hiding, look him in the face, and defeat him. But you must understand that you cannot defeat your enemy without defeating your own ego. Your ego is the face of the enemy. Your ego is a phantom soul that you have created, whether you know it or not, and it is a fake and a fraud. You may think that it is the real you, but it isn't. Your wife probably knows this, and she wants to be married to the real you, not the phantom you. Let your ego take a beating; let it be destroyed, and let it die. Your wife will help! In this battle she is your ally. When your ego is finally conquered, you will be free to be the man, the husband, and the father God calls you to be—and that you want to be.

If you have not picked up on it yet, you must lay hold of one foundational principle before you read further. It is this: you cannot change your wife. Let me say that again—you cannot change your wife. Trying to change her will only create walls between you, inflict pain and scarring that will take years to heal, and maybe destroy your marriage. You can change only you. And you can change. God requires it. The question is, are you willing to work on your soul? Are you willing to suffer the pain that truth will inflict upon your ego? Are you willing to become a valiant warrior and fight the dragon that wishes to destroy the woman you love? This battle is your battle, and its victory is your glory.

As a child, I enjoyed (and even now enjoy as an old man) reading books about knights going on quests to slay dragons, discover new lands, and win glory in battle. This battle to win your marriage and be your wife's knight in shining armor is the adventure of a lifetime. If you and I can win these battles, the tales of our glorious victories will be recounted for eternity. Remember, marriage is the grand theme of the Bible, and it should also be the grand theme of our existence. Let us purpose in our hearts to walk in truth and humility. Let us put on our armor and take up our swords and defeat the enemy that seeks to destroy us.

There is one additional detail in *The Accolade* that I wish to describe. In the background of the painting is a crowd of onlookers, both young and old, standing quietly and in admiration of what they are witnessing. But the figure that captures my attention is a young boy at the front of the crowd holding the knight's shield. I can almost read his thoughts: he wants to grow up to be just like the knight—to walk in the knight's footsteps and someday to be honored just as the knight is.

You see, the battle for your marriage is not just about you. It is not just about you and your wife. The victory you seek is for you, your wife, your children, your grandchildren, and everyone else in your realm of influence. You are being watched, and what you do matters. Many are pulling for you and wishing to hear your tales of victory in battle, because the grand theme of the Bible—the battle for the bride—is also the grand theme of your life. Your marriage, in its own way, is a part of the great marriage of the Lamb and his bride.

It is time for us as men and husbands to arise to war. It is time for us to put on our armor, take up our swords, and go into battle for the wives we have committed our lives to loving and serving. It is time for us to turn away from distractions and focus on the battle at hand. The battle is spiritual. It is fought in the mind. And the enemy is the ego. And, like war, this fight is an adventure.

INTRODUCTION FROM
FIRST FRUITS OF ZION

This is a book for men only—specifically followers of Jesus, especially if they are married men, and especially if they are finding marriage to be perplexing and more difficult than they expected. This is a book about how God's instructions in the Bible can make a man's marriage better.

Before getting married, most men think that marriage will be easy. The man assumes that if he finds the right woman, he will be an excellent husband. She will love him; he will love her. What could be simpler? The Bible teaches a different message. The Bible commands men to love their wives as the Messiah loves his people:

> Husbands, love your wives, as Christ loved the church and gave himself up for her. (Ephesians 5:25)

This verse from Paul's letter to the Ephesians means that, according to the Bible, a man must crucify himself, so to speak, for the sake of his bride. That's how Christ loved the assembly of his people.

If you are happily married, you might not understand Paul's picture, but if you are struggling in a distressed marriage, you might identify with the metaphor a little too readily. Husbands enduring unhappy marriages might think crucifixion is preferable to the torment of an abrasive home life. This is a book about how you can carry out the Bible's instruction to "love your wife just as the Christ loved the assembly and gave himself up for her."

> Husbands, love your wives and do not be embittered against them. (Colossians 3:19 NASB)

If you agree to prayerfully read and study this book and implement its teachings into your marriage, the state of your marriage will improve. Happy marriages will become happier. Unhappy marriages will become happy marriages. Men in really difficult marriages will feel as if they have moved from the torment of crucifixion to the bliss of the resurrection. Even if you think your marriage is dead and almost over, there is still hope for you and your wife. With God's help, your marriage may even come back from the dead, and you and your wife will experience the bliss of Adam and Eve in the garden of Eden. It all starts with reading this book—the whole thing. Don't skip around. Read it from one end to the other, from cover to cover. It's important to read the whole book in the order in which it is written.

Maybe you already feel that you have a blissful, Edenic marriage. Congratulations! This book will help you preserve that marriage. Don't make the mistake of assuming you already know it all. Read this book from cover to cover, and pray over it, asking God, "Search me, O God, and know my heart! Try me and know my thoughts! And see if there be any grievous way in me!" (Psalm 139:23–24). The typical husband obliviously assumes that his marriage is healthy and strong, unaware of his wife's true feelings. Don't make the mistake of assuming you already have your marriage relationship all figured out.

Maybe you are a single man preparing for marriage. This book could mean the difference between a bad marriage and a good marriage. You still have time to do things right from the beginning. Many men in distressed marriages would trade all they have in this world in order to be in your place. They would pay any price to be able to start all over with their wives, implementing the godly counsel in these pages from the beginning of their marriage. I often hear men say, "If only I had known then what I know now." This book is your opportunity to know now what it takes most of us a lifetime to learn. The majority of us never do learn the principles explained in the book. Read this book. Study it, and refer back to it frequently as you begin your married life.

This book is not for women. If you are a woman, you should not be reading this book at all. To do so might cause your marriage harm rather than good. Think of the book as if it is medicine specially formulated for men but toxic to women. If a doctor gave a man a prescription for some malady that afflicts only men, his wife would not insist upon taking the medicine as well. If she did so, the medicine might cause her physical harm because it was not formulated for a woman's body.

Assuming that you are not a woman, do your part to keep this book out of the hands of your wife. This is not a book for husband and wife to read together. We will be speaking candidly about a lot of issues that might cause you discomfort and embarrassment, perhaps open old wounds, or even create some sense of friction (God forbid) because of the different ways men and women think about things and see the world.

THE GOOD AND THE BAD

A good and happy marriage is a tremendous gift from God. In a good marriage, a man's wife brings him good, not harm, all the days of her life.[1] The Bible advises men, "Enjoy life with the wife whom you love, all the days of your vain life … because that is your portion in life" (Ecclesiastes 9:9). In other words, God has given us a simple recipe for a happy life:

> A man should enjoy life with the wife he loves. Nothing in life can be more satisfying than full and happy days with the woman you love.

To the same proportion that a marriage has the potential to bring blessing, goodness, and fulfillment, however, it also has the potential to bring curse and misery. An unhappy wife tears her home down with her own hands.[2] The Bible says, "A wife's quarreling is a continual dripping of rain" (Proverbs 19:13), which means that it seems as though her complaints and affronts never cease.[3] The Bible says, "It is better to live in a corner of the housetop than in a house shared with a quarrelsome wife" (Proverbs 25:24), a saying that is the ancient equivalent of, "Better to live in the garage than under the same roof with that woman."

A MESSIANIC JEWISH PERSPECTIVE

This book will offer you a fresh perspective on marriage that can make all the difference in the world. At First Fruits of Zion, we are Bible teachers, not professional counselors. We have no credentials in marriage counseling. The words of this book are not built on any particular theory of marriage or family counseling, nor should they be considered to take the place of professional marriage counseling. This book does not offer counsel; it offers the Bible's perspective on how to be a better husband and obtain a better marriage.

First Fruits of Zion (FFOZ) brings Messianic Jewish teaching to Christians and Jews. We are Bible teachers in Messianic Judaism, the faith practice of many Jewish believers in Jesus. Our teaching role in Messianic Judaism places us in the unique position of being able to draw insights from both the New Testament and the wisdom of the Jewish people.

As is common in Messianic Jewish teachings, we might occasionally use the Hebrew name Yeshua instead of the Anglicized name "Jesus." We will also frequently refer to something called "the Torah." The Torah is God's Law. It consists of the Old Testament books of Genesis, Exodus, Leviticus, Numbers, and Deuteronomy—the first five books of the Bible. The Torah is the foundation for the rest of the Bible, including the New Testament. The Hebrew word *Torah* actually means "instruction." The laws in God's Law are supposed to be his instructions for his people. When you see the word "Torah" in this book, just remember that it's God's instructions for his people from Genesis, Exodus, Leviticus, Numbers, and Deuteronomy.

Because we write from within the spheres of Messianic Judaism, we also employ rabbinic commentaries such as the Talmud, an early Jewish commentary on Torah and Jewish law. We cite teachings from famous rabbis, insights from Hebrew exegesis, and quotes from Jewish sources, which might sound strange to you unless you are familiar with Jewish methods of Bible study. Don't let the unfamiliar terms and Jewish sources put you off. Don't let them dissuade you from studying this book. You can feel confident that everything in the book is based squarely on the Bible, even when we choose to bring in supporting teachings from the rabbis.

Although we are teachers in the field of Messianic Judaism, that doesn't mean that this book is meant only for Messianic Jews. The teachings in this book are Bible teachings, and they apply equally to every Christian husband who wants to obtain a better marriage relationship with his wife.

ATTRIBUTIONS

This book is not the creation of a single author. We compiled much of the material in this book from First Fruits of Zion's popular Torah Club commentaries. Some of the material in this book comes from the personal anecdotes and advice of Messianic Jewish rabbis and congregational leaders, including First Fruits of Zion staff members. Special thanks goes to Grant Luton, the congregational leader of Beth Tikkun Messianic Fellowship in Hartville, OH.

This book was inspired by Rabbi Shalom Arush's *The Garden of Peace: A Marital Guide for Men Only* (Diamond Press, 2008), a book that has helped many men overcome the obstacles to a peaceful home. We saw that *Garden of Peace* contained many truths that would be better expressed in the words of the New Testament, and we felt that Christians and Messianic believers needed a similar book grounded on the teachings of Rabbi Yeshua and the teachings of our apostles rather than on the teachings of Reb Nachman of Breslov (זצ״ל), on whom Rabbi Arush heavily relies. *Adam Loves Eve* translates the core teachings expressed in *Garden of Peace* into terms appropriate for those of us who are disciples of Jesus. The writings of C. S. Lewis have also influenced this book, particularly *The Four Loves* and the devilishly clever *Screwtape Letters*. We were pleased to find corroboration for many of the ideas in *Adam Loves Eve* in Shaunti and Jeff Feldhahn's helpful book *For Men Only: A Straightforward Guide to the Inner Lives of Women* (Multnomah, 2013). Most importantly, however, this book speaks from a foundation of solid Bible bedrock: the Torah of Moses and the teachings of Jesus and his apostles.

SWEEPING GENERALIZATIONS

Throughout this book we indulge in sweeping generalizations. We say things such as, "Men behave in this way, but women behave in that way," or, "Men are like this; women are like that." These are not always accurate statements, since human beings do not have an identical or universal gender-specific pattern of behavior. We are all individuals, and every individual is unique. Some readers might find themselves saying, "This description of men does not sound like me at all." Or they might say, "This characterization of women does not sound like my wife whatsoever." That's all right; it can't be helped. It's impossible to write a book of this nature that does not make sweeping generalizations, over-simplifications, and broad characterizations. A book that tries to address every potential permutation on human behavior would be useless to everybody. In order to write a useful book, we had to make statements about how we perceive and understand the behavior and psychology of the majority of men and women struggling in troubled marriages.

Naturally, there are many exceptions to every generalization. We are dealing in broad characterizations of gender differences for the sake of simplicity and ease of communication. The generalizations help us trace out the lines of the big picture, even if they do not account for all the details in the picture. When you find that the generalization does not fit your specific situation, look past it, and keep reading.

A NOTE FOR MEN WHO HAVE BEEN DIVORCED

If you have ever been through a divorce, you know how traumatic it is. You don't ever want to experience that again. The instructions in this book will protect you from going through another divorce. If you are recently divorced and neither you nor your wife have since remarried, this book might help you put things back together. If your wife has remarried, the Bible says that she's no longer eligible for you to remarry, even if her new marriage ends.[4] Likewise, if you have remarried, your focus now needs to be on protecting the marriage in which you currently are. As you read this book, you might start to recognize how things went wrong with your previous wife. Use those hard-earned life lessons to make a better marriage with the woman to whom you are now married.

WHY YOU WON'T LIKE THIS BOOK

We wrote this book primarily for men who find themselves in a distressed marriage, but, ironically, men in distressed marriages are the least likely to enjoy the book. An obese person does not want to hear the truth: The only way to lose weight is to change one's eating habits. The obese person wants a magic pill or miracle diet. He does not want to do the real work to recover his physique. The same is true of the man in a troubled marriage. He wants a miracle cure, a weekend-long marriage encounter, or some other trick that will restore peace to his home with a minimum investment of time and effort.

We anticipate that most men won't like this book because it calls upon us to become Christlike, and that's a tall order. We expect that most husbands will chafe under this book's instruction and complain that it is unfair, idealistic, and unbalanced. They might claim that the instructions are not biblical. Their human sin nature will try to convince them that the advice in the book is idiotic. They will look for every possible excuse to ignore the truths in this book, not because the principles herein are wrong, but because they are offensive to the male ego.

Don't listen to those guys. Your marriage is at stake. Don't wait until your wife says to you, "I am dead inside. I don't love you anymore." When a man's marriage comes crashing down, then he will say to himself:

> How I hated discipline, and my heart despised reproof! I did not listen to the voice of my teachers or incline my ear to my instructors. I am at the brink of utter ruin in the assembled congregation. (Proverbs 5:12–14)

So don't listen to the other guys. You don't want to be like them. You're the type of person who takes his faith and his marriage seriously, otherwise you would not be reading this book in the first place. You still have hope. All you need to do is believe, pray, and implement the things you learn in these pages.

FIXING YOUR MARRIAGE

Here is a final word for all husbands looking for a way to fix their relationships with their wives: No book can fix your marriage. That's in God's hands.

In the same vein, this book definitely will not help fix your marriage unless you implement the instructions you read in these pages. Additionally, it will not be sufficient to read through the book once. You will need to study it again and again, reviewing its contents and implementing them into your life.

Imagine a man who thinks he will lose weight from reading a book about a diet plan. It does not work that way. Unless he consistently and diligently applies the dietary guidelines he reads in the book, he will not lose weight.

Does this book sound as if it's going to be a lot of work? A real man is not afraid of hard work. A real hero is eager to embark on a quest and slay a dragon for the sake of his beloved. Are you willing to be a hero for your beloved?

Any lazy, selfish man can have a mediocre or troubled marriage, but a diligent man of God will work hard for the prize. If you put your effort into it, Jesus himself (the Bridegroom of all bridegrooms) will be with you to strengthen you on the way. With prayer, faithfulness, and real, sincere effort, your work will pay off. God will reward your efforts. You can do it. Think good, and it will be good. Believe in yourself, believe in your wife, and believe in God. With God's help, you can go the distance and win the prize.

We pray that you find this book to be helpful. More than that, we pray that this book revolutionizes your marriage beyond your wildest dreams and, with the help of our Master, ushers you and your wife into the bliss of Eden. If you do find the book to be helpful, please send us a note and tell us your story. Write to us or send us an email at: adamloveseve@ffoz.org

In addition, pass the book around to your friends. Recommend it to your brothers in Christ so that you can share in the great blessing and mitzvah (good deed) of bringing peace between a husband and a wife: "Blessed are the peacemakers, for they shall be called sons of God" (Matthew 5:9).

Finally, we pray, by the merit and favor of our holy Master and Savior, Jesus of Nazareth:

> May the LORD reward every man who diligently studies this book and implements its teachings into his life. May the LORD reward him with a happy marriage, a peaceful home, and the spiritual bliss and unity of our first father and mother in the garden of Eden.

1

NOT GOOD FOR MAN

Have you ever considered a divorce?

Most people get divorced because their marriages make them unhappy. A man in an unhappy marriage thinks, "I'd be happier if I were single."

Maybe being single would make him happier, but would it make him more godly? The Bible does not command husbands to be happy about their marriages, it commands them to love their wives: "Husbands, love your wives, as Christ loved the church and gave himself up for her" (Ephesians 5:25). In order to love his wife as the Messiah loves his church—the assembly of his people—the true disciple must take up his cross daily in imitation of his Master and lay down his life for his wife. This is the obligation of discipleship.

Divorce and remarriage is not a good option for disciples of Jesus. If we are followers of Jesus, the word "divorce" should not even be in the vocabulary of our marital relationships. Our Master forbids divorce except in tragic situations in which infidelity has occurred. Jesus made this clear to his disciples when he said, "Whoever divorces his wife, except for sexual immorality, and marries another, commits adultery" (Matthew 19:9). The disciples immediately objected, "If such is the case of a man with his wife, it is better not to marry." In other words, they said, "If a person is going to be stuck with a woman who makes him miserable his whole life, it would be better to stay single."

Maybe you are considering a divorce. You might think, "I will get a divorce and just remain single." Or maybe you are a single person thinking about whether or not to get married, and perhaps you agree with the sentiment expressed by the disciples: "If such is the case of a man with his wife, it is better not to marry!"

Is the single life a viable option? Is it better to stay single? If so, why did God say, "It is not good for man to be alone"?

SINGLE OR MARRIED?

When God made the first man, he made him single. He lived alone in Eden, serving the Creator. He had no worries or concerns. He did not worry about what to eat, what to drink, or what to wear. His Father in heaven provided all he needed.

He enjoyed the radiance of the splendor of the presence of God. He served God with his whole being, and he loved God with all his heart, all his soul, and all his strength. God had his undivided attention. It was Paradise.

Then came Eve. After Eve, everything changed.

Did Adam make a mistake? Had it really been so bad for man to be alone?

There were times when Adam must have wondered, "What is wrong with this woman? She is always unhappy. She rarely, if ever, says anything nice to me. She flies into a rage for no real reason at all. She never admits she is wrong. She has never apologized for anything in her life. She blames every mistake she has made on someone or something else (usually me)." After he found himself and his wife locked outside the gates of Eden, Adam must have thought, "I should have remained single."

Is it better to be single or to be married? Men who are single often look at married men with envy. Likewise, men in troubled marriages are sometimes jealous of single men.

Most marriages are not happy marriages. Christian marriages are not exceptions to the rule. Believing couples tend to have higher expectations of marriage than their secular neighbors, and higher expectations lead to deeper disappointments. Statistics say that around half of all marriages end in divorce. A fair number of the other half are barely holding it together.

The holy Apostle Paul encouraged his single disciples to remain single. He said, "Those who marry will have worldly troubles, and I would spare you that" (1 Corinthians 7:28). Everyone who marries has worldly troubles and concerns of some sort. The Talmud (a rabbinic commentary on the Bible and Jewish law) says that a married man has a millstone tied around his neck.[5] How much more so for men in bad marriages! A bad marriage must feel like a heavy millstone indeed. Without a doubt, a painful marriage is deeply troubling, difficult, and emotionally exhausting for both the husband and the wife.

Paul explained, "I want you to be free from anxieties" (1 Corinthians 7:32). The unmarried man has few anxieties. John the Immerser remained unmarried. He lived in the wilderness, eating and wearing only what he found in nature. He had no financial concerns or worries. He did not have to worry about how to afford health insurance or provide for a family. He did not have to worry about appeasing an angry spouse. He did not have to tiptoe around someone else's mood swings. Likewise, our Master, Jesus, did not take a wife. He was able to wholly commit his life to the service of the Father. He chose a path of celibacy, which he called "becoming a eunuch for the kingdom of heaven."

Paul explained that the single man is able to serve God with all his heart, soul, and strength because he does not have to be concerned for his wife. He said, "The unmarried man is anxious about the things of the Lord, how to please the Lord. But the married man is anxious about worldly things, how to please his wife, and his interests are divided" (1 Corinthians 7:32–34).

SEEK THE KINGDOM FIRST

Being single seems to make sense for disciples of Jesus. After all, every disciple of Jesus is obligated to seek first the kingdom of heaven. All other concerns that pertain to this material world are irrelevant when compared to that one single overarching goal. We seek the things of the kingdom by seeking those things that are pleasing to the LORD. We seek the kingdom by serving God.

Jesus warned us that worries and concerns about the material world are an impediment to seeking the kingdom:

> Do not be anxious, saying, "What shall we eat?" or "What shall we drink?" or "What shall we wear?" For the Gentiles seek after all these things, and your heavenly Father knows that you need them all. But seek first the kingdom of God and his righteousness, and all these things will be added to you. Therefore do not be anxious. (Matthew 6:31–34)

If worries and concerns are an impediment to seeking the kingdom, and marriage brings with it many troubles, worries, and concerns, it seems as though it would be better not to get married.

Jesus' disciples came to the same conclusion. They said, "If such is the case of a man with his wife, it is better not to marry" (Matthew 19:10). But the Master warned them that the single life is not for everyone—only for a select few to whom it has been given:

> Not everyone can receive this saying, but only those to whom it is given. For there are eunuchs who have been so from birth, and there are eunuchs who have been made eunuchs by men, and there are eunuchs who have made themselves eunuchs for the sake of the kingdom of heaven. Let the one who is able to receive this receive it. (Matthew 19:11–12)

The "eunuch for the sake of the kingdom of heaven" is the man who voluntarily chooses a life of celibacy. He chooses to remain single so that he can serve God with an undivided heart and undivided attention. He remains single "for the sake of the kingdom of heaven," the very thing that the Master told us to seek first.

WHAT IS THE KINGDOM OF HEAVEN?

Every disciple of Jesus is obligated to seek the kingdom of heaven first; but what is the kingdom of heaven? The kingdom of heaven is the reign and rule of God through his righteous Son the Messiah. The kingdom refers to the Messianic Era when the knowledge of the LORD will be universal. All nations will ascend toward the light of Messianic Jerusalem. The kingdom will bring an era of universal peace. "The wolf shall dwell with the lamb, and the leopard shall lie down with the young goat, and the calf and the lion and the fattened calf together" (Isaiah 11:6).

The Messianic Era will blossom in an age of miraculous fertility. "In that day the mountains shall drip sweet wine, and the hills shall flow with milk, and all the streambeds of Judah shall flow with water" (Joel 3:18). In that day, there will be no poverty because everyone will sit under "his vine and under his fig tree" (Zechariah 3:10), meaning everyone will be self-sufficient. The LORD will make the land "like Eden ... like the garden of the LORD; joy and gladness will be found in her, thanksgiving and the voice of song" (Isaiah 51:3). The kingdom of heaven is like the garden of Eden, the first Paradise of creation.

In the kingdom of heaven, God will raise the righteous to eternal life, and man will be able to reach his true potential. The evil inclination within us will be subdued, and Satan will be bound with chains. The kingdom represents what Eden was meant to be.

Our holy teacher, rabbi, and Lord, Yeshua of Nazareth, taught us to seek to enter the kingdom. Every disciple of Jesus should be living for the sake of passing through those gates of Eden and entering the kingdom. Our Master taught us that if we will believe in him and cling to him—like a branch growing from a vine that does not let go—he will bring us into the kingdom. Not only in the future to come but right now as well. We can take hold of the kingdom of heaven immediately. We do not need to wait until the Messiah comes to enter the kingdom; we can experience the power, peace, and perfection of the kingdom right now. He said, "The kingdom of heaven is at hand" (Matthew 3:2, 4:17, 10:7).

The true disciple of Jesus lives his whole life for the kingdom—both for the future and for the experience of the kingdom right now. Every day he prays, "May your kingdom come and may your will be done on earth as it is done in heaven" (Matthew 6:10). He seeks to prepare himself for the reward of the kingdom by his service of God in this age, and he seeks to bring the kingdom into this world through his attachment to the Messianic King and the presence of the Holy Spirit of God. This is a full-time endeavor.

THE SINGLE LIFE

If we are obligated to seek the kingdom first, it would seem as if that goal can best be attained by remaining single. That is why Paul says that a single man is better able to serve God with an undivided heart and undivided interests. That is why the Master taught that some men are called to take the path of celibacy for the sake of the kingdom. Some men are.

But most men are not.

Most men are not of the spiritual caliber to benefit at all from the single life. Very few men are on the level of Paul, John the Baptist, or Jesus. Except for Paul and the Apostle John, so far as we know, all the apostles had wives. Paul said, "Do we not have the right to take along a believing wife, as do the other apostles and the brothers of the Lord and Cephas?" (1 Corinthians 9:5).

Most single men use the single life to indulge their own selfish desires and inclinations. They do not submit themselves to serve the kingdom; they rather serve their own appetites and egos. They collect toys and play games. They spend their free time chasing amusements and pleasures. They waste the potential that God has invested in them on vanity and idleness. That is why God designed marriage—to correct men and make us whole. Except in rare cases, the single man does not serve God, he serves himself.

A married man, on the other hand, must learn to live like Messiah by dying to self and sacrificing for another. Marriage is God's higher education in spiritual maturity. Only an exceptional man will be able to achieve even a portion of the spiritual disciplines incumbent upon the married man.

The married man learns to serve God by serving his wife, and as he serves his wife, he serves God. This is one reason it is not good for man to be alone.

MARRIAGE IS A TEST

Marriage is God's primary testing ground of faith and spiritual growth. The sages say that God tested Abraham with ten trials to prove his faith. Rabbi Moses ben Maimon (Maimonides) enumerated a list of the ten trials that Abraham endured. Five of them have to do directly with his relationship with Sarah.

A man can maintain a pretense in front of people who do not live with him. Perhaps you appear to be full of the fruit of the Spirit. You appear to be full of love, joy, peace, patience, kindness, goodness, and self-control. A single person can fool the world into thinking that he is pious. A married man, however, cannot fool his wife. She knows the real man. She knows the sinner.

Marriage tests a man's character. The way you treat (or mistreat) your wife and the way you react when she mistreats you reveal your inner person. Your devotion to Jesus is all theoretical until God tests it in the crucible, and marriage is one of the most common testing grounds of faith. A difficult marriage is even more telling. It will reveal what you are really made of: "If you faint in the day of adversity, your strength is small" (Proverbs 24:10).

Sure, it would be easier to live alone, never having to apologize, never having to back down, never having to defer to someone else, but a disciple in such a situation will never become more like his Master.

He will never learn to be a servant. He will never learn humility. He will never learn to sacrifice.

Marriage reveals the real you. The real you might not be pretty, but it's the true person. If your wife doesn't like you, it's probably because you have a lot of sin and sinful attitudes that need to be fixed. This is how marriage helps to usher us into the kingdom of heaven. Marriage can be full of tribulation, but Paul says, "Through many tribulations we must enter the kingdom of God" (Acts 14:22).

These marital trials and tests, however, are to a person's advantage only if he passes through them successfully. He passes the test by letting marriage's difficulties refine his character to be more like Messiah and by obtaining the glittering prize of a peaceful home (*shalom bayit*). If a man does not work on himself and use marriage to improve his character as he strives to obtain a peaceful home, his marriage is senseless. Why bother?

NOT GOOD TO BE ALONE

God declared everything he created to be good. "And behold, it was very good" (Genesis 1:31). The only thing in creation that God declared to be "not good" was man's loneliness. Then the LORD God said, "It is not good that the man should be alone; I will make him a helper fit for him" (Genesis 2:18).

No suitable partner could be found for the man among all the creatures of creation. Despite his innocence, his capacity for fellowship with God, and all the pleasures of Eden, man experienced an inconsolable loneliness. He sought a partner. That's the way God made him. The Almighty hard-wired the desire for love and companionship into human beings.

A married man receives extra favor and grace that a single man does not need. In the Proverbs we read, "He who finds a wife finds a good thing and obtains favor from the LORD" (Proverbs 18:22). The Talmud echoes the same sentiment:

> Any man who has no wife lives without joy, without blessing, and without goodness. "Without joy," for it is written [in Deuteronomy 14:26], "And you shall rejoice, you and your household." "Without blessing," for it is written [in Ezekiel 44:30], "So that a blessing may rest on your household."

"Without goodness," for it is written [in Genesis 2:18], "It is not good that the man should be alone." (Talmud, b. *Yevamot* 62b)

This teaching states that God gladdens us, blesses us, and bestows his goodness on us through our wives and on account of our wives. This does not mean that a single person will never have joy, blessing, or goodness. All those things come to us through our relationship with God by means of his Son. But the married man experiences a certain quality of joy, blessing, and goodness that a single person simply cannot. These are gifts of God that can come to man only through his wife.

SUITABLE PARTNER

The Bible says that Adam could not find a "helper fit for him" (Genesis 2:20). The Hebrew behind the term "a helper fit for him" literally translates as "a helper opposite him" (*ezer kenegdo*, עזר כנגדו). The Talmud explains why the Torah calls your spouse a helper "opposite" you: "If man is worthy, the woman will be a helper. If he is unworthy, she will oppose him."[6]

This means that a man's wife functions as a spiritual barometer. The closer you walk with God, the closer she will want to draw to you. The further you walk away from God, the more repulsive you will appear to her. She may not know about your secret sins, but the Spirit within her does.

A wife reflects a man's inner self like a mirror. The LORD uses a man's wife to speak to him. For example, Abraham thought that his wife Sarah was acting petty, jealous, and spiteful when she told him to send away Hagar and Ishmael, but the LORD said to Abraham, "Listen to your wife Sarah." This is one of the key principles in this book. A man who does not listen to his wife closes his ears to the voice of God. A man without a wife loses the opportunity to hear God speak to him through his spouse, and that means losing some of the revelation of the kingdom.

In the kingdom of heaven, everyone will hear from God. God will pour out his Spirit on all flesh. Sons and daughters will prophesy. Old men and women will dream dreams. Young men and women will see visions. God will pour out his Spirit on everyone.[7]

Seeking the kingdom means seeking God's voice right now. In this era we can hear God's voice through the study of the Scriptures, but if we are really listening, we will hear God speaking to us through our wives. After all, God made your wife to be a "helper fit" for you, a suitable partner. If you are worthy, she will be a helper. If you are unworthy, she will let you know about it!

MARRIAGE MAKES NO SENSE

Marriage is a divine institution. It's a God thing.

Think about it. What is marriage really for?

God made Eve because it was not good for man to be alone. What does that mean?

Was it merely man's loneliness God wanted to solve? No. Marriage is not just for companionship. If marriage is simply meant to solve the problem of man's loneliness, a dog would make a better solution.

Marriage is not for help with life's tasks. A wife is not just man's "helper." Domestic servants would be better suited for the job and less expensive.

Marriage is not about sexual gratification. Men routinely find marriage to be more about sexual frustration than gratification—and the marital bond continues even in the absence of sexual gratification. Most men could find better sexual solutions outside the constraints of marriage.

Marriage is not just biologically convenient. Lots of animals successfully mate without any kind of relationship resembling marriage or monogamous fidelity. We are not biologically programmed for marriage. Other mammals similar to human beings do not mate a single spouse for life.

Marriage is not just for the purpose of raising children. Lots of married couples do not have children. Perhaps a father-mother team can provide a good environment for raising children, but that is not always the case. Plenty of families with both parents in the home are dysfunctional. Besides, if marriage were just about the kids, why not end the marriage after the children have started their own families? Marriage continues even after children are grown and gone.

No matter how you view it, marriage makes no natural sense, and when something defies the laws of nature, we call it "supernatural." Marriage is a supernatural institution. It exists because God ordained it. It's a divine relationship.

TWO HALVES

If God did make Eve after he made Adam, as the Bible indicates, why does Genesis 1:27 say, "Male and female he created them"? It sounds as if he made both male and female at the same time.

The rabbis explain that God originally made Adam both male and female—a single being with attributes from both genders. A parallel text in Genesis 5:2 says, "Male and female he created them, and he blessed them and named them *Adam* when they were created." The Hebrew name *Adam* (אדם) means "man." In other words, God created male and female as a single being—two halves of the same person. This means that a man is actually only half a man without a wife.

This also explains why the LORD had to remove Eve from Adam's body, and it explains why the male and female are attracted to one another—they seek to return to the original state, as it says: "They shall become one flesh" (Genesis 2:24). Like the polar opposites of a magnet, the soul of a man draws the soul of a woman, and the soul of a woman draws the soul of man:

> Rabbi Eleazar said, "Any man who has no wife is not a complete man [*adam*]; for it is said [in Genesis 5:2], 'He created them male and female and ... named them Adam.'" (Talmud, b.*Yevamot* 62b)

> It is written: "And God created man in his own image," and it is written, "Male and female created he them." How is this to be understood? In this way: In the beginning it was the intention of God to create two human beings, and in the end only one human being was created. (Talmud, b.*Ketubot* 8a)

Our Master taught the same understanding of the male-female relationship. He cited Genesis 2:24, which says that a man will "be joined to his wife; and they shall become one flesh" (NASB). He understood marriage as a return to the Edenic and primal perfection of the first Adam. Just as God mysteriously formed Eve by separating her from Adam, so too, he mysteriously joins a man and a woman into one being at marriage: "They shall become one flesh."

The mystics explain that husband and wife are two halves of the same soul. In that regard, marriage is not so much a spiritual union as it is a spiritual reunion. In addition, the sages viewed the marital union as a step toward spiritual union with God. The rabbis said, "Man does not fulfill his destiny without woman, neither does woman fulfill her destiny without man, nor do the two of them together without the Divine Presence between them."[8]

WOMAN AND MAN

Rabbi Akiva, a famous second-century Torah teacher, taught that "when husband and wife are worthy, the Dwelling Presence of God abides with them, but when they are not worthy, fire consumes them."[9] Rabbi Akiva had in mind the letters of the Hebrew words "man" and "woman." The Hebrew word for "man" is *ish* (איש). The word for "woman" is *ishah* (אשה). Both words have common letters and unique letters. If we recombine the unique letters from the two words, taking the *yod* (י) from *ish* (איש) and *heh* (ה) from *ishah* (אשה), the two letters spell *Yah* (יה), which is the first half of God's holy name. Removing those unique letters from both words changes the words to *eish* (אש), which means "fire."

Rabbi Akiva uses the unique letters to illustrate that when a marriage is godly, God is present with husband and wife. When a marriage is godless, the marriage becomes a consuming fire that will destroy both husband and wife.

Man	*Ish*	איש
Woman	*Ishah*	אשה
HaShem (God)	*Yah*	יה
Fire	*Eish*	אש

When a marriage is godly and a man walks in godliness with his wife, the presence of God dwells with them, just as Adam and Eve used to walk with God in Eden during the cool of day. When a man conducts his marriage out of kilter, poisoned by selfishness, pettiness, anger, rage, abusive speech, lust, and other sins, the presence of God withdraws from the home, and the fires of Gehenna burn hotly around husband and wife.

Maybe you feel as though your marriage has a lot more devouring fire in it than the presence of God. Maybe it feels as if you are living in the fire of Gehenna right now. If you would like to switch that around so that your marriage becomes like the garden of Eden, where Adam and Eve walked together with the presence of God, read and study this book cover to cover, and work hard to follow all its instructions. Set aside the many objections that your male ego will raise. With God's help this book will assist you on the quest for marital peace, and more than that, it will bring you a long way toward your quest for the kingdom.

FIND A GOOD THING

> Two are better than one, because they have a good reward for their toil. For if they fall, one will lift up his fellow. But woe to him who is alone when he falls and has not another to lift him up! Again, if two lie together, they keep warm, but how can one keep warm alone? And though a man might prevail against one who is alone, two will withstand him—a threefold cord is not quickly broken. (Ecclesiastes 4:9–12)

The Bible presents the single life as a viable option for those select individuals whom God has specifically called to that purpose, but as a general rule, "It is not good for man to be alone." Instead, "He who finds a wife finds a good thing." A single man has to make his way through life with half his soul missing, so to speak. He forfeits the opportunity to spiritually grow in maturity through the trials and disciplines of married life. The single man will find it difficult to enter the kingdom because he has no wife to challenge his ego and teach him the art of selflessness. He forfeits the special blessing and unique portion of the presence of God that rests only upon a married couple.

Therefore, if you have been considering divorce, drive that thought out of your head. It's not for you. If you have been considering staying single for the sake of the kingdom, pour a lot of prayer into that, and seek God's will. Maybe you are called to live out your life as a single man serving the kingdom, but most of us serve the kingdom better with the help of a suitable partner.

Now that we've learned how valuable a wife is, let's learn about how to keep her.

2

THE GREATEST COMMANDMENT

Which commandment in the Bible is the most important of them all? If you are a married man, your most important obligation before God is to love your wife.

You are probably objecting, "That's not what Jesus said!"

Our Master taught us that the most important commandment in the Bible is to love the LORD our God with all our hearts, souls, and minds. He said that the second most important commandment is like it: A man must love his neighbor as he loves himself:

> You shall love the Lord your God with all your heart and with all your soul and with all your mind [Deuteronomy 6:5]. This is the great and first commandment. And a second is like it: You shall love your neighbor as yourself [Leviticus 19:18]. On these two commandments depend all the Law and the Prophets. (Matthew 22:37–40)

Jesus never told us to love our wives, did he? The only thing he said about loving one's wife was a warning against prioritizing her higher than him. He said, "Anyone who loves his wife more than me cannot be my disciple."[10]

If Jesus taught us that loving God is the most important commandment, that loving our neighbor is the second most important commandment, and that anyone who loves his wife more than him cannot be his disciple, how can we claim that a husband's most important obligation before God is to love his wife?

LOVING GOD AND ONE'S FELLOW

The most important commandment is to love God with all one's heart. The apostles explain that we show our love to God by keeping his commandments.[11] The Bible also commands a husband to love his wife.[12] This means that if we do not show our wives proper love, we break God's commandment for marriage, and if we break his commandments, we are not keeping the commandment to love God. Therefore, a person who does not properly love his wife does not properly love God. He breaks the most important commandment—his obligation to love the LORD.

The apostles also state that anyone who says he loves God but does not love his neighbor or his brother is a liar. A man's closest neighbor is his wife. The Bible calls her "a friend who sticks closer than a brother" (Proverbs 18:24).[13] Paul explains that the commandment to "love your neighbor as yourself" especially applies to one's wife. He says, "Husbands should love their wives as their own bodies. He who loves his wife loves himself" (Ephesians 5:28); "Let each one of you love his wife as himself" (Ephesians 5:33).

If a man is obligated to love his neighbor as himself and to love his brother as Christ loved us, how much more so is he obligated to love his wife—his closest neighbor who sticks closer than a brother?

To better illustrate the point, we have substituted the word "brother" with the word "wife" in the following passage:

> If anyone says, "I love God," and hates his *wife*, he is a liar; for he who does not love his *wife* whom he has seen cannot love God whom he has not seen. And this commandment we have from him: whoever loves God must also love his *wife*. (1 John 4:20–21)

A man who does not love his wife breaks the two most important commandments in the Bible—the commandment of loving God and the commandment of loving his neighbor.

SERVING GOD

A godly man might mistakenly assume that serving God is more important than meeting the needs of his wife. This is a serious spiritual blunder. A man's relationship with his wife is the most important thing in his spiritual life. It serves as his spiritual barometer. It is God's greatest test of a man. The man who sacrifices his marriage for the sake of serving God destroys both his marriage and his service of God. He fails the test.

Nothing is more important than serving God. God made men to serve him, but the Apostle Paul also teaches us that pleasing our wives has the same priority as serving God. The apostle says that if a man is not married, he should devote his whole life to pleasing the LORD, but if a man is married, he must divide his efforts between pleasing the LORD and pleasing his wife.[14]

Maybe the idea of dividing your priorities between both God and your wife sounds like serving two masters. Jesus said, "No one can serve two masters" (Matthew 6:24). To reconcile this contradiction, a man must make his efforts to please his wife a part of his spiritual service to the LORD. One who expends his energy on making his wife happy is, at the same time, pleasing the LORD. He must realize that his love for his wife, his kindness to her, and all the ways that he gladdens her are not merely for her benefit but also a service to God who commands a husband to love his wife. Therefore, the man who loves and serves his wife is loving and serving God. He does not love her more than God. He does not serve her instead of God. He loves her because he loves God. He serves her because he serves God.

SHALOM BAYIT

What is the most important thing in marriage? The most important thing a husband and wife can share is not romantic love or intimacy. Emotions and sexuality are only the outer manifestations of a much deeper inward spiritual need. The most important thing a man and woman can share is selfless love and spiritual unity.

A husband and wife who live together in selfless love and spiritual unity create a peaceful home. In Hebrew a peaceful home and marriage are called *shalom bayit* (שלום בית). Nothing on earth can be more fulfilling and beautiful for human beings than a marriage of *shalom bayit*. The man in such a marriage finds spiritual power and energy to accomplish great things for God. He rejoices in his wife, and his wife rejoices in him.

On the other hand, the marriage without *shalom bayit* can be hell on earth. A husband who finds himself in a troubled marriage or married to an unhappy woman will discover that there is nothing more stressful and difficult in life. A bad marriage creates pain and pressure in every area of a person's life. A home characterized by shouting voices, angry words, slamming doors, and cutting insults is no home at all. The husband in a home without shalom feels the spiritual life sucked out of his body. He feels helpless. Every day of his life is just more misery. He thinks to himself, "It would be better to die." The Bible says that it would be better for him to live on the corner of his roof than with an angry, unhappy wife.

When a man does not have *shalom bayit*, there is always a good reason for it. And it can usually be fixed. If a husband does not have *shalom bayit* with his wife, he must make the quest for such a peaceful marriage his first and highest priority. He must devote his time, his studies, and his prayers to achieving it. He must make it his spiritual focus. He must read and pray over this book and take its words to heart. He must read this book over and over and continually work to implement every word. As long as a person lacks *shalom bayit*, he must make it his most urgent objective to obtain it. He should consider it to be his call to ministry.

The man who does possess a happy, peaceful marriage and an abundance of *shalom bayit* need not be so focused on the matter. He might not understand this book, and he may even find that this book offends his sensibilities. Skinny people do not need to read books about weight loss. That blessed man with a happy wife might read this book and say to himself, "My wife is not like that. This does not sound like my marriage at all." If that is really true, he should sincerely thank God for the gift of a peaceful marriage, and he should acknowledge that he received an unmerited gift from God—not something that he earned or deserved.

At the same time, he should beware of spiritual pride. Perhaps his male ego has deceived him. Perhaps, if someone privately asked his wife for her honest opinion, she would not have the same positive assessment of the marriage. Perhaps his ego has blinded him to how his wife really feels.

Most men do need to work at marriage. Being a good and godly husband is not something that comes naturally to us. We are not naturals at being good husbands any more than we are naturals at golf.

A good golfer practices and improves his game. A good husband must do the same.

The Bible asks, "An excellent wife who can find?" She might be hard to find, but an excellent husband is even rarer.

LOVE YOUR WIFE

Which commandment in the Bible is the most important of all?

For married men the answer is clear: "Husbands, love your wives, as Christ loved the church and gave himself up for her" (Ephesians 5:25). When a man loves his wife, he fulfills both his obligation to love the LORD and his obligation to love his neighbor.

It's not hard for a man to love his wife, but sometimes it's hard for a husband to show his wife that he loves her, and sometimes it's hard for a wife to believe in her husband's love. Don't worry. You've done hard things before, and so has your wife. Stay positive, and ask God to help you show your love through your actions. He will be glad to help you. After all, loving your wife is the Bible's most important commandment for you.

3

EDEN OR GEHENNA

In Jewish terminology Eden corresponds to Paradise. Jewish sources refer to "heaven" as "the garden of Eden." When the righteous die, the angels escort their souls to the garden of Eden, where they enjoy their reward. When the wicked die, their souls descend to the fire of Gehenna, where they receive punishment for their wicked deeds.

When Jesus taught about marriage, he pointed his disciples to Adam and Eve in the garden of Eden as the perfect example "from the beginning." When a marriage is good and functioning well, with both partners loving and respecting one another, mutually supporting one another, it feels like the paradise of Eden. When a marriage is distressed and full of dysfunction, however, it might feel like the tortures of Gehenna.

The decisions we make in life will determine our ultimate destiny—whether we end up in Gan Eden or Gehenna. The same principle applies to our marriages. The decisions we men make will determine whether we live in a home full of the pleasures of Eden or consumed by the flames of Gehenna. The decision is in our hands.

The first and biggest mistake most men make is to assume that they and their wives share an equal responsibility for making the marriage work. To some extent, of course, this is true, but as a general spiritual principle, the responsibility falls to the man. The Bible commands him to love his wife as the Messiah loves the assembly. The Bible says that the husband "is the head of the wife" even as the Messiah is the head of the assembly.[15] Does this sound like a fifty-fifty relationship to you? Did God send his Son to halfway die on the cross and then ask us to pick up the slack?

Even marriage counselors will admit that fifty-fifty marriages do not work. If you are one of those men who are willing to do your part in being a good husband and working hard on the marriage only so long as your wife is doing her part, your marriage is doomed. That's not the self-sacrificing, heroic, "I am willing to die for you" kind of love demonstrated by Jesus. It sounds more like an arrangement between two college roommates: "If you wash the dishes, I'll clean the bathroom." Marriage is not a business arrangement.

THE BAD WIFE

But what if you just get stuck with a bad wife?

Most marriages don't reach the point of total dysfunction, but when they do, the husband comes to his rabbi or counselor in distress, at his wits' end, utterly at a loss as to how to deal with his wife.

Every man in a dysfunctional marriage thinks that his wife is a special case and that she is the problem. He thinks that his wife is abnormal. He tells about how she allows her emotions to dictate her behavior. She bursts into fits of rage with the slightest provocation and sometimes with no provocation whatsoever. He says that she is moody and depressed, sometimes in tears, but when she is asked to explain, she has no rational explanation to offer, and just asking her might incite her displeasure. He might attribute her mood swings to hormones, or he might question her sanity. From his perspective he is simply the victim of bad luck. He got hitched to a defective woman.

The husband in the dysfunctional marriage says, "She is so selfish and self-centered that she never gives a single thought for me. She expects me to make the money, but she can't even afford a single kind word to me."

His rant against his wife is just getting started. He goes on, "What's more, she blames me for everything. She finds some way to make her problems into my fault. She, on the other hand, never admits to a single fault. She never apologizes or admits it when she is wrong, and she never forgives. That woman can hold a grudge forever! I mean, she still brings up stuff from even before we were married!"

The unhappy husband says, "Rabbi, my wife constantly criticizes and nags me about every tiny little thing, but if I say one thing to her, she goes into a rage. She can dish it out, but she sure can't take it. I tell her that people who live in glass houses shouldn't throw stones. Living with her is like constantly walking on egg shells."

Maybe the husband of this woman feels as if he drew an unlucky card. Maybe he looks at other marriages and thinks to himself, "Why can't my wife be like so-and-so's wife?" He wonders, "What did I do to deserve this woman?"

THE TORMENTED WIFE

In reality, the woman described above is not at all unusual or defective in any respect. Women operate from an emotional core. When a woman is unhappy, she feels that unhappiness deeply, and it affects her behavior and poisons interactions with her husband in predictable ways.

The husband described above thinks that he is a victim of bad luck and that his wife has an unusual, dysfunctional personality. He thinks that God played a mean trick on him by putting such a woman into his life. The truth is just the opposite. The woman he is living with is not the woman God gave him, and she is not the woman he married. She is the woman he created through pig-headed and insensitive behavior.

She is a completely ordinary girl who has had the life and the joy stomped out of her by a man she used to love. The symptoms described above are those of a woman in emotional distress over her marriage. Years of emotional abuse have so battered her soul that she no longer dares to feel anything but bitterness. She might not even know why she behaves the way she does; she certainly will not be able to articulate the problem, but she feels it deeply in her heart. It twists in her heart like a knife, wrenches her guts, boils in her blood like black poison. She is in despair. She wishes she could die. She would rather die than go on living in her marriage. She has so much hurt and so many deep wounds that she does not even know how to breathe. She does not understand how her husband, who claims to love her, can hurt her so deeply, so repeatedly, and so callously. She wonders what great sin she committed to deserve such a cruel and insensitive man. When he is not around, she weeps until her tears run dry. She hates herself, and she feels utterly unloved and unlovable.

Meanwhile, her baffled husband has no idea that he is the cause of her distress. He does not even realize that he has emotionally hurt her. "Sure, we've had some fights, but who doesn't?" he says. "Besides, I apologized." He has no idea how damaged she is, and he has no clue about a woman's heart.

His obliviousness is not really his fault. No one ever taught him how to take care of a woman. His father might not have even known, and if he did, he probably never communicated the fine art of nurturing a woman's soul to his son. His pastor or rabbi probably did not tell him how to deal with a woman's heart because pastors and rabbis usually get involved after things have already fallen apart—they are usually not the source of preventative care in a marriage. Marriage counselors could not tell him how to properly care for his wife because they are focused on improving communication between couples and working through issues—not the spiritual needs of a woman. His wife certainly did not tell him; she would not have been able to put it into words. Even if she did say something to him, what good would it do? He would have just shut her down, arguing with her and telling her that she needed to grow up, toughen up, and get a grip on reality.

THE WEAKER VESSEL

Men pride themselves in being logical and rational. They express frustration with their emotion-driven wives, and they try to use their cool and rational logic to direct their wives. When the wife does not respond to his reasoning, the man becomes more insistent, disputes her more heatedly, and presses his position with stronger proofs and arguments. He brings her to tears and then shakes his head in exasperation.

The rabbis say, "One should always be careful not to upset his wife, for her tears come frequently and she is easily hurt."[16] The Bible refers to the wife as the "weaker vessel" in the marriage. This does not imply that she is a lesser vessel; it implies that she is more fragile and precious. A man is like a cast-iron pot. A woman is like fine china. If the cast-iron pot is not careful, he can easily crush the fine china. He can do it without even noticing that he has done it. The holy Apostle Peter says, "Husbands, live with your wives in an understanding way, showing honor to the woman as the weaker vessel, since they are heirs with you of the grace of life" (1 Peter 3:7). When a man fails to show his wife honor, he crushes her spirit, like a heavy cast-iron pot crashing down on a piece of fine china.

A wife relies on her husband for her sense of vitality, self-worth, and self-respect. Even though she might not realize it or want to admit it, he is everything to her because, when she married him, she gave everything she had to him. His opinion of her means everything to her. She looks to him for physical, emotional, and spiritual sustenance. She needs him to affirm her and believe in her. If he criticizes her, reprimands her, or corrects her, even though he means to do it in a constructive manner, he crushes her sense of dignity and self-respect.

God made women in such a manner that their dignity and sense of honor is as vital to them as oxygen. Criticisms and nasty-spirited snarky remarks should roll off a man like water off a duck's back, but those same things lodge deeply in a woman's heart like barbed and poisoned arrows. When a woman feels disrespected or dishonored by her husband, she feels as though she is suffocating. She feels the life and vitality drain out of her body. Her love for him grows colder and colder, and she becomes spiritually, emotionally, and sexually despondent.

God appoints men to a role of priesthood in their homes: "I want you to understand that the head of every man is Christ, the head of a wife is her husband, and the head of Christ is God" (1 Corinthians 11:3). This means that a husband is supposed to be the conduit of God's infinite, forgiving grace and love. God bestows his grace upon the Messiah; the Messiah bestows the grace upon his disciple, and the disciple bestows the grace upon his wife. A woman does not necessarily understand this hierarchy, but her godly soul within her intuitively comprehends it and needs it. When the man becomes an obstacle in that chain of transmission, he obstructs his wife's experience of God. Not only that, his behavior toward her severs his own relationship with God. The holy Apostle Peter says that if a man does not live with his wife in an understanding way, showing her honor as the weaker vessel, his own prayers will be obstructed.[17] If you are not showing your wife honor and understanding her as a delicate and fragile woman, God will not hear your prayers.

On the other hand, the rabbis warn men not to make their wives cry because those tears ascend straight to heaven to accuse the man who inspired them. Even when the gates of prayer are locked, the gates of tears are still standing wide open.[18] This means that God hears the painful cries of a wife's heart and sees her many tears, while at the same time he shuts out the prayers of the man who makes her cry:

> Live with your wives in an understanding way, showing honor to the woman as the weaker vessel, since they are heirs with you of the grace of life, so that your prayers may not be hindered. (1 Peter 3:7)

THE NORMAL DYSFUNCTIONAL MARRIAGE

Are you one of those men who have been telling yourself that your wife is the problem? A wife is rarely the source of the problem in an unhappy marriage. At the same time, a husband almost never realizes or freely admits that he is the source of his wife's unhappiness. He says, "I guess she was damaged goods when I married her. I just didn't know it then." The husband never takes responsibility for his wife's unhappiness. He blames her. He blames her insecurities. He blames her hormones. He blames her mother. He blames her friends. He blames her counselor. He blames the devil. He blames God. He blames everyone except the real culprit: himself.

Many times, the wife's unhappiness, anger, and bitterness catch the husband completely by surprise. He never saw it coming. He never imagined that he was hurting her or doing anything except being a normal husband. His wife's unhappiness blindsides him. It leaves him confused and resentful because he cannot, for the life of him, see what he could possibly have done to make his wife so unhappy. This is the normal dysfunctional marriage: a bitter, unhappy woman married to a blind, self-righteous man.

THE WRONG WOMAN

Mr. Self-righteous begins to wonder if he married the wrong person. He thinks about getting a divorce and finding a nice, normal woman. But this plan will not work because he is already married to a completely normal woman. His wife is not the least bit abnormal. She is exactly the way the Almighty God designed all women.

If he marries another "normal" woman and treats her the same way, he will end up with the same results. He will reduce her to a prickly, bitter, resentful, and emotionally toxic person—just as he did with his first wife. This time things will fall apart faster because the second marriage does not have the same spiritual glue and traction of the first. It does not matter how many times he gets married. As long as he marries normal, healthy women, he will destroy them one at a time.

THE SHATTERED HEART

Mr. Self-righteous not only fails to see how he has damaged his own marriage in the past, but now he fails to see that the embittered, mean-spirited woman who lives with him is actually the same tenderhearted, blushing bride who married him. Before they were married, she used to secretly practice signing her first name with his last name. Over and over again she wrote out her new name just to see it in print, and it made her heart race to think about being Mrs. So-and-so. She dreamed about how romantic the wedding day would be. She fantasized about how idyllic life was going to be with the perfect man whom God had chosen to be her husband. Lying alone in her bed at night, she prayed earnest prayers for the man to whom she had given her whole heart. She counted off the days until she could finally be together with her one true love.

Yes—that's still the same woman. The only difference is that he has crushed that precious flower under his foot. He has battered her with sharp-tongued criticism of everything she does; he has trampled her heart with "rational" arguments in which he meticulously and logically shows her the errors in her thinking; he has broken her heart by ignoring her while she talks with him; he has shattered her sense of self-worth by making her feel stupid and inadequate; he has smashed her self-image by looking at other women or commenting negatively about her appearance; he has betrayed her trust by publicly making remarks about her—sometimes even while she is present; he has stabbed her soul to death with insults and cutting words. And this is just the beginning of his insults to her dignity.

He does not recognize or admit to any of it. He has a perfectly reasonable explanation and excuse for all of it. He complains, "She is always making mountains out of molehills! She always blows things way out of proportion!" These statements indicate that he does not understand anything about women.

Although his wife is married and shares the same bed with him every night, she feels utterly alone in the world. She has no one to turn to, and every day and night are filled with agonizing loneliness. If she had the chance to go back to her wedding day and do it all over again, she would flee from him as fast as she could.

THE HOUSE ON THE SAND

As if all this was not enough, the poor woman is driven to exasperation because everyone else thinks her husband is such a great guy. Everyone else thinks of him as a godly man. She sees him as a hypocrite. He calls himself a disciple of Jesus, but she does not see anything particularly Christlike about him. She knows that a disciple of Jesus is supposed to be gentle spirited and slow to anger, but this woman's husband is always seething at her. A disciple of Jesus does not look at other women with lust, but this man can never keep his eyes off other women, and she notices. A disciple of Jesus turns the other cheek, but this man is always ready to verbally hit her back. A disciple of Jesus does not return evil, but this man always retaliates against his wife's verbal attacks. A disciple of Jesus forgives others their sins, but this man keeps bringing hers up in every argument. A disciple of Jesus does not judge others, but this man never stops judging her or criticizing her. A disciple of Jesus takes the log out of his own eye before taking the speck out of someone else's, but this man does not see the log in his own eye as he claws at her eyes. A disciple of Jesus treats others as he would be treated, but this man does not treat her as he would want to be treated.

Our Master warned us, "Everyone who hears these words of mine and does not do them will be like a foolish man who built his house on the sand. And the rain fell, and the floods came, and the winds blew and beat against that house, and it fell, and great was the fall of it" (Matthew 7:26–27).

In the language of the ancient rabbis, a man's wife was called his "house." In Biblical Hebrew the term *house* is used idiomatically to speak of a man's family, his home, his children, and his wife. Without a wife a man has no children, no home, and no family. He does not have a household; he does not need a house. Therefore, the ancient rabbis used to refer to a man's wife as his house. One early rabbi said, "I have never called my wife 'my wife.' I have always called her 'my house.'" [19]

The disciple who does not conduct his marriage according to the teaching of Jesus builds his house on the sand. Maybe the house looks pretty solid, and maybe it even stands straight and true for the first few years of marriage. Then come the troubles. The rain of marital discord falls. The waters of emotional turbulence erode the sand beneath the house. The wind of life's stresses and worries blow against the house.

Since the man did not conduct his marriage according to the teaching of Jesus, it collapses around him.

DIVORCE IS NOT AN OPTION

In Jewish law husbands are allowed to divorce their wives, but women cannot divorce their husbands. Jesus forbids us from divorcing our wives except for the grave sins of infidelity, adultery, and sexual immorality.[20] He forbids men from divorcing their wives for any other reason. If a man does divorce his wife for any other reason, he bears the responsibility himself. The Bible does not consider the divorce legitimate. If the woman remarries, Jesus charges the ex-husband with the sin of causing her to become an adulteress. The ex-husband bears her guilt; she is innocent. If the divorced man himself remarries, the Bible charges him with the sin of adultery.

In view of these difficult teachings of Jesus, it should be perfectly clear to every disciple that divorce is not an option for the follower of God. A disciple of Jesus should never even consider divorcing his wife any more than he would seriously entertain the notion of committing murder or some other heinous crime. He should certainly never allow the word "divorce" to leave his lips. He must never, ever use the threat of divorce as a way to manipulate his wife. He should consider divorce to be far outside the realm of possibility.

A disciple of Jesus cannot legitimately divorce his wife unless she has committed some act of infidelity (God forbid). Even in such a terrible situation, the man holds the moral high ground to divorce her only if he himself has not also engaged in some act of infidelity: "Let him who is without sin among you be the first to throw a stone at her" (John 8:7).

Since Jesus does not offer divorce as a viable option for his disciples except in these cases mentioned, this leaves only two possibilities for the man in a troubled marriage. He can choose to live in Gehenna, or he can choose to live in Eden. He can choose to let his marriage continue to go from bad to worse, or he can start turning things around by doing the hard work of repairing his marriage and nurturing his wife's soul. He can keep living in a house built on the sand, or he can rebuild on the solid rock.

The choice is yours: Eden or Gehenna? It's really not a choice: "I have set before you life and death, blessing and curse. Therefore choose life" (Deuteronomy 30:19). If you commit yourself to a path of repentance and carefully implement the things you learn in this book, your marriage will go from spiritual death to spiritual life. You will become a blessing to your wife instead of a curse, and she will become a blessing to you.

On the other hand, if you insist on continuing to blame her and cursing your bad luck for ending up with such a woman, then you might as well get comfortable on the corner of the roof. Things are not going to get better, and you will never have back that sweet, innocent, blushing bride you married. You can settle in for the rest of your life in a house of pain.

Why would any sane person belligerently choose to live in Gehenna when he could be living in Eden?

THE GOOD NEWS

If your wife is unhappy, don't point the finger of blame at her or at anyone other than yourself. Your wife might seem to you ungrateful, mean spirited, and spiteful, but if she does, it does not indicate that she is in any way unusual. Instead, it indicates that she is a normal woman suffering from emotional distress in an unfulfilling and hurtful relationship.

That's good news because it means that the situation can be remedied and reversed if you commit yourself to the difficult task of becoming a true disciple of Jesus in regard to your marital relationship. Since divorce is not an option for you, you have no other reasonable choice. So keep reading. Keep believing. And keep praying.

4

SHE'S NOT A DUDE

M en make the biggest marital mistakes when they assume that
women are the same as men. Of course we know that women
are different from men—*vive la différence*. Aside from the obvious ana-
tomical differences, men joke all the time about how incomprehensible
they find women to be. As one popular secular title put it, *Men Are from
Mars; Women Are from Venus*. Despite all this, most men still think
of women as if they are men repackaged in attractive female bodies.

BOYS AND GIRLS

Most of the critical mistakes a man makes in his marriage come from
this unconscious, underlying assumption that his wife is the same as
him. He assumes that beneath that attractive female layer, she thinks
and reasons like he thinks and reasons and that she processes information, conversation, humor, horseplay, sarcasm, verbal jabs and pokes,
and all human interactions in the same jocular, lighthearted manner
as his college roommate or best friend from high school. He assumes
that he can have an amicable, low-investment, easygoing relationship
like any two guys might share. He does not actually consciously think
through these assumptions, and if he would, he might realize their
intrinsic folly.

A husband operating under such assumptions lives in a completely different world than his wife does. Things that he assumes
are funny pranks, such as those that two good buddies might play on
one another, deeply offend and wound her. Innocent roughhousing
seriously frightens her. Offhanded remarks, offered lightheartedly or
simply thoughtlessly, strike her heart as if they are serious, calculated,
cutting remarks intended to wound her. Sarcastic statements that he

assumes she will dismiss as mere sarcasm strike her literally and make her doubt his intentions.

Later, when he attempts to figure out what has gone wrong, she rejects all his attempts to defend himself by explaining those things away as simply boyish behavior, childish pranks, silly talk, and so forth. Just as the limitations of his male perspective prevent him from correctly anticipating how she will react to all his boyish charm, the limitations of her female perspective prevent her from actually believing that his behavior is anything less than intentionally malicious and carefully calculated to communicate hatred.

Don't make the mistake of assuming that living with a woman is the same as working with another man on a job or living with a brother or roommate. Men have low-maintenance relationships with one another. The unspoken agreement between men is simple: "If I don't have a problem with you; you don't have a problem with me." That works fine between men, but it does not work with women at all. To live with a woman, you have to know how she thinks. You have to understand the spiritual and psychological forces at work in her soul—what makes her tick. You have to understand that women are not men.

WOMEN AND MEN

At this point we are diving into more of those sweeping generalizations about gender differences. We are saying things like, "Men behave in this particular way, but women behave in that particular way." Obviously, broad statements like that are not going to be universally accurate. Human beings are individuals, and every one of us is unique. But we need to speak in broad generalizations in order to communicate some essential points about the common differences between men and women and what happens when we forget those differences.

Ironically, almost every woman identifies herself as an exception to the generalizations about women. She sees how other women do match the characterization, but she does not feel that it describes her. Instead, she sees herself as different from other women. She says she prefers the company of men because she is not like most of the other human beings who share her gender. She almost certainly *is* unique in some ways, but for the most part, and "generally speaking," she isn't.

All women say that they aren't like other women, and men say that they aren't like other men.

BOYS WILL BE BOYS

Men get away with a lot of misbehavior under the excuse "Boys will be boys." It's true that boys will be boys, but a boy who marries a woman better grow up and become a man really fast. No woman wants to be married to a boy.

A man's boyish behavior ranges from the clutter he leaves behind him as he walks through a room to the lazy type of procrastination that typifies a teenager more interested in video games than responsibilities. None of that is going to work in marriage. A boy enjoys rowdy, bawdy behavior knocking around with his buddies. Boys compete with belches and farts and entertain one another with crudity and vulgar talk.

When a man behaves that way around his wife, however, she does not react like one of his schoolyard buddies because she is not a dude. Those behaviors communicate a completely different message to her: complete and total disrespect. He chastises her for her reaction because he expects her to laugh along the way any of his old buddies would do. A husband's farts and belches indicate to his wife that he does not regard her worthy of the respect he would show to other women. His rude behavior, ill manners, and base observations speak to her only of disdain and disregard. If he dresses like a slob, it says to her that he is not interested in her. As he chews with his mouth open and wipes his face with his sleeve, she feels the spark of sexual attraction die within her. She wonders how she will live the rest of her life with this barbarian. If you treat your wife the way you treat your buddies, she will quickly learn to hate you. Maybe it's true that boys will be boys, but your wife is not a boy. The sooner you figure that out, the better.

SHRUGGING IT OFF

When men take verbal shots at each other, things can get tense very quickly, but ordinarily, a few minutes later, both fellows blow it off and move on. After letting off a little steam, they are back to laughing and having a good time. If they are good friends, neither one will give the prickly exchange a second thought. Men can shrug off criticisms and even insults. They do not ordinarily dwell on them or even necessarily remember them the next day. They don't usually demand an apology. Men prefer to pretend that an uncomfortable moment never took place.

That system might work fine for men. It's good discipleship too. That's the real meaning of what Jesus meant when he instructed his disciples to turn the other cheek and refrain from repaying evil with evil.

Women are not like men. Women are not able to shrug off critical remarks and hurtful comments. Their brains don't work that way. They are neurologically unable to just blow stuff off.

Instead, hurtful words lodge deep in a woman's heart and echo in her mind for years to come—probably forever. She can't help it. If she could blow the memory off and forget about it, she would, but her brain does not work that way. This does not mean that women are poor disciples; it means that women are different from men. Men are warriors. Males cavalierly exchange challenges, instinctually posture around one another, flex their muscles, snarl threats, and mark territory in various verbal and non-verbal ways. They understand verbal sparring as normal guy stuff, so they do not take it too seriously. Most of the time it's just machismo, and it's rarely meant seriously at all.

Women are not wired like that. They have no frame of reference for understanding male bravado, especially when it turns against them. They feel threatened and attacked by the men to whom they look for protection and nurture. What seems like harmless fun or a few meaningless jabs to the husband feels like ruthless emotional battering to the wife.

Don't take shots at your wife. Even friendly little barbs, sarcastic quips, and humorous zingers (such as might be common in the dialogue of television sitcoms) will hit your wife like a slap in the face. She does not have your built-in male ego to deflect those remarks. They cut her to the quick.

When guys are together, they commonly make deprecating remarks about one another for the amusement of the whole company: "Hey, you putting on a little weight there, Al? Might want to start mixing in a few salads." Everyone laughs. Al shoots back, "I got a long way to go to catch up with you, chubby." Everyone laughs again, and the guys exchange a few backslaps. A good time is had by all. Now imagine shooting the same zinger at your wife in mixed company. That would not go over so well, would it?

Nevertheless, this is exactly what happens all the time. Over and over again, a husband makes critical remarks about his wife in front of other people as if she were a guy and should just laugh it off. The poor woman might put on a fake smile, but inwardly the public humiliation absolutely crushes her. The wound to her dignity is so deep that her husband (who probably is still trying to get a few laughs at her expense) cannot begin to fathom the damage he has just done to their marriage. How can she ever trust this man? How can she ever believe him when he says he loves her? Would a man who loves his wife publicly humiliate her?

Here's another thing that commonly happens in social situations: A man's wife says something or does something that embarrasses him. He responds by making a sarcastic remark about her in order to distance himself a little bit from her behavior. For example, she accidently tips over her drink. He rolls his eyes and says, "Maybe you've had too much." Another example: She says something that sounds ignorant to him. He shakes his head to others in company with them and says, "Don't get her started. She doesn't know what she's talking about." These kinds of remarks and comments might be all right between men, but when lodged against one's wife, they are a betrayal of trust. You are supposed to be her source of self-confidence, self-worth, and dignity. She is the weaker vessel, and you are to honor her and protect her. A man should be warding off any incoming insults, not launching them. Instead, you publicly shamed her. You just threw your wife under the bus. She won't forget. Women do not shrug it off. They can't.

FIREBRANDS, ARROWS, AND DEATH

Guy humor usually involves some form of deprecation or humiliation. From a man's perspective, that's playful fun. From a woman's perspective, it sounds fiendish and demeaning. If you find yourself saying a lot of things that are only "half serious," look out. Your wife takes it all completely seriously, and it alarms and wounds her.

Most women struggle with issues of self-esteem in a way men can scarcely guess. The inner voice of their insecurities constantly whispers accusations: you're not pretty enough, you're not clever enough, people are laughing at you, you made a fool of yourself, no one likes you, and so forth. The demonic assault never stops. This inner turmoil creates a special filter in a woman's head that deflects words of praise and affirmation but amplifies every negative comment, criticism, or cutting remark.

Men do not understand this at all. Most men have the opposite type of filter working in their heads. A man's ego is honed for conflict. He needs to be thick-skinned to compete in the world of men. The praise-hungry male ego deflects and disregards criticism and amplifies words of affirmation. As a result, men assume that women have the same capacity for deflecting negative comments and retaining positive comments, when in fact women deflect praise and retain insults. Your wife has a remarkable capacity to vividly remember every unkind word you have ever spoken to her. In fact, her memory has dramatically amplified the sinister intentions behind each remark. Meanwhile, most of your nice words have fallen on deaf ears. Moreover, a man is not accustomed to doling out a lot of praise because his own mind amplifies praise. He tends to be sparse with words of affirmation.

This disparity between the way men and women filter and deflect words makes the male sense of humor extremely dangerous to a woman. If a man gets a chuckle out of making his wife squirm or hitting her with a witty zinger, he thinks of it as a little harmless fun. She thinks of it as a ruthless, cold-hearted assault.

Perhaps you are smart enough not to make your wife the target of your sense of humor, but even if you target only others with cheap shots and crass remarks, you will come off to your wife as sounding cheap and crass. A woman does not respect a man for his witty ability to deprecate others. She respects a man who comes to the defense of others.

All this explains why men constantly find themselves beseeching their offended wives with the words, "I was only joking!" The Bible says, "Like a madman who throws firebrands, arrows, and death is the man who deceives his neighbor and says, 'I am only joking!'" (Proverbs 26:18–19). To your wife, your insulting and mean-spirited jokes are firebrands, arrows, and death. Jesus says, "On the day of judgment people will give account for every careless word they speak, for by your words you will be justified, and by your words you will be condemned" (Matthew 12:36–37). That ominous warning rings especially true in marriage.

MISCONSTRUING EVERY WORD

The filtering problem described above helps to explain how husbands and wives can be so adept at miscommunication. A distraught husband says, "It's like she turns everything I say backward in her head. If I say, 'I love you,' she hears, 'I hate you.' If I say, 'Let's spend time together,' she hears, 'I want to be alone.' If I say, 'You win,' she hears me say, 'You lose.'" The distraught husband is not alone. Many couples with distressed marriages share similar stories of communication break-down. Men exclaim in frustration, "My wife has the unique ability to misconstrue every word I say and put a malicious spin on it. I can make a completely innocent remark, and she takes it as a personal insult."

Most remarks are not completely innocent, but even if they are, a wounded wife will try to "read between the lines" in order to find the hidden dagger. Pretty soon she takes every word her husband speaks as some sort of dig at her. At this point Satan offers his services as a translator. He interposes himself in a marriage and begins to translate conversations between husbands and wives. His subtle poison manages to twist words into unintended meanings in the heads of both parties. It's amazing to watch. Before long the husband and wife completely lose the ability to communicate, and any attempt at communication brings disaster.

Another difference between men and women further stymies communication. Men tend to take things at face value without looking for deeper meanings. They tend to say exactly what they are thinking (even when they are not thinking at all, as is often the case) with no hidden messages. Women tend to look for underlying, implied meanings. A wounded wife tries to read between the lines to determine what a husband's remark *really* meant. Since he has wounded her so often before, she suspects some concealed malice. She treats her husband's words as if they are a secret code language that must be passed through an internal cipher—namely her own insecurities. The decoded message she derives from that process might have no relationship to her husband's intended meaning. This exasperates her husband. He throws his hands up in the air and says, "That's not what I meant." She is not apt to believe him.

Men with quiet and compliant wives are often completely unaware of the wounds they inflict on their wives every single day. They have no idea that their wives are continually misconstruing their words. Such a husband has no clue that his wife's insecurities have twisted and turned his words backward.

A wounded woman with a particularly low self-esteem might feel that she deserves the abuse, so she simply internalizes it and stores it away in her heart where it poisons all affection for the man to whom she is married. Later, if that man probes into his wife's heart for an explanation, he will be shocked to discover years and years of recordings of his own voice stored away there, grossly distorted, played backward, and echoed with demonic reverb. He will never be able to untangle that mess.

If you feel that your wife misconstrues your words, this indicates that this process is already well underway inside her. You need to change your patterns of communication immediately. The first step involves realizing that she is not a guy. She does not hear things the way a guy does. She does not deflect things the way a guy does. She does not process things the way a guy does.

SARCASM AND CRUDE REMARKS

In their conversations with other guys, men employ sarcasm to make a point. Sarcasm is the use of words that mean the opposite of what you really want to say. We use sarcasm especially in order to insult someone, to show irritation, or to be funny. It's a bad idea to use sarcasm with your wife. Her internal filters are already flipping your words around and playing them backward. A sarcastic remark just aggravates that process. The wounded wife finds sarcastic remarks utterly baffling. The sarcastic husband tries to explain, "I meant the opposite. I was only joking." Too late. Your sarcasm has taken lodge in her heart like a deadly poisonous arrow.

In their conversations with the boys, men often resort to crude jokes and immodest speech. That might get a few laughs from your locker-room pals, but don't try it with your wife. Even if she smiles politely, the godly soul within her recoils from it. A disciple of Jesus should not be trading crude remarks: "Let there be no filthiness nor foolish talk nor crude joking, which are out of place, but instead let there be thanksgiving" (Ephesians 5:4).

DEAL WITH IT

Thanks to our natural psychological defenses, most men have the ability to get over hurts, deal with personal slights, and move on quickly. We are not easily offended, and when we are offended, we are quick to let an affront go and forget about it. God has given men that ability so that we can effectively compete in the world to provide for our families. A warrior who sits down on the battlefield to nurse every scrape and cut will not survive long.

Women do not possess that same capacity, but men do not realize this. Husbands assume that their wives can just "get over it" the way they do. When a woman does not just get over it and move on, the man becomes frustrated with her and tries to prod her along: "You need to quit being so thin-skinned. Toughen up. You just need to let it go and move on." Such a husband is asking his wife to be a man. His prodding does not help her to get over it at all. Instead, he sounds to her like an insensitive bully. It sounds as if he has no concern for her feelings. His words pour salt into her open wounds.

Does a man really want a thick-skinned warrior wife? Probably not. God made women tenderhearted, nurturing, and compassionate because they need to nurture their families and show compassion and concern for their children. The same softness and sweetness that attracts a man to a woman makes her thin-skinned and vulnerable. In this regard the Apostle Peter refers to her as the "weaker vessel." She is fragile like fine china. She is not a cast-iron pot. A man should not expect his wife to be simultaneously feminine and masculine. Expecting her to simply shove emotional pain aside and move on as if nothing has happened will not help. She is not a dude. She is not a warrior. If a woman has been hurt, the man's job is to stop, acknowledge the wound, and show her compassion. Telling her to forget and forgive only wounds her more.

CONVERSATIONS

Men don't need to talk much. They don't need to lock eyes with one another as they engage in conversation. They keep their conversations with each other on the surface, and they exchange few words. Men don't spend hours on the phone talking with their best friends. A man and his college roommate might go for days without exchanging words and never think twice about it. They mind their own business and do just fine.

Most women are just the opposite. Women are verbal. That's how their brains work. They need to talk—a lot. When they talk with other women, they find affirmation in a friend's attentive ear. They make eye contact while speaking. The contents of their conversations might sound like meaningless prattle to a man, but the women are communicating for the sake of communication. They find intimacy and affirmation in the process.

When a husband treats his wife as if she is a man, he inadvertently communicates disdain and disrespect. His silence sounds ominous to her. His inattentive ears are insulting. His failure to look her in the eye when she is speaking communicates complete disregard. He seems uninterested in her. She feels unvalued and unloved.

The man does not intend any disrespect at all. He is simply treating his wife as if she is any other guy. The problem is that she is not a guy.

THE WANDERING EYE

Men are naturally attracted to women's bodies. When some men hang out together, they let their eyes follow women's bodies, and they comment on attractive women: "She's hot. She has a nice ..." Men understand each other. They know that this type of behavior does not imply any disloyalty to one's spouse. It's an idle amusement for them.

Women are not men. If a woman sees her husband's eyes following another woman, she immediately takes it as an offense to her dignity, an insult to her marriage, and a deprecation of her body. It makes her feel ugly and unattractive. She feels that her husband has committed an act of infidelity, and, in some sense, she is right, because Jesus teaches us that anyone who looks at a woman with lust commits adultery in his heart. When a man does this, his wife's insecurities flare up, and she suddenly feels completely inadequate and utterly disrespected. Her heart goes cold, and she wants to die. Meanwhile, her husband is happily and thoughtlessly checking out some complete stranger's assets, indulging in what he considers to be completely harmless and normal behavior. It certainly is normal behavior, but it's not at all harmless. A wife takes it like a punch in the stomach.

If your wife has caught you gazing at other women, you have already breached the sacred unity that she expected from you. If she has caught you leering at photographs of women or feasting your eyes on pornography (God forbid), she cannot help but see you as a spiritual adulterer, philanderer, and traitor to the marriage. She wonders how she can live another day with such a pervert, and she feels as though now she needs to compete with other women for you. She despairs of ever being pretty enough or attractive enough to you.

If a husband does not realize that his wife is not a man, he might even go so far as to make the mistake of commenting on other women. He might say to his wife, "Ellen looked good tonight, didn't she?" He might say, "That blonde at the cash register is a head turner." Since he assumes that he is married to man, he does not think twice about the impact his words will have on his wife. Those words go off in her head like a nuclear bomb, utterly devastating her spirit, blowing away all shreds of self-respect, vaporizing her heart, and shattering her very bones. She might react sharply, surprising her husband who expected her to nod and chuckle in agreement. Or she might say nothing at all as she internally disintegrates.

This same principle holds true regarding any and all comparisons with other women. Remarks like "Why can't you be like so-and-so?" are cruel to a woman. They strike her like a sledgehammer and make her wish she could die. She already felt inadequate around other women. Now she feels that her husband—the one person who is supposed to be on her side in the world—also thinks of her as inferior to other women. Even innocent remarks like "Mrs. So-and-so sure knows how to cook a meatloaf" can wound your wife. As a rule, never compare your wife to any other woman, and never praise another woman in the presence of your wife. This applies doubly in regard to another woman's physical features.

As a disciple of Jesus, you have no business at all looking at any woman other than your wife. If you are foolish enough to leer at women in your wife's presence or, even worse, to comment on their attractiveness, you will lose your wife's heart and her respect. Worse yet, you will destroy her sense of self-esteem and sever her desire for intimacy with you. You can expect your sex life to begin an immediate cool down because she is not man. She is not your buddy. She is a woman.

LINEAR LOGIC

Most men tend to think and reason in a linear fashion—at least we think we do. We apply logic and deduction to troubleshoot situations, calculate strategies for success, and fix problems. If a man thinks his wife is actually another man in a woman's body, he will expect her to think in the same way he does. He will constantly be using logic and linear thought to argue with her. He will run circles around her arguments, ruthlessly pointing out flaws in her thinking and her faulty conclusions. If he was arguing with another man, this tactic might be successful. He is not arguing with another man.

His wife is not impressed with his logic. She probably does not follow it all, and in any case, it does not persuade her. Women do not think the same way men do. Their minds do not necessarily follow a flowchart of linear progressions. God has given them a broader capacity to factor in emotional and spiritual content, intuition, and intangible values. She sees flaws in his logic to which he is utterly blind because they are outside his narrow scope of vision. Her skills are critical in child rearing because children are not rational equations. Husbands do not understand this about their wives. They complain, "She makes no sense! She won't listen to common sense!"

The collision between the male thought process and the female thought process becomes clear when a man asks his wife, "What's wrong?" She tells him the problem. He immediately begins to explain how to fix the problem. She retorts that he does not understand her trouble at all. He tries again. She rebuffs him. Now he is angry. Why is she being so unreasonable? He begins to point out flaws in her thinking. In reality, she was not looking for a fix to the problem, she was looking for sympathy and understanding. The man does not see how sympathy will help improve the situation. The woman does not see how "thinking things through" will change anything.

A wounded wife is further stymied by desperate attempts to defend herself from her husband's logic. The more he presses her with cold, rational facts and obvious conclusions, the more desperately her mind flails for an avenue of escape. To him she seems utterly irrational, so he tries to help by reasoning for her. She does not want him to reason for her; she wants him to listen and understand, support her and back her up.

The husband who does not understand this disparity in cognitive processes will assault his wife with his rational, logical arguments and use his clear thinking to batter her into a corner. He keeps pressing her to admit that she is wrong and he is right, and he keeps bringing stronger and stronger proofs to try to wrest that admission from her lips. She cannot, however, admit to being wrong. God made women with an internal sense of dignity that recoils from bullying and force. A man who forces his wife to admit some fault or admit that she is wrong and he is right shatters her sense of self-worth and dignity. He wins the argument, but he loses his wife. He did not treat her as a woman.

MANHANDLING AND STRENGTH

God has given men physical strength to defend their families and provide for them. Boys enjoy sparring with one another, exchanging punches on the arm, wrestling, and good-natured horseplay. When boys get angry with each other, they exchange blows, but within a few minutes, they return to being best friends.

Women did not grow up that way. Most women grew up dressing dolls, hosting imaginary tea parties, and playing house. If a man thinks of his wife as if she is like any other guy, he is apt to frighten and repulse her. Consciously or unconsciously, she looks to him for protection. She knows she is vulnerable, and she relies on her husband's strength to shelter her from harm. When he turns that strength against her, man-handling her, wrestling her down, or overpowering her in any way, it breaks her trust in him. Even if he thinks he is just funning around with her, pinning her down to tickle her or picking her up to spin her about while she protests, from her perspective he engages in a form of physical abuse. She feels scared and vulnerable, frightened by the very man she looked to for protection.

If (God forbid) he ever strikes her or in any way threatens her, he shatters her trust and permanently scars her soul. A physical bruise might heal over time, but the emotional bruise never heals. A disciple of Jesus must absolutely never raise his hand against his wife. He should never even raise his voice, much less wield his physical strength against her.

A man who strikes his wife is no man at all. He is a brute and bully not fit to be married to a woman. A man who slams doors, punches walls, and kicks chairs is not much better. All these actions speak clearly to the wife, "That's what he wants to do to *me*, and next time, maybe he will." His "blowing off steam" breaks her heart, kills her affection for him, and makes her distrust him. She will immediately begin to emotionally shut down toward him as she attempts to protect herself from the monster living in her house. She may pretend to forgive the outbursts and blows because she is afraid and not because she actually forgives them. Inside her heart, those acts of rage against her will live on forever.

Men sometimes claim to strike their wives in self-defense. "She was attacking me," he simpers. A man who needs to strike a woman in self-defense is truly a coward and a simpleton and not worthy of the name of Jesus. Our Master taught us to turn the other cheek to blows. How much more so if those blows come from one's wife!

A man who thinks of his wife as one of his schoolyard playmates expects to be able to knock her around a bit and then be best friends a few minutes later, just the way he does with his friends. She is not one of his buddies. She is a woman, and she expects to be treated like a woman. A man who turns his physical strength against his wife—for any reason—is no longer acting the way a husband would act. He is acting the way a brute would, the very thing from which he is supposed to be protecting her.

SHE'S NOT A MAN

Women are not men repackaged in attractive feminine bodies. Women are completely different creatures from men with completely different psyches. A man needs to patiently learn to understand and appreciate both his wife's weaknesses and strengths so that he can support her in the areas in which she needs affirmation and help and applaud her in her feminine capacities.

A man must refrain from impish behavior with his wife. He should not expect his wife to shrug off criticism and insults, forgive, and move on. He must be careful to govern his speech, realizing that her internal filters deflect his compliments, amplify his criticisms, and involuntarily invert the meaning of his words. He must remember that she needs intimate conversation and an attentive listening ear. He should never gaze on other women or praise the virtues of other women at all—especially in the presence of his wife! He must not try to bully or coerce his wife with persuasive, logical arguments. He must never turn his strength against her, even in play, and he should certainly never lift a finger to harm her (God forbid). A man who assumes that his wife is one of the guys and treats her accordingly will quickly shipwreck his marriage.

Luckily for you, you aren't like that guy—or at least not anymore. From now on you're going to treat your wife like woman. She's going to notice the difference.

5

CLEAVING TO YOUR WIFE

Our teacher, rabbi, and master never married, but Jesus knew where to find the recipe for a successful marriage. He pointed his disciples back to the story of Adam and Eve in Eden. He said, "Have you not read that he who created them from the beginning made them male and female, and said, 'Therefore a man shall leave his father and his mother and hold fast to his wife, and the two shall become one flesh'? So they are no longer two but one flesh. What therefore God has joined together, let not man separate" (Matthew 19:4–6).

GET OUT THE GLUE

> A man shall leave his father and his mother and hold fast
> to his wife, and they shall become one flesh. (Genesis 2:24)

According to Jesus, God made male and female as two opposite halves that join to form a whole. In order for that union to work, however, the man must leave his father and mother and "hold fast" to his wife. The Hebrew word "hold fast" is *davak* (דבק). It's difficult to translate: "cleave to," "cling to," "stick to," "hold fast to," etc. In Modern Hebrew, the word means "glue." A man must leave his old life behind and glue himself to his wife. That's the essential idea.

Notice that the Bible does not say that a woman must glue herself to her husband. That's not her job.

Learning the difference between a man's role and a woman's role in marriage will spare you a lot of pain and frustration. As we observed in the previous chapter, your wife is not a man. Women are completely different from men. As the Apostle Peter said, a woman is the "weaker vessel," and she must be handled delicately and with great care.

God made men and women different from each other in order to complement one another's weaknesses and shortcomings. When a man understands the respective roles of a husband and wife, he and his wife will form a powerful team with vast spiritual potential. They will be able to weather the storms of life and prevail in the strength of the LORD.

It's a husband's job to cling to his wife, not her job to cling to him. How does he practically do that? He must set aside his personal goals, his amusements, his recreations, his ambitions, his dreams, and anything else in his life that might impede him from sticking to his wife. He must set aside his family, his mother, his father, his friends, and his buddies in order to be glued to her. If he is glued to anything else, he will not be able to properly adhere to her, and a competition will ensue.

Men usually expect the opposite. They expect their wives to set everything aside and glue to them. They expect their wives to sacrifice for the husbands' needs, desires, ambitions, and amusements. That does not work. Women are not spiritually equipped to glue themselves to a man. God has equipped women to glue themselves to their children.

When a man fails to understand this, he feels jealous of everything. He does not understand why his wife always seems to have time for other things but no time for him. He pouts and throws tantrums to get her attention. He criticizes and cajoles her and tries to focus her on his needs. That behavior does not help. She will never glue herself to him. God did not make her with spiritual glue that sticks to a man. God made her with glue that sticks to her children. The despondent husband will say, "You dote over your cats, but you have no interest in me." His wife has glued to the cats because they are in the role of her children, and she has glue for that.

Rather than pout about it, a man needs to recognize that this is how God has made men and women. Problems erupt when the man fails to let go of other things in his life for the sake of gluing to his wife and when he expects the woman to set aside her things and glue herself to him. This man has turned things exactly backward of how they actually work. He wants to be the woman, and he wants her to be the man.

This does not mean that a married man has no life. It just means that he has no life of his own. His life belongs to his wife. When a woman feels confident that her husband is glued to her, she is happy to give him the freedom and latitude to engage in his own interests and pursuits. The moment that she feels he has glued himself to those interests and pursuits instead of her, she begins to fight him. If a woman does try to glue herself to her man, he quickly begins to take her for granted. He feels stifled. He loses interest in her. His heart starts to wander toward other women who are not glued to him so tightly.

There's no use protesting and arguing about it. God himself designed men and women to function this way. Jesus said, "What therefore God has joined together, let not man separate." When a man glues himself to his wife, she reciprocates by receiving his attention, affection, and singular devotion, and the two become "one flesh."

In the Bible, the term "flesh" means "human body." This is the amazing mystery of marriage. When a man and a woman are married, they spiritually and physically unite to become one new human body. Henceforth, neither one is complete without the other. That's why marriage can be so wonderful. That's why divorce is traumatic and tragic. This also explains why infidelity and sexual relationships outside of marriage are so damaging. The apostles say, "Let marriage be held in honor among all, and let the marriage bed be undefiled, for God will judge the sexually immoral and adulterous" (Hebrews 13:4).We are not designed for multiple partners. We are physically and spiritually designed for a committed, monogamous relationship as one flesh.

GLUED TOGETHER

The Bible also commands us to glue ourselves to God: "You shall serve Him and *cling* to Him" (Deuteronomy 10:20 NASB, emphasis added). It's the same word in Hebrew as the one Jesus quoted in Matthew 19:5. This helps us understand what God requires of us when he tells us to *cling* to our wives. In a similar way that we must "cling" to God with singular devotion, serving him and attending to his commandments, we must cling to our wives. The word "cling" cannot mean "serve" in one place and "lord it over" in another place.

When a man has properly glued himself to his wife, she has no doubt about where his loyalties and priorities lie. She knows that she is the most important thing in his life, and her insecurities vanish. She becomes free to blossom into the godly woman God has designed her to be.

A man who has glued himself to his wife makes her priorities into his priorities. Her needs are his first concern. Her family is his family.

Her interests, desires, and hopes are the things that interest him, that he desires, and that he hopes for—not for their own sake but for hers.

A properly glued man has no interest in anything that will separate the union he shares with his wife. Other women do not exist. Intruding family members are of no consequence. Financial stresses, pressures from work, and the worries and concerns of life cannot weaken his adhesion to her. Even ministry does not separate him from making his wife his first priority. He knows that God has joined him to his wife, and since God has done the joining, he will not let anything separate him from her.

The glue of clinging to his wife requires him to treat her with appropriate respect. He never criticizes her or insults her. He is quick to defend her. He does not raise his voice with her. He does not hesitate to forgive—even if she never asks for forgiveness—and he carries no grudges against her.

He does not expect her to cling to him that way. He knows that is not her job. Instead, he is happy to fulfill his God-given role and be the one with the glue. Again, this does not mean that a man must roll over and play dead for his wife. He will find that when she is confident that he has glued himself to her, she will be happy to give him plenty of slack to pursue his own interests, hobbies, and ambitions. On the other hand, if she ever feels that he has allowed those things to tear him away from clinging to her, she will resent them and resent him for pursuing them.

ON HER SIDE

A man who is glued to his wife is on her side. He's got her back. That means he does not stab her in the back. He does not complain about her to others—not to his parents, not to his friends, not to anyone. She does not need to fear that he is bad-mouthing her with his buddies.

A story from the Torah illustrates this principle. In the book of Genesis, we read that the Egyptian Pharaoh was delighted when he heard that Joseph's brothers had come to Egypt. He immediately made provision to bring the entire family to Egypt so they could survive the famine in safety and comfort. He provided wagons for the move. He promised them the best of the land of Egypt.

Pharaoh's warm welcome of Joseph's brothers reveals an important detail about Joseph's time in Egypt. Apparently, the entire time he had been in Egypt, he had never told anyone the story of what his brothers had done to him. Pharaoh, at least, had never heard the tale of how Joseph's brothers had abducted him and sold him. Had he known the story of the villainous deed, he would not have extended the warm welcome.

When someone wrongs us, it is natural for us to tell others about it. We want to tell others about how it happened to garner their sympathy and support. For some reason it soothes the wound to know that others are aware of the injustice committed against us. We seek out sympathy and simultaneously commit a small act of retaliation. By telling people about another person's misdeeds and unkindness, we turn opinions against that person. While it gratifies us to turn others against the person who hurt us, it is wrong. Even though every bit of the story is true, when we tell others about how we have been wronged, we are in danger of indulging in the sin of evil speech, and we are returning evil with evil.

Joseph loved his brothers and his family so much that he could not bear the thought of having them defamed. He did not want Egyptians saying to one another, "Did you hear about the nasty thing that Joseph's lowlife brothers did to him?" Joseph kept the entire episode to himself. The only thing he ever said about his past was the vague explanation, "I was indeed stolen out of the land of the Hebrews" (Genesis 40:15). His love for his brothers compelled him to protect their reputation.

Instead of emulating Joseph, who was concerned about protecting the dignity of his loved ones, it seems we do just the opposite. A man is out with his friends when they begin discussing the frustrations of marriage. Taking the opportunity to unload his hurt feelings, the man lets his friends know how unfairly he suffers from his wife's nasty and irrational behavior toward him. Why would we sell out the person we love this way? The husband who does this has higher regard for a little bit of sympathy from his buddies than he does for the reputation of his wife. That's not being on her side. That's not being glued to her.

COMPLETE THE CIRCUIT

The Torah says that when a man clings to his wife, the two will become one flesh, that is, a new, single creature. The man is the head of this one-flesh new creature. The woman is the body. The holy Apostle Paul says, "I want you to understand that the head of every man is Christ, the head of a wife is her husband, and the head of Christ is God" (1 Corinthians 11:3). This means that when a man is properly glued to his wife, he can function as her spiritual head, just as the Messiah is his spiritual head, and God is the spiritual head of Messiah. Headship implies leadership and authority, but in this equation it also implies completing a spiritual circuit. The man receives God's spiritual vitality, grace, and blessing through his relationship to the Messiah because Messiah is his head. The Messiah receives it from God, then he passes it to the man, and the man passes it to his wife. With the circuit complete, the wife spiritually lights up like a light bulb and radiates godliness and true spiritual beauty.

If the husband is not properly glued to his wife, the two of them will not properly become one flesh, and the husband will not be a proper head. He will still act as if he is the head and she is the body, but he will be trying to exercise authority and leadership over a body to which he is not properly attached. That can't go well. She will resist him every step of the way. Moreover, he will not be able to pass God's spiritual vitality, grace, and blessing on to his wife. His misplaced headship will spiritually starve her, and she will circumvent her husband to find spiritual life. She will find spiritual headship in other places: her pastor, her rabbi, her Bible teacher. Or (God forbid) she will look outside the faith for vitality and begin to feed off the things of this world. She might become a slave to materialism or even (God forbid) look for other men to satisfy her craving for true masculinity.

SUBMITTING TO THE HEAD

As the head of his wife, the husband feels he has the right to exercise authority over her. Paul says, "Wives, submit to your own husbands, as to the Lord. For the husband is the head of the wife even as Christ is the head of the church, his body" (Ephesians 5:22–23). The husband will probably show his wife this Bible verse and others like it. If he is not properly glued to her, however, he cannot expect her to submit to him. Imagine a body walking around with its head lolling off, hanging by a few threads. That head will not have much control over the body's movements.

The man gets angry and demands his wife's submission. He tells her that she is in disobedience to the Scriptures because she is not submitting to his authority. This brings up an important point that seems to be completely missed in most Bible teaching: submitting to one's husband is an obligation addressed to wives, not men.

Not every commandment in God's Law applies to everyone universally. For example, certain commandments apply to priests and not to laymen. Some commandments are incumbent upon Jews but not Gentiles. Some commandments apply to men but not to women. Each person stands before God responsible for the commandments given to him, not for those given to someone else.

The apostles addressed the injunction that requires a wife to submit to her husband only to wives—not to husbands. The Bible does not say, "Husbands, make your wives submit to you." You will never find a commandment in the Bible that says, "Men, subjugate your wives." Ultimately, it's your wife's business whether she submits to you or not. It's her responsibility before God, not yours. If you try to force her to submit, you are overstepping your bounds. You will break the glue and make things worse for yourself.

You are the head of your wife as Jesus is the head of you. Ask yourself, "Do I always submit to him?" Before verbally beating up your wife for failing to bow down to your authority, you should check to make sure that you do not have a big log in your own eye. How can you say to your wife, "Let me take the speck out of your eye," when there is a log in your own eye (Matthew 7:4)?

Jesus does not force us to submit to him. God respects every individual's right of freedom of choice. He does not subjugate us as slaves. He gently calls us into the paths of obedience, but he never forces us. When we disobey him, he is quick to forgive us when we repent. He does not stand over us, glowering and snarling. He speaks gently to our souls with persuasive words of love and grace, but he does not terrorize us.

If a man takes it upon himself to try to force his wife to obey the commandment of submitting to him, he will certainly inspire rebellion and resentment in her heart. Though he may strong-arm her into submitting to his will, she will store that offense away in an increasingly bitter heart. She will learn to see her husband as her enemy instead of her lover. She will grow cold toward him and, perhaps, cold toward the Scriptures, which he has used as a weapon against her. She may even turn her back on God.

A man should imagine how he would feel if someone ruthlessly trampled over his free will and took him prisoner. Would he feel love for this person? Would he want to share a bed with this person?

The husband who demands submission from his wife makes her feel disrespected and unvalued. She wonders why her husband, who claims to love her, treats her as if she were a child. She does not feel like his partner at all anymore, and she wishes for a way out of the marriage.

On the other hand, if a husband has properly glued himself to his wife, he will not demand something contrary to her will, and she will not resent his leadership. He will not need to point out her obligation to submit to him because she will reflexively do so. When she fails to do so (and she will, unless she is perfect, like you), she will regret it and correct her course herself. Even if she does not, however, the husband must remember that her submission or lack thereof is between her and God. It's not his problem.

GIVERS AND RECEIVERS

A man shows that he is glued to his wife by giving everything he has to her and bestowing gifts upon her. Jesus said, "It is more blessed to give than to receive" (Acts 20:35). This is good news for men because we are natural givers. Men find their greatest fulfillment in life through contributing and giving. A man on a team delights in being the one to give the rest of the team an advantage. A man serving a king takes great pride in the gifts and tribute he offers to his lord. A man working for an employer finds fulfillment in a job well done.

Men delight to shower gifts on the women they love, and women delight in receiving gifts from the men they adore. There is a spiritual dimension to the idea that males are the givers and females are the receivers. The idea manifests in our physical bodies. Physiologically speaking, men are the givers and women are the receivers.

In every functional relationship, one person needs to be the giver and the other person the receiver. Between God and men, God is the giver, and men are the receivers. Between men and women, men are the givers, and women are the receivers. Between women and children, women are the givers, and children are the receivers.

In the spiritual realm, men receive from God and pass the gift of spiritual beneficence to their wives. Their wives receive it and pass it on to the children. This is the natural order of spiritual headship.

When a man understands his role as a giver, his joy will know no bounds as he seeks more ways to bestow goodness on the woman placed under his charge. He will take it as a personal challenge to out-give himself. For example, in the realm of merely physical gifts and provision, the rabbis give this sagely wisdom:

> A man should always eat and drink less than his means allow, cloth himself in accordance with his means, and honor his wife and children more than his means allow. Why? Because they lift their eyes to him, but he lifts his eyes to the one who spoke and the world came into being. (Talmud, b.*Chullin* 84b)

God designed women to function as receivers. Biologically, they must receive from men in order to beget children. In conventional arrangements, they rely on receiving sustenance and provision from their men, which they can pass on to the children.

The Torah says that a man cannot be drafted for military service or mandatory civil service for the first year of his marriage. Why? Because he needs to remain at home for that first year to gladden his wife: "He shall be free at home one year and shall give happiness to his wife whom he has taken" (Deuteronomy 24:5 NASB). This law reveals God's intention for the marital arrangement. The man's job is to make his wife happy. The Hebrew literally says, "He shall gladden his woman that he has taken." Too often men think that their wives are there to gladden them. According to the Bible, it's just the opposite. The man is supposed to be the one making her happy.

Problems erupt in a marriage when a man expects his wife to function emotionally as the giver. He wants to be the receiver. He expects her to meet his emotional needs when God has made him to meet hers. He expects her to fulfill his sexual needs (as if it were possible to satiate a man's libido) when God has made him to fulfill hers. He expects her to affirm his ego and prop him up when God has made him to affirm her and dispel her insecurities. In such a situation, the man wants to be married to a man. He wants to be the woman.

Obviously the man receives a lot from his wife, and along the way, she does meet his emotional needs, fulfill his sexual needs, affirm his ego, and prop him up. When the man expects these things and demands them from his wife, however, she pulls away from him, leaving him more frustrated and desperate than ever. She finds him repulsive because, deep inside, she realizes he is acting like a woman.

When a man thinks only of satisfying his own needs and appetites, he fails to be the giver that God designed him to be. No matter how much he takes to satiate himself, it will never be enough because a man cannot find fulfillment in taking. He finds meaning, purpose, and validation only when he acts in his capacity as a giver.

A man who thinks that marriage is a fifty-fifty give and take is in for a grave disappointment. Marriage is not a business arrangement. The man who wants to take from his wife and use her to fulfill his needs will fail to fulfill hers. He will be so focused on himself and his needs that he will scarcely even notice her own emotional and spiritual needs. In his greed for her love, affection, attention, submission, and sexual intimacy, he will trample her. If he forces her to become the giver in the relationship, he will leave her feeling spiritually empty, dry, and lifeless. She was not designed to be the giver.

The worthy disciple of Jesus seeks to emulate his Master: "A disciple is not above his teacher, but everyone when he is fully trained will be like his teacher" (Luke 6:40). The Son of Man came to give his own life for his bride, not to demand anything from her to meet his needs. A man should learn to pray, "Father! May I receive from you and give to her, and protect me from thinking that I need anything from her at all!"

SERVANTS

A man shows that he has glued himself to his wife by serving her and protecting her. God made men to be his servants. The Bible says, "The LORD God took the man and put him in the garden of Eden to work it and keep it" (Genesis 2:15). The Hebrew more literally translates to say, "He put him into the garden of Eden to serve her and protect her." (The word "garden" is feminine, so the pronouns are as well.) Unless a man is doing his job of serving and protecting, he feels unhappy and unfulfilled. He might try to fulfill his psychological emptiness with all sorts of toys, amusements, games, and entertainments, but these all leave him feeling frustrated. Men are not happy unless they have some form of service to perform. This is why the Bible says, "There is nothing better than that a man should rejoice in his work, for that is his lot" (Ecclesiastes 3:22).

When a man understands this and quits trying to fill his time with vanity and foolishness, he comes alive in his service to God. He finds joy and satisfaction in keeping the commandments, serving his Creator, and laboring for the sake of the kingdom of heaven. Suddenly all his days are filled with meaning and purpose. He is eager to get up in the morning and return to his service. He derives satisfaction from a job well done, and he falls into bed at night, exhausted. He sleeps well in the contentment that he has served well that day.

Boys in today's world grow up removed from the chores and labors of an agricultural society. Many turn to all sorts of trouble, vices, sins, and addictions to fill the emptiness because, without work, they have no purpose. Nothing can be more frustrating for a man's soul than lack of purpose.

The Bible refers to us as God's servants. Jesus taught several parables in which he compared his disciples to servants. He himself said, "The Son of Man came not to be served but to serve" (Matthew 20:28).

Men become unhappy when they reverse this and desire to be served. Ironically, men always think that they will be happy if others serve them. In reality, men find fulfillment only in being of service to others—not in being served. A married man who expects his wife to be his servant has turned the biblical value of servanthood upside down. He wants to be the woman in the marriage, and he wants his wife to be the man.

The Bible places a man in a position of headship over his wife, but biblical headship involves servanthood. Jesus told his disciples, "The rulers of the Gentiles lord it over them, and their great ones exercise authority over them. It shall not be so among you. But whoever would be great among you must be your servant, and whoever would be first among you must be your slave" (Matthew 20:25–27). This means that as the head over your wife, you need to consider yourself to be her servant. Like Adam in the garden of Eden, your job is "to serve her and protect her." If a man can internalize this principle, his frustrations with marriage will melt away. He will take joy in his career because he sees it as a service to his wife. He will take joy in household tasks and family responsibilities as a good servant serving his master. He will cease procrastinating and putting off projects and home improvements that his wife nags him about because he will realize that, as a servant, he has to obey her wishes.

As he begins to serve her with enthusiasm and consistency, he will find the satisfaction that men derive from servanthood. Moreover, her nagging will taper off as she tries to figure out who this guy is and what he did with her real husband. Through his service to his wife, the man demonstrates that he adheres to her, just as the Bible says regarding the LORD: "You shall serve Him and cling to Him" (Deuteronomy 10:20 NASB). The two cannot be separated. A man cannot cling to God without serving him. Neither can he cling to his wife without serving her.

When a man tries to impose his authority as the biblical head of the family without first proving his right to that authority through biblical servanthood, he places the cart before the horse. His wife and children will not respect a man who demands to be served and demands their submission. That sounds like a dictator, not a disciple of Jesus.

BE A MAN

Marriages turn into war zones when a man tries to take a woman's role. When the man wants his wife to glue herself to him, and he wants her to be the giver so he can be the receiver, and he wants her to serve him, he is trying to be a woman. Unfortunately, that's exactly what happens in most dysfunctional marriages today. The man worries about how his wife is failing to meet his needs. He throws emotional tantrums, pouts around the house, slams doors, and feels sorry for himself as if he were a woman. A godly woman does not want to be married to another woman.

A woman needs a man who will remain rock steady through her emotional turbulence. Contrary to pop psychology, women do not want men who are in touch with their feminine side. They do not want men wrapped up in emotional problems and insecurities. A woman has enough emotional problems and mood swings of her own without having to worry about her husband's inner psychology.

Peace in the home depends on both men and women fulfilling their respective roles. A man glues himself to his wife; he does not expect her to cling to him. A man gives. A man serves. A man sets aside his desires and his needs for the sake of others. A man forgives. A man does not seek honor and respect from his wife; he gives those things to her. A man sympathizes with his "weaker vessel," handling her like the fragile, precious flower that she is.

A man can accept humiliation and criticism patiently without retaliating with a barrage of self-defenses and accusations. A man does not need to raise his voice or slam a door. He provides the calm in the midst of his wife's emotional ups and downs. Like Jesus in the storm at sea, he can speak a word and still the wind and the waves. He does not need his wife's affirmations because he knows that, while she lifts her eyes to him, he lifts his eyes to God. A man acts as the head of his wife by serving her and prioritizing her. He stands in the gap between her and the Almighty as Messiah does for him.

You are that man, a high priest over your household. You can do it. Just keep your eyes fixed on Jesus, and make it your goal to be the closest thing to Jesus that your wife will ever know.

6

THE CRITICAL SPIRIT

A re you ready to learn how to revolutionize your marriage? This chapter will give you one of the most important secrets to turning your marriage around and finding your way to shalom in the home, but this secret is also the most difficult challenge in the entire book.

Don't think that one reading of this chapter will do the trick. You are going to have to come back to this chapter and read it again and again and again, praying over every paragraph. In fact, this chapter is going to ask you to do something that you will say is impossible. But it's not impossible with God's help: "Is anything too hard for the LORD?" (Genesis 18:14).

THE DIFFERENT SPIRIT

When Moses sent out the twelve spies to explore Canaan, ten came back with a negative report. They accurately described massive fortifications, armies of gigantic men, and all the obstacles to success. They recommended calling off the whole invasion and returning to Egypt. Two spies, however, Joshua and Caleb, ignored all that and delivered a good report. They said, "The land, which we passed through to spy it out, is an exceedingly good land. If the LORD delights in us, he will bring us into this land and give it to us, a land that flows with milk and honey" (Numbers 14:7–8). But the people listened to the ten spies instead of Joshua and Caleb. So the LORD punished them by consigning them to forty years of wandering in the wilderness. He declared that they would never see the promised land that they had rejected. Instead, their bodies would be buried in the wilderness. Their children, however, would be privileged to enter the land.

Only Joshua and Caleb were given permission to enter the land. The LORD said that Caleb would be allowed to enter the land because he had "a different spirit" (Numbers 14:24).

Caleb demonstrated his different spirit when he gave his report about the land. He and Joshua had seen the same Canaanites, the same fortifications, and the same difficulties as the other spies had, but they had come to a different conclusion. The other spies saw those things as obstacles. Caleb and Joshua saw them as opportunities for God to demonstrate his glory.

Some people like to regard themselves as "realists." You may have heard someone say, "I'm not a pessimist; I'm a realist." Maybe you have said that yourself. This saying infers that an optimistic person is not realistic. Accordingly, the only honest and correct way to view the world is to point out the deficiencies, difficulties, and inevitable failures.

There is nothing special about having a "realist" attitude. Anyone can point out problems. Everyone can criticize. It takes no talent to be a naysayer. Maybe you know someone who is a rigid realist. Such a person is usually not realistic at all. Instead, a person like that demonstrates a tendency to emphasize the negative, ignore the positive, and disregard miracles. To that person, answers to prayer are mere coincidences. Words of encouragement are irritating. Behind the realist's veneer of cynicism, a life of dark self-absorption and self-pity lurks.

The ten spies were such realists. They assessed the situation in terms of their own reality—a faithless reality. From that perspective, things looked pretty dismal. They felt that a quick march back to Egypt was probably the best solution.

Caleb and Joshua were a different kind of realist. To them reality was not as big as God. They assessed the situation in terms of a reality that included faith. The difference between Caleb's spirit and the spirit of the ten spies is the difference between seeing life through the eyes of faith or faithlessness.

The optimist says the cup is half full. The pessimist says the cup is half empty. The man of faith gives thanks that the cup is half full, and he marvels that God will either make the half cup sufficient to meet his need or miraculously fill the cup completely.

People say, "Every cloud has a silver lining." The optimist sees the silver lining. The pessimist sees the cloud. The man of faith sees both the cloud and the silver lining. He gives thanks to God who made the cloud, provides the rain, and clears the sky.

God said he heard the grumbling and the complaints of the children of Israel:

> How long shall this wicked congregation grumble against me?
> I have heard the grumblings of the people of Israel, which
> they grumble against me. (Numbers 14:27)

The Talmud comments on the story of the ten spies and their evil report by saying, "One who spreads evil reports almost denies the existence of God."[21] God hears *our* complaints too. Complaints, criticisms, and murmuring destroy our quality of life, and they will destroy a marriage as certainly as fire devours dry kindling.

If a man ever hopes to have *shalom bayit* (household peace) in his home, he must strive to have a different spirit such as Caleb did. He cannot settle for being a "realist." He needs to be a man of faith, and a man of faith is something extraordinary.

TRIP TO THE ZOO

Imagine going to the zoo with a cranky and undisciplined five-year-old. You take the child to see the lions, but he is sulking because you did not buy him candy. You take him to see the zebras, but he is angry because he does not want to hold your hand in the crowd. You take him to see the monkeys, but he is having a tantrum because he wanted French fries. You buy him French fries, but he complains that they are soggy and leaves them uneaten. At the end of the day, he did not see lions, zebras, and monkeys, nor did he eat French fries. He has had a miserable day, and so have you. The child transformed what could have been a wonderful experience into a horrible experience for no good reason.

As an adult, it is easy to look at a situation like that and realize how foolish the unruly child is being. It's harder to realize that our own complaints, grumbling, and murmuring sound just as petty to the Almighty. Adults are usually sophisticated enough to disguise their childish tantrums and inner discontentment. We disguise them as serious adult issues, concerns, and complaints. On closer investigation, many of those issues tend to be no more than sulking over soggy French fries.

The worst part is that this is not a trip to the zoo. This is your marriage and your life. If you spend it fussing and sulking, you will never enjoy the good things God is continually doing for you. You will never even notice them—and you will be spiritually killing your wife.

CRITICISM AND COMPLAINTS

God has invested human beings with skills in critical thinking for the sake of problem solving and improving things. If we did not have a healthy critical apparatus, we would never create, invent, solve, or improve. In this sense the critical thought process is a gift from God. Men are particularly adept at seeing problems, diagnosing causes, and attempting solutions. These are problem-solving skills. We use these skills to fix the furnace, diagnose a mechanical problem, balance the budget, avoid a traffic jam, and undertake a thousand other daily tasks. When we apply the same skills to try to fix our wives, however, we run into problems.

A man sees something wrong with his wife's behavior. He sees some way she could improve or something she could do to achieve a better outcome. He sees a problem and tries to solve it. He tells her. She reacts badly. This happens over and over again, until soon he is resorting to sarcasm to point out her deficiencies to her. Nothing is getting fixed. More things are breaking.

Imagine if you decided to fix your car by changing the water pump. In the process you broke the fan and damaged the radiator. Trying to fix those things, you snapped a belt and sheared off several mounting bolts. Every time you tried to fix one thing, you damaged another, making the mechanical problems worse and worse. If that happened, maybe you should not be trying to fix your own vehicle. Most men would have the common sense to realize that they are not making things better.

Quit trying to fix your wife. It's not your job. That's God's job.

The most important skill that a man must master if he ever hopes to have a happy marriage is the ability to refrain from criticizing his wife. Peace will never rest in his home so long as he offers his wife criticism, corrective comments, or any derogatory remarks. Even so-called constructive criticism must be avoided at all costs.

A godly man would never dream of physically striking his wife, but what he does not realize is that, for a woman, every comment, correction, criticism, and remark feels like a slap in the face. An insult or derogatory remark feels like a punch in the face. Don't expect to have a happy wife if you keep verbally slapping her around and punching her out.

THE THIN-SKINNED WOMAN

Remember that, in previous chapters, we learned that women are different from men. This is especially true when it comes to the ability to receive criticism. No one likes to be corrected or criticized. A man bristles with anger when anyone, especially his wife, criticizes him. But generally speaking, men cool off quickly and forget about the insult to their dignity. We rationalize and tell ourselves that the person offering the comment simply had it wrong, or perhaps, if we are spiritually mature, we even accept the criticism and attempt to correct our behavior. Most men are not still mulling over the comment the next day, the next week, or the next year.

Women are completely different in this regard. A woman's brain works completely differently. She does not have the same type of internal wiring, and she can't just forget about it or get over it, even if she wants to.

Most of the time a woman's dignity, self-respect, and ego are incredibly fragile. She derives a great deal of her sense of worth from the opinion of the men in her life—particularly her father and her husband. This is how God designed her. Remember, Messiah is the head of the man, and the man is the head of his wife. God created the marital relationship in this manner. If the head turns against the body, it disrupts the whole order and damages the relationship. If a man criticizes his wife, he is no longer "clinging" to her, nor is he acting as "one flesh." Every negative remark severs those bonds.

Women are not designed to withstand criticism and correction. Critical remarks do not slide off women like water off a duck's back, and women cannot shrug off derogatory remarks. Every negative comment lodges in a woman's heart like a poison dart. There it remains. It stays there forever, continually injecting its poison. Your wife might not be able to remember her shopping list or the balance in her checkbook, but she can remember every unkind thing you ever said to her. She can recall remarks you made twenty-five years ago—word perfect.

Don't blame her. This is how God made women. Do you want to be married to a woman or to a man? Don't tell your wife that she is thin-skinned or immature. Don't expect her to grow up and start taking it like a man. She's not a man, and she will never get used to your critical remarks. They will never do her any good. They will never improve her behavior. They will never correct her in any manner. They will only batter her soul and kill her love for you.

SHE CAN DISH IT OUT

Husbands always object, "She can dish it out, but she can't take it." The typical unhappy husband says, "My wife criticizes every little thing I do. She never stops criticizing me. But if I say one little thing to her about something she does, she flies into a rage." That's not at all unusual. In fact, it just proves the point about the difference between men and women. God has made men broad shouldered and strong enough to endure criticism with patience and fortitude. He has not made women that way, so don't expect your wife to be any different from other women.

A woman derives her spiritual and emotional vitality from honor. This is why the Apostle Peter says, "Live with your wives in an understanding way, as with someone weaker, since she is a woman; *and show her honor*" (1 Peter 3:7 NASB, emphasis added). Her happiness and spiritual well-being depend on her husband's honor for her. Therefore, any disrespect or dishonoring remark spiritually wounds her, drains her vitality, and emotionally destabilizes her.

Even if a man delicately attempts to correct his wife with the most gentle and respectful words possible, she feels devalued and suffers internally. When a man unleashes vicious and brutal words at his wife, those cutting words lacerate her soul.

A woman wants to be perfect in her husband's eyes. If she does not feel that way, feelings of jealousy, insecurity, self-hatred, rage, and despair overwhelm her. She feels unloved by the only man who is supposed to love her. Her husband's insults, sarcastic remarks, and "constructive criticisms" shatter her self-image and sense of value. Wives do not have a sliding scale of self-appraisal. A woman either feels perfect in her husband's eyes, or she feels worthless and hated. Her self-esteem has only a two-way switch. It's either on or it's off, and it can't stay on when her husband's criticisms and ugly remarks keep flipping the switch off.

A wife with a critical husband finds life miserable and unbearable. She has no joy, and the light in her eyes goes out. She goes through the dreary routine of life, day after day, without hope or radiance. She waits for death.

SHOW HER HONOR

Simon Peter, speaking of the wife, tells the husband to "show her honor" since "she is a woman." Jewish law teaches that criticism is the opposite of honor. For example, the Ten Commandments say, "Honor your father and mother." Jewish law interprets this to mean that one must not criticize, correct, insult, or in any way shame one's parents. To do so is to dishonor them. The same principle holds true in regard to one's wife. If the Bible commands us to "show her honor," then we must refrain from negative comments that will dishonor our wives.

The Apostle Paul says, "Outdo one another in showing honor" (Romans 12:10). This calls for chivalry. It is appropriate to open the car door for a woman, to stand aside and open a door as she passes through, to rise in her presence, to offer her a seat at a table, and so forth. All these antiquated manners communicate honor for a woman. How much more do the standards of chivalry call upon a man to honor his wife by refusing to allow negative words about her from escaping his lips?

Godliness requires us to learn how to bridle our tongues. James says, "If anyone thinks he is religious and does not bridle his tongue … this person's religion is worthless" (James 1:26). If a man can't refrain from making critical remarks about his wife, what good is his religion? James says, "Do not speak evil against one another, brothers. The one who speaks against a brother or judges his brother, speaks evil against the law and judges the law" (James 4:11). The same rule applies to your wife. "Do not grumble against one another, brothers, so that you may not be judged; behold, the Judge is standing at the door" (James 5:9).

IDEALISTIC AND UNREALISTIC

Many men claim that this teaching is unbiblical and out of balance. They say that the prohibition on criticizing or correcting a woman is idealistic and unrealistic. Then they return to their unhappy marriages and carry on with their barrage of corrections as they attempt to fix their wives. Now who's being idealistic? Your wife does not meet your ideals, so you are going to fix her with cutting remarks? Now who's being unrealistic? Watch those marriages go from bad to worse.

On the other hand, men who take this advice to heart and make a serious effort to implement it see an immediate improvement in their home life.

"But surely there are those occasions when it is absolutely necessary to say something to correct one's wife." Yes, there are such occasions, but not nearly as often as one would think. In later chapters we will discuss the criteria that define such a situation, and we will learn positive ways to influence a wife and correct her—without words.

The fool thinks that with a well-placed comment here and a clever remark there, he can steer his wife and correct her. In reality, a man cannot change anyone, much less his wife. Face it. We cannot even fix ourselves. How many times have you made a commitment to repent or fix some area of your own personal life and failed? True repentance is a gift from God. We hardly have the power to correct ourselves, much less someone else.

You cannot change your wife. The more you try, the worse you make your relationship, and the less likely the possibility for any improvement whatsoever. Only an idealistic and unrealistic idiot would continue to use negative remarks and corrective comments to change his wife.

REACTION TO CRITICISM

When a husband criticizes his wife, he makes matters worse. For example, suppose a husband criticizes his wife for her tardiness. He is tired of waiting for her while she gets ready to go out the door, so he says, "You are always making us late!" Now he has made his point, and he feels better about things.

She does not stop to think, "He might have a good point there. Perhaps I should try to be more punctual. Next time I will begin my preparations fifteen minutes earlier so that I do not make my husband late for his appointment." Not one of those thoughts passes through her head. Instead, when she hears the criticism, she cannot understand it. It sounds like a foreign language to her. She does not hear him at all. She only thinks, "Why is he attacking me? Why is he always angry with me? Can't he see I'm doing my best? Why is nothing ever good enough for him?" She feels her insecurities rise up to choke her, and her self-confidence crumbles. She immediately tries to defend herself. She might blast back at him with a barrage of hostility and arguments, or, worse yet, she might retreat into a shell of silence. The negative comment does nothing to improve anything. It does not fix the problem; it only damages the marriage.

Husbands in difficult marriages complain that their wives constantly blow things out of proportion, make mountains out of molehills, and continually attack them over the smallest things. These are all symptoms of a wounded spirit. When a wife feels as though she needs to defend her own dignity, she does so by retaliating to his criticism. Oftentimes her retaliations seem completely irrational and unreasonable to him. The truth is that she is sad and brokenhearted from her husband's unkind words. She cannot forget them and move on. They haunt her day and night, and she cannot find any way to escape from the emotional pain that her husband so cavalierly inflicts upon her. She strikes at him out of despair.

GOD'S DAUGHTER

What made Caleb and Joshua different from the other ten spies? All twelve saw the same land. They saw the same Canaanites. They saw the same obstacles, but somehow Caleb and Joshua came back with a positive, faith-affirming report, while the other ten spies came back with a negative report. Surely the other ten spies were just being "realistic." But the man of faith is not "realistic"; he is spiritual, he is supernatural. Caleb and Joshua deliberately chose to see only the good instead of the bad. They saw the bad in light of God's power and promises as opportunities for the Almighty God to demonstrate his glory. This is why the LORD said, "My servant Caleb has a different spirit."

A husband of faith needs to have a different spirit the way Caleb did. He must deliberately choose to see only the good in his wife and never to look at the bad. He must not even acknowledge the bad, but rather he should leave it with the LORD, who made his wife according to his purpose. After all, the man is married to God's daughter.

Imagine if your daughter married a young man, and after a few months of marriage, your new son-in-law said to you, "Your daughter is full of flaws. She's a real case. I try to straighten her out, but she won't listen to me. She's always complaining, and she's completely irrational. She drives me crazy." Would you sympathize with that complaining son-in-law? Instead, you would be more inclined to box his ears and tell him to either shape up or ship out. By the same token, your wife is God's daughter! Are you going to complain to your Father-in-law in heaven about his daughter, or are you going to get down on your knees and thank him for the precious gift he has given to you?

Remember that in the garden of Eden, the LORD made Eve as a "suitable helper" for Adam. In the Psalms, the psalmist says, "From where does my *help* come? My *help* comes from the LORD, who made heaven and earth" (Psalm 121:1–2, emphasis added). This refers to one's wife, his "suitable helper." A man should read the psalm to say, "From where does my *wife* come? My *wife* comes from the LORD, who made heaven and earth." Judaism teaches that God selects a man's wife for him. There are no accidents or mismatches. God selected exactly the one woman in the whole earth that you need for the sake of your soul and your mission on earth. God's ways are not our ways. His thoughts are higher than ours. He knows what we need, and he makes no mistakes.

If a man complains about his wife or makes negative comments, he is actually complaining against God who has selected this perfect woman for him. He is saying, "Almighty God, you made a mistake when you gave this woman to me. You must not realize that I deserve something better." Such an arrogant and spiritually blind man is not worthy to stand in the presence of the Almighty whatsoever. So who are you to complain about your wife or make negative comments to her? Are you wiser than the LORD?

SATAN'S LITTLE HELPER

Caleb and Joshua chose to see the good instead of the bad. You need to deliberately choose to see only the good in your wife and not even acknowledge the bad. The LORD says, "Should not you have had mercy on your fellow servant, as I had mercy on you?" (Matthew 18:33). You claim to love your wife, but pointing out her deficiencies and dwelling on her weaknesses is the exact opposite of love. In fact, you are speaking the language of Satan, the accuser of the brethren. If you criticize your wife, you do the devil's work for him.

You claim to love your wife, but real love "bears all things" and "endures all things" (1 Corinthians 13:7). "Love covers all offenses" (Proverbs 10:12). "Love covers a multitude of sins" (1 Peter 4:8). If you are criticizing your wife, pointing out her deficiencies, or trying to "fix" her, you are certainly not loving her. Instead, you are exposing her sins and weaknesses. In this capacity, you act as Satan's helper, tearing her down and stripping away her dignity.

THE LOG IN YOUR OWN EYE

The Bible says, "You shall surely rebuke your neighbor, and not bear sin because of him" (Leviticus 19:17 NKJV). This rule encourages us to hold one another accountable to the standards of God's Word, even going so far as to rebuke our brother in order to turn him from sin. One might suppose that this obligation includes rebuking one's spouse. On the contrary, the Master warns us, "Why do you see the speck that is in your brother's eye, but do not notice the log that is in your own eye?" (Matthew 7:3).

Since a husband and a wife are one flesh, a wife's sins and weaknesses are not hers alone, they also belong to the husband. The speck he sees in her eye is a log in his own eye. In this regard, God uses a man's wife to show him the log in his eye. If a husband sees a weakness or deficiency in his wife, he should immediately use that as an occasion to search his own heart for a corollary weakness or deficiency.

For example, a man feels his wife dresses immodestly. Does he let his hungry eyes feast on immodestly dressed women? A man feels his wife does not fulfill her sexual obligations to him. Has he kept himself sexually pure for her, or has he defiled himself by gazing at other women or pornography (God forbid) or masturbation (heaven forefend)? A man feels his wife gossips. Has he kept himself from the sin of evil speech? A man feels his wife spends money frivolously. Has he been a proper steward of his finances, or has he been indulgent with himself? In every area, a man should use any deficiency he happens to detect in his wife as a message from God that he himself needs to repent in some area. This simple exercise keeps his criticisms and critical attention focused in the right place: his own sinful ways.

The Bible tells a man to glue himself to his wife, but he cannot glue himself to her so long as he takes note of her shortcomings and trumpets them aloud. Instead, that behavior necessitates both a psychological and emotional distancing from his wife. If a man truly glues himself to his wife, he will repent on her behalf and beseech God to be merciful toward her.

NOT HER RABBI

Sometimes men misconstrue the Bible's principle of a husband's spiritual headship to imply that a man has the responsibility of spiritually steering his wife. He thinks of himself as her rabbi or her pastor. He must point out her errors, sins, and deficiencies and put her on the right path. He imagines that he is her spiritual guide, and as such, he has the authority and the responsibility to constantly correct her. This man is a fool.

You are not your wife's rabbi. You are not your wife's pastor. You are her husband, and you are supposed to be one flesh with her. Her weaknesses are your weaknesses. Her sins are your sins. You are supposed to be on her side, covering for her, not correcting her. You cannot be one flesh and glued to your wife while taking a spiritual and psychological position of higher authority over her, looking at her with condescension.

Think about it. Would you want to be married to a clergyman who was constantly watching you and correcting your every mistake? You bristle when your wife tells you to clear your dishes from the table! How is she supposed to handle a husband who thinks he is her spiritual boss?

Your wife cannot take that kind of correction from you. Aside from the fact that women do not take correction well, your wife knows you too well to respect you as a spiritual guru. She has seen you naked, so to speak. She knows you too personally and intimately to think of you as a spiritual giant who has the right and authority to speak into her life and reprimand her. As soon as you attempt to do so, her mind fills with all your shortcomings. She thinks to herself, "Who does he think he is to tell me how to behave when I know all about his misdeeds and weaknesses?" And she is correct.

Instead of trying to be your wife's spiritual superior, try being her friend. Remember that you are supposed to be on her side. You are supposed to be glued to her and one flesh with her, defending her and speaking on her behalf, not condemning her.

If a husband is supposed to be to his wife what Christ is to his assembly, that means forgiving her sins, interceding for her in prayer, and sheltering her from judgment. A husband who points out her sins and judges her is not acting the way Messiah would, he is acting like Satan.

WORDS OF AFFIRMATION

> When words are many, transgression is not lacking, but whoever restrains his lips is prudent. (Proverbs 10:19)

An old adage says, "If you can't say something nice, don't say anything at all." That's good advice for social situations but not good advice for marriage. If you can't say something nice in marriage, you need to try harder.

This chapter has one simple message: Don't criticize your wife in any way whatsoever. As it says in the prophecies of Micah, "Guard the doors of your mouth from her who lies in your arms." Instead of making comments to your wife or trying to correct her with your so-called constructive criticism, from now on you must commit to speaking words of affirmation into her life.

God has given you the gift of speech with the power to curse or to bless. From now on, commit to using your tongue only to bless your wife with positive words of affirmation that build up her self-esteem. Look for every possible opportunity to speak well of her. Praise her for the little things she does. Praise her for the big things. Laugh at her jokes, and tell her how charming she is. Thank her for everything that you ordinarily take for granted: the dishes, the laundry, the diapers—whatever the case may be. If she falls behind in domestic duties, don't point it out. Find something else to praise her for. Look for opportunities to sincerely praise her in public, in front of other people. Build her up in every possible way. Tell her how attractive she is—not as a ploy to get her into bed but genuinely for the sake of building her self-esteem. Smile at her. Look her in the eye when she is talking to you. Listen to her, and acknowledge her thoughts and affirm them.

THE SCALE OF MERIT

One of the maxims of Jewish wisdom instructs us to "judge every man in the scale of merit."[22] That means we should consider a person's good qualities and not his or her bad qualities. Judging a person in the scale of merit is the same as giving someone the benefit of the doubt. It's a big principle in Jewish ethics. Rather than assume the worst about a person, one should always try to assume the best.

For example, if your boss at work says something to you that seems rude and insensitive, you should not think to yourself, "What a jerk!" Instead, you should remind yourself, "He's a human being like me. He has good days and bad days. He probably has something on his mind. He did not mean to insult me." That's what it means to judge in the scale of merit.

It takes just a little bit of effort, but it can transform your whole life. It's sort of a game you can play throughout the day in every encounter with other human beings. Whenever you have an interaction with another person, find some positive virtue about the person. Whenever you have a negative interaction, take a mental step back and give the person the benefit of the doubt. There is always more to the story, and since you don't know the whole story, you are not in a position to cast stones.

The same rule applies even more to your wife. Rather than assume the worst about her, try assuming the best. Rather than assuming that she acted irresponsibly, assume that she did her best in the circumstances and simply made an innocent mistake. Rather than assuming that she intentionally wants to irritate you with that sarcastic comment, assume that she really is trying to communicate something important, but she doesn't know how to do so without feeling vulnerable. Rather than assuming that she is withholding sexual intimacy from you to frustrate you or reject you, assume that she has a lot on her mind, is exhausted, and simply isn't in the mood as often as a man is. Rather than assuming that she dislikes you, assume that she loves you deeply, but she is having difficulty expressing that love because it is buried under layers of emotional pain.

You get the idea. By giving your wife the benefit of the doubt and judging her in the scale of merit, you demonstrate the "different spirit" of Caleb.

THE HUSBAND WITH CALEB'S SPIRIT

The man of faith has a "different spirit," as Caleb and Joshua had: a spirit of optimism that sees the good in everything and refuses to engage in complaints, criticisms, and murmuring. A husband with a Caleb spirit deliberately chooses to see only the good in his wife and never to look at the bad because he knows that he is married to God's daughter. He knows that God selected exactly the woman he needs.

Men are great problem solvers, but when men try to fix their wives, they create far more serious problems than the ones they were trying to solve. A husband is not his wife's rabbi, pastor, or source for spiritual correction. The most important skill a man must master if he ever hopes to have a happy marriage is the ability to refrain from criticizing his wife because women are not designed to withstand criticism and correction. Every negative comment lodges in a woman's heart like a poison dart. The wife of a critical husband feels no joy, and the light in her eyes goes out.

Fortunately, that's not going to be the case for you or your wife. If you make an absolute commitment to dispense with negative remarks, criticism, corrections, and insults, and if you replace all that satanic communication with godly words that communicate your love, affection, and steadfast devotion, your marriage will immediately improve. Think good, and it will be good. Your wife will wonder who you are and what you did with her real husband! She will never want the old you back. She will love you the way the LORD loved Caleb: "He has a different spirit ... I will bring [him] into the land" (Numbers 14:24).

7

PRIORITY NUMBER ONE

Human beings take things for granted until they lose them. A person never thinks about being grateful for his good health until he suffers sickness. A person takes for granted that he will have another paycheck at the end of the month until he unexpectedly loses his job. We take for granted that our loved ones will always be there until a sudden death (God forbid) shatters that illusion.

Husbands take their wives for granted. Usually by the time the blissfully unaware and self-absorbed husband realizes that his marriage faces jeopardy, he has traveled far past the point at which he could have done something to save it. He has ignored years of warning signs, and now, as his marriage collapses around him, he suddenly realizes that his naïve negligence has cost him the most important thing in his life.

A rabbi has the unpleasant job of meeting with husbands in the midst of marital crisis. The distraught man comes to meet with his rabbi or counselor. He tells him that his wife has left or kicked him out. She wants a divorce. He can't eat. He is dehydrated because the stress of the situation has so physically wrenched his body that he has diarrhea. He can't sleep. He is desperate. He is stalking his wife online and on the street. He can't concentrate. He is missing work. His life has fallen apart. Money flies at his command as he tries to buy her back with expensive presents. He has no interest in anything other than getting his wife back. He is so desperate and emotionally raw that when he does finally have the opportunity to speak with her, his desperation frightens her away even further. It's an ugly picture.

How ironic that now, suddenly, the man's wife is the center of his universe, but for the previous years of his marriage, he hardly noticed she existed. Previously he thought everything was more important than her. Now nothing matters except getting her back.

As explained in previous chapters, God has designed marriage in such a way that a man must leave his own world and pursuits and glue himself to his wife in order to become one flesh. The Bible does not say that a woman must leave her world and glue herself to her husband. The man glues himself to her. In order to glue himself to her, he needs to make her his first priority.

Paul teaches that a married man must divide his priorities between pleasing God and pleasing his wife.[23] This indicates that a man should prioritize nothing other than God himself above his wife, and pleasing his wife ranks on par with serving God. If he places anything above his wife (other than God), he damages the adhesion and separates himself from the one flesh. If he prioritizes his career, work, hobbies, entertainments, friends, or ministry above his wife, he risks losing her and all those things as well.

If you want to be married to a happy woman, make her the center of your life—the most important thing next to God. If a woman believes that her husband cherishes her above all other things, she will find joy and delight in her union with him. She will repay his devotion with her love, fidelity, affection, and kindness. She will honor him and cherish him because he honors her.

A woman's sense of honor and dignity depends upon her husband's devotion. Unfortunately, men are not naturals at offering singular devotion. We are easily distracted, quickly bored, and more than a little bit self-centered. Those failings do not make for a happy wife.

This chapter focuses on making your wife the top priority in your life, but as a man, you will probably rebel at this idea. It's not that you don't love her; it's just that you love a lot of other things, too. To successfully love your wife and give her top honor as first priority in your life, you will need God's help. Your evil inclination will work hard to make sure that, despite your good intentions, your wife and her needs never come first. You will need to sincerely and regularly pray, "Father, please help me place my wife ahead of myself and ahead of other things, and help me place her first in my heart."

Many husbands go through the motions of placing their wives first, but their hearts are not in it. A wife can intuitively sense when her husband is merely playing along for the sake of avoiding confrontation and argument. She is not looking for disinterested, passive cooperation; she is looking for passionate commitment. To truly prioritize your wife and get beyond your own male ego, you will need God's help.

THE INSULATED MAN

Marital happiness depends upon a woman's confidence that she occupies the center of her husband's devotion and that she need not compete with anyone or anything for him. If a man wants a peaceful home (*shalom bayit*) and an Edenic marriage, he needs to communicate to his wife that she is his number-one priority, the center of his universe. It will not be sufficient for him to simply say, "Honey, you are number one to me! The most important thing in my life." She knows better. A man should certainly say things like this at every opportunity, but he needs to back them up with proof.

A husband must leap at every opportunity to show his wife that she takes first place. When she needs something, he immediately attends to that need with alacrity. When she says something, he should fix his attention on her as if she were about to utter the most important thing he will ever hear.

If your wife calls you during work, do you stop what you are doing to take her call? If not, it indicates to her that your work is more important. If your wife is overwhelmed with household chores, do you help out? If not, you clearly communicate to her that her needs are irrelevant to you. If your wife asks you to fix something around the house, do you do it promptly, or do you procrastinate? Procrastination indicates that you do not prioritize her. If your wife asks you to do something with her, such as go out on a date, go shopping, take a walk, or watch a movie, do you make excuses? If so, she knows that you do not value her. If your wife asks you to do something with the children, do you comply with her request, or do you find some excuse of being too busy? If you do, she knows that your schedule is more important to you than she and the children are.

Men are professionals at insulating themselves with important busyness, business, and urgencies that preclude the possibility of spending meaningful time with their families. We excuse ourselves under the pretense that we are doing it all for our wives and children. "I have to work late and over the weekend because I need to provide for my family." "I can't be at my son's softball game because I have scheduled a meeting." "I can't get to that project my wife has been nagging me about because I have important ministry work to do for the congregation." Over and over again we find that everything in life is more important than the things that are most important. When it comes time for our own personal playtime and self-indulgence, however, we are adept at rearranging our schedules, letting a few things slide, and making room for fun. We excuse ourselves by saying, "I deserve the break. I need a little time off for my own mental health."

Our wives observe this pattern of behavior day after day and year after year. They clearly see where they rate on our list: near the bottom. This is not the marriage that your wife imagined when she used to practice appending your last name to her first name. This is not the marriage she dreamed about. She feels like your doormat.

THE INSULTED WIFE

Why does a man need to prioritize his wife? A woman needs to be the center of her husband's life. Women are perfectly capable of living alone, but when they do get married, the spiritual and emotional center of their life shifts. Wives need their husbands' complete loyalty and attention. God designed the chain of spiritual authority in this manner. The Apostle Paul clearly states, "Man was not made from woman, but woman from man" (1 Corinthians 11:8). Therefore the woman derives her essential sense of being from the man. Paul explains, "Neither was man created for woman, but woman for man" (1 Corinthians 11:9). Sometimes men misunderstand the implication of this teaching to suggest that God created Eve to wait on Adam and meet all his needs. On the contrary, he created the woman for man as his opposite—his suitable partner. In other words, without her husband, the married woman's life feels as if it has no meaning—no purpose.

Paul says that man was not created for woman. The man does not need his wife to find purpose in life. Just as Adam lived alone before the creation of Eve, busy with the work of the garden, the man is completely capable of finding purpose, satisfaction, and meaning outside of his relationship with his wife. He can fill his life with all sorts of hobbies and pursuits that have nothing to do with her, and he feels completely fulfilled by them even without her. This is why it is so easy for men to set their wives aside, putting them on a shelf, so to speak, while they stay busy with their own pursuits, interests, responsibilities, and obligations.

That works for husbands, but it does not work for their wives. The wife was made from man and for man. If the man in her life has no time for her or interest in her, her sense of purpose and self-worth deflates like a leaking balloon. The color bleeds out of her life, and soon she lives in a dismal world of disillusionment and constant unfulfilled longing. She might not even be able to explain why she feels so lifeless and constantly angry. She lashes out at her husband over the tiniest provocations without even being able to explain why she behaves that way.

She derives her self-esteem and her sense of value from her husband. If her husband does not prioritize her or make her the center of his life, he robs her of her self-esteem and makes her feel as if she has no value. Her life feels empty.

"The head of every man is Christ, the head of a wife is her husband, and the head of Christ is God" (1 Corinthians 11:3). This hierarchy of spiritual headship means that the disciple of Jesus derives his vitality directly from God through Jesus. The woman derives her vitality through her husband because the husband is the head of the wife. As the rabbis say, "She lifts her eyes to her husband, but he lifts his eyes to the one who spoke and the world came into being."

If other things are more important to her husband than she is, the wife feels spiritually and emotionally destabilized, devalued, vulnerable, and insecure. Feelings of jealousy rise up in her. She wonders if he loves her any longer. She begins to resent those other things that are competing with her for her husband's time, attention, and affection. She feels a quiet anger burning in her all the time. She begins to seek his attention in negative ways, challenging his loyalties, and calling his behavior into question. These are her cries for help.

Husbands react badly to these signals. They turn on their wives and say, "What's the matter with you? Why do you have to be so selfish?" Of course, these assaults exacerbate her feelings of insecurity. She feels unloved, and her heart turns bitter toward her husband.

THE REAL REASON SHE'S UNHAPPY

Many men feel as though their wives constantly barrage them with complaints. She is always demanding this and that. She wants him to spend more time at home, but when he is home, she goes on the warpath with complaints about everything under the sun. He has no idea what she really wants, and neither does she. He says, "She's just an unhappy woman. Nothing is good enough for her." He's right about one thing. She is an unhappy woman. She probably does not even know why she feels so unhappy.

Her complaints and nagging are only symptoms of her wounded heart. Deep in her psyche, she knows that she rates low on her husband's list of priorities. This wound to her dignity festers invisibly inside her, poisoning her whole world. She criticizes her husband and hurls sharp words at him because she intuitively feels that something is out of balance, but she does not know how to express what she is feeling.

The husband fails to recognize these cries for help. Instead, he scolds her and tells her to improve her attitude. That puts her on the defensive. Now she needs to offer a justification for her bad attitude, so she looks for something else to complain about. She does not know why she feels so unhappy, so she keeps grasping at straws.

The real source of her unhappiness springs from her husband's disregard for her.

For example, consider the wealthy man who showers his wife with gifts. She has expensive clothing, jewelry, her own car, and everything she could possibly want. None of it makes her happy. Instead, she feels as if the gifts are bribes trying to buy her happiness and compensate for the disregard that her husband otherwise shows her. The husband scoffs, "I give her everything, and nothing makes her happy." But he does not give her the one thing she actually wants: him. The Bible says that a woman's desire is for her husband.[24] Unfortunately for men, this does not necessarily refer to sexual desire, it refers to psychological need. She desires her husband's friendship, companionship, and undivided attention. No number of gifts can fill that need.

A FOOL AND HIS BRIDE

A Messianic Jewish rabbi was providing Andrew with some premarital counseling, and he asked the young man how things were going. The wedding was coming up in a month. Andrew admitted that he and Dinah had been in a stupid fight over wedding shopping. It all started when she asked him to come with her to pick out colors and fabrics for the wedding. He said in all innocence, "Honey, I don't need to come with you to do that. You go pick whatever you want. Whatever you like is good with me." Inexplicably she blew up at him. He protested, "Dinah! If it was up to me, we would just get married by the Justice of the Peace.

I don't care about the wedding; I just care about you." Naturally this made things worse.

The rabbi said, "Andrew. What are you thinking? Of course you aren't interested in color swatches and fabric samples. You're a man, but Dinah isn't. Dinah has been dreaming about her wedding day since she was little girl. She has imagined it a thousand times. By showing your disinterest in something so precious to her, you crushed her heart. You weren't willing to spend two or three hours of your week on her. Of course she was upset. When you said you would prefer to elope, you broke her heart. She wonders how you could be so insensitive. I know you are just being a guy, but she's not a guy."

Andrew looked stunned. He said, "Wow! I never looked at it from her side."

This is the problem. We never do look at it from her side. Instead, we carry on with our boorish male disregard for the feminine, and we expect our wives to love us for it. Our consistent patterns of selfish disregard for our wives' feelings continually transmit the message: "I don't care about you. You do not matter to me."

ACTIONS SPEAK LOUDER

Most wives suffer from a nagging insecurity about their marriages. Deep inside, sometimes even unconsciously, the typical wife wonders, "Does he still love me?" It's a question that rarely occurs to men. Men assume that their wives naturally love them. But women do not make that assumption. A woman assumes the opposite. She assumes that her husband no longer loves her (or perhaps never did love her) unless she sees that he is prioritizing her as the number-one thing in his life. This is a default state deep in a woman's psyche. She can't help it. Even if she knows better, her natural feminine insecurities whisper, "He doesn't love you." The only thing that can dispel those insecurities is the evidence of her husband's love—evidence that she takes top priority in his life.

Picture it as an on-off switch for some sort of voice track. The "he doesn't love you" voice is always playing in her head until you switch it off by making it clear to her that she is number one in your life. If you neglect her, however, it switches back on by itself.

A husband who is serious about marital peace and his wife's well-being should sincerely pray every day, "Help me to show my wife that she is the center of my life and my first priority. Help her to believe in my love for her and in your love for her."

It does not work for a man to tell his wife, "Honey, you are my top priority." The Apostle James says, "As the body apart from the spirit is dead, so also faith apart from works is dead" (James 2:26). Actions speak louder than words.

A woman's natural insecurities filter out a husband's vain attempts at flattery. Words are cheap when they are not backed up by deeds. Gifts are nice, but they don't mean much in terms of real relationship. Even if you immediately begin to make your wife the center of your attention and the top of your priorities, it will take a long time before she believes it is anything more than a phase. It can't be just a few flowery words, favors, and gifts. You need to permanently move her to the top of your priority list, not for a few weeks or months alone but for the rest of your married life.

A man should think of himself as a servant to his wife. If something is important to her, it should be important to him. If she indicates that it is important for him to be home by a certain time, he needs to make sure that he is home by that time. If she feels that he should be at dinner at six, he needs to set aside any other pull on his time that might make that impossible. A husband who loves his wife is willing to drop everything and rearrange his schedule at a moment's notice if she needs him to do so. A man who tells himself that he needs to prioritize his job or career over his wife so he can provide for her is a fool. Soon he might not have a wife to provide for—except in alimony payments. A man who places his wife second to his religious obligations will inspire his wife to hate and resent his religion and his God. A man who goes to hang out with his buddies when his wife wants him home tells her that he values his friends more than her. She will resent his buddies.

Many wives complain that their husbands do nothing around the house to fix things. The living room needs to be painted, the plaster is cracked, the leaves need raking, the gutters are plugged—the list goes on and on. Men reply that they are too busy with work and other important things to keep up with it all. The list gets longer and longer. That type of procrastination frustrates a wife because she intuitively realizes it means that her husband does not value her. It's not really the dripping faucet that makes her so angry, it's the fact that her husband promised to fix it weeks ago and still has not done so. This proves to her that he does not take her seriously or care about her requests.

ALACRITY

Most men do not mean to disrespect their wives or demote them in any way. It's just that men tend to procrastinate. A woman says, "Please take out the garbage." The husband agrees to do so, but he does not do so immediately. He wants to finish what he is doing first. A few minutes later, he forgets. The next day, the garbage still has not been taken out. This simple pattern of behavior repeats itself a thousand times over in every area of life. Procrastination tells a wife that her needs and requests do not matter to her husband and that he perceives her as a nuisance.

Procrastination sours a relationship by placing a wife's needs, concerns, and requests behind whatever random thing the husband might be occupied with at the moment. For example, a wife says to her husband, "I'd like to go out for an evening." He says, "Let's do that some time." He does not mean to put her off, but as the days go past, he never makes the plans, and it never happens. A wife says, "You should spend some time with the children." The husband thinks, "I'll do that as soon as I have time." He will never have time.

When it comes to serving God and serving one's wife, a man must act with alacrity. Most men do not even know the meaning of the word. Alacrity means "a quick, cheerful readiness to do what is required." Alacrity requires a person to immediately set aside what he is doing and attend to the matter at hand without delay or procrastination. When we do not attend to our wives with alacrity, we communicate disrespect. It's the same as saying, "I hear you, but you and your needs are not as important as my other interests and responsibilities."

Alacrity also requires him to serve his wife cheerfully and without grumbling. Many husbands are adept at communicating their displeasure as they carry out their wives' requests. Deep sighs, rolling eyes, and sulking body posture tell a wife that her husband resents her for intruding on his time. Then the husband says, "I did what she wanted, and she still isn't happy!" His bad attitude speaks louder than words: "You have no right to ask something of me!"

TIME FOR TALK

How does a man show his wife love and respect? A talmudic adage says, "If your wife is short, bend down and hear her whisper."[25] This piece of marital advice from the Jewish sages teaches us how to honor our wives.

One of the most important things a man can do to demonstrate his love for his wife is listen to her. Most women are verbal, and they emotionally connect through conversation. It does not necessarily need to be deep or meaningful conversation. It can be about anything at all or nothing at all.

Women need conversation. Many men can go through a day perfectly happy not to speak a single word. Women need to communicate. To show your wife that she is important to you, that you value her, and that you respect her, you need to spend time listening to her and talking with her every day. It does not matter if you are not interested in what she has to say. The point of the conversation is not necessarily the contents or subject matter. Women seek the intimacy of communication. Women rate communication with their husbands above sexual intimacy. How would you feel if your wife treated sexual intimacy with you with the same vapid level of polite but lifeless enthusiasm that you show her in conversation?

As a man, you are probably a professional at tuning out your wife while she speaks to you. You probably have the natural male ability to completely disengage your mind from the conversation and think about something else or do something else while she speaks. While she is telling you all about her day at work or the latest funny thing that one of the kids did or how things went while picking the kids up from school and so forth, you are able to think about something completely different, occasionally nodding to indicate that you are listening. Actually, you are not listening at all.

After talking for a while and not getting much in response or feedback from you, your wife might ask, "Are you listening to me?" You lie and say, "Yes, of course I am." Then she tests you, "What was I just saying?" The remarkable thing is that, although you were not listening whatsoever, your devious male brain has a short-term playback mode, so you can immediately repeat the last few sentences she uttered. All men have this ability. The truth is, you were not listening at all.

If you want intimacy with your wife and want her to feel valued and cherished, change that mode of communication immediately. When she speaks to you, stop what you are doing, stop what you are thinking about, and listen to her. Look into her eyes while she speaks, and then reply to her thoughts. Participate in the conversation. Don't just nod. Don't watch TV or look at your computer or your smartphone while she is speaking. Be there with her in the moment, and make the effort to be a genuine friend to her.

Sometimes a man with young children comes home after work looking for peace and quiet, but his wife has been penned up with the children all day, longing for adult conversation. A husband needs to recognize this basic female need and honor it if he wants his wife to feel loved and respected. Would you rather have her find an intimate emotional connection somewhere else or with someone else (God forbid)?

IN-LAWS

Jesus teaches, "No one can serve two masters, for either he will hate the one and love the other, or he will be devoted to the one and despise the other" (Matthew 6:24). Does this mean that a man cannot serve both God and his wife? Not at all. The Bible teaches us to honor our wives and love them as part of our service of God. On the other hand, the Master's words teach us that we cannot be devoted to two different masters simultaneously.

Men commonly make the mistake of trying to remain loyal to both their parents and their wives at the same time. This is a recipe for disaster. The Bible clearly says that a man shall leave his father and mother and glue himself to his wife. If a man continues to defer to his mother against his wife's wishes, he will create war and hostility between the two women. A man most often makes this mistake when he takes his mother's side in an argument or defends his parents in conversation with his wife. For example, a woman says, "Your mother was cold toward me at dinner." The husband says, "You're imagining it. She wasn't cold toward you. Why are you always on her case?" When a man reacts this way, it sends a clear message to his wife that she takes second place behind her mother-in-law. This is a nearly fatal error. You don't have to live with your mother anymore, but you need to live with your wife. Your wife comes first.

The relationship between a wife and her mother-in-law can be prickly under the best of circumstances. Every family event becomes tense. The desperate husband tries to make peace by pacifying both women, but his peacemaking attempts add fuel to the fire. The two women will compete for territory and exchange barbs so long as the husband tries to divide his loyalties between the two. The sooner you make it clear to your mother, your father, and your family that your loyalties are 100 percent with your wife, the sooner you will have peace with both your wife and your family. You need to make it completely clear to your wife that you are on her side, no matter what. You are a team—one flesh. An insult to your wife's dignity is an insult to you.

Naturally, a man wants to honor his father and mother in keeping with the commandment, but he must not do so at the expense of honoring his wife. Your parents have to take second place to your wife.

By the same token, a man should not try to defend his in-laws from his wife. Many women have rocky relationships with their own mothers and fathers. When this is the case, a man might feel tempted to try to correct his wife, telling her that she needs to honor her parents. That's her problem, not his. He has no place trying to play peacemaker between his wife and her parents. His attempts at peacemaking will only escalate the hostilities. His job is simply to stand behind his wife and offer her the moral support she needs. When a wife feels confident because her husband is firmly on her side, she will not feel threatened by her parents, and the hostilities will ease.

On the other hand, the husband must tactfully resist the urge to pile on his wife's troubles with her parents. He must govern his tongue and resist defaming her parents at all. A husband who take shots at his in-laws will quickly find his wife switching sides to defend them. Critical comments directed against a wife's family are in extremely poor taste and will wound a man's wife. They are her family. This type of delicate situation requires intense prayer.

Ask God for wisdom, and do your best to stay out of it. The only remark you ever need to make about your in-laws is to say that they raised an excellent daughter.

THE CHILDREN

Fathers often make the terrible mistake of taking the side of their children, as if they need to defend the child against his or her mother. Nothing could be more humiliating to a woman than to be abandoned and betrayed by her husband in front of her children. The husband who sticks up for the kids, taking their side against their "irrational mother," thinks he is a hero, but unless he is intervening to prevent physical abuse, he has overstepped his boundaries and is doing immense damage to both his wife and his children. By taking the kids' side against their mother, he clearly communicates to his wife that he values her less than the children and does not respect her as a mother.

For example, a young mother reaches the point of exasperation with her unruly five-year-old and launches into a loud verbal scolding. Her tirade might be completely out of balance and disproportionate to the offense. Her husband comes to the defense of the child, reprimanding his wife in front of the child. He feels as if he is doing the right thing. On the contrary, he tears the family apart with his own hands. He humiliates and infuriates his wife, and he plants seeds of distrust, disrespect, and sedition in the children. These types of confrontations have a tendency to become worse as the children grow older and learn to manipulate their parents against one another.

The Ten Commandments tell us to honor our fathers and mothers, but we cannot force our children to honor us. Children learn to honor their mother only by observing their father as he honors her. They learn to honor their father only by observing their mother as she honors him. Husband and wife need to present a united front to their children. Even though they will disagree about child rearing, appropriate forms of discipline, and a hundred other matters relating to the children, they need to maintain at least a pretense of agreement in front of the children. If they turn against each other, the children will become pawns in a ruthless spat with one another. The children will learn to disrespect both parents and pit them against one another. In the end, the children will sustain much worse damage from the breakdown between mother and father than they would ever have sustained by a mother's disproportionate outburst.

Divorce and remarriage with stepchildren involved makes this relationship even more tenuous and difficult. If a man chooses to take the side of his children against their new stepmother, he will be looking at a second divorce pretty soon, and that will only make things worse for his children.

On the flip side, mothers sometimes reprimand their husbands for being too harsh with the children. This is a more normal and appropriate type of relationship. Children naturally perceive Father as the sterner, stricter disciplinarian and Mother as the compassionate caregiver. When your wife tells you to back off from the children, back off. She probably has a much better perspective on the situation. The children will not disrespect their father when their compassionate mother comes to their rescue, but they will learn to disrespect both father and mother if the father takes her role as compassionate defender.

HANGING WITH THE GUYS

Many young men seem to think that marriage should not present any obstacle to their ordinary routine of hanging out with their friends, enjoying sporting events, playing video games, or going drinking with the boys. They carry on as if they were still single men. These behaviors indicate that they have not yet matured enough for marriage. This type of man communicates disrespect to his wife, placing her in the awkward position of coming between him and his fun.

When you married your wife, you made a commitment to glue yourself to her. If you intend to go out or attend some entertainment event, your first thought should be to do so with her. This is not to say that you cannot have social time with the guys. That might be important, too, but not nearly as important as your wife.

Never make her feel as though she is an obstacle to your good times. Never let her imagine that you would rather be with your friends than with her. There will be plenty of times to hang with your friends and for her to spend time with her friends, but as a married couple, these occasions will be exceptions to the rule, not the norm. You prefer each other's company because you are glued together, one soul and one flesh. You do not enjoy the freedom of the single life any longer because you are not single.

If your wife feels as though she must compete with your hobbies and your friends for your attention, she will try to keep you from them. If she feels confident that she is your first priority and the center of your attention, she will be happy to give you plenty of time to spend with your friends and pursue your hobbies.

THE WORKAHOLIC

When a man's family scores low on his priority list, everything else comes first. He might spend a few hours of "quality time" with them here and there, but his wife and children know that they are not as important as his work. He is an achiever, a most-valuable employee, with a schedule simply jam packed. He chases success and constantly aspires to achieve more.

Some husbands claim, "I do everything for my wife. I work hard to support her. I buy her gifts and presents. I take her out for dinner. Nothing makes her happy." That's true. Gifts and special gestures ring hollow to her because she knows that she is merely an afterthought in her husband's busy schedule. Is she supposed to feel grateful when her husband manages to squeeze her into his life? She gave her life to this man, but he does not seem to appreciate that gift. A few trinkets here or a reluctant night out on the town there do not compensate.

The busy man tells his wife and children that he must work so much to provide for them. He stays so busy for their sake, but that's not really the case. A closer look reveals that even his busyness with work is all selfish.

Generally speaking, men derive their sense of dignity and self-worth from work and service. Generally speaking, women derive their sense of dignity and self-worth from their husbands and children—especially if they are not in a career of their own. A man can find total fulfillment in his job or career. His role as a valued employee or an important part of a business stokes his ego and grants him the type of affirmation and fulfillment that his soul craves. By contrast, his wife's nagging, critical remarks and dismissive behaviors deflate him and make him feel unloved and unvalued. For this reason, whether consciously or unconsciously, he throws himself into his work, career, or even religious ministry where he can receive the constant morphine drip of accolades and congratulations.

His wife quickly learns that she takes second place behind her husband's important work and priorities. This saddens her. The "he doesn't love me" switch goes back on. Infuriated, she rewards him for his disinterest in her with more negativity. Her emotional assaults inspire him to bury himself even deeper in his work where he finds his affirmation. The cycle spirals on until husband and wife become virtual strangers.

A husband can save his marriage from this ugly outcome if he intentionally places his wife and her needs ahead of his work, career, or ministry. He can achieve no greater success in life than a happy marriage. As he continually demonstrates to his wife that she takes first place in his life—far ahead of projects, promotions, and applause—she will begin to provide him with the positive affirmation he seeks outside the home.

A man needs to remember that his affirmation comes from God alone. He should not seek the applause of men at all. He should find his fulfillment and self-actualization in God. Then he will not need the love of men or the praises of his wife to feel good about himself. He will be able to serve both his work and his wife in appropriate measure because he does not depend upon either one for his own sense of validation.

DON'T SMOTHER HER

A man must work hard to continually show his wife that she takes first place in his life, but at the same time, he should be careful not to smother her with his affection and attention. Just like men do, women also need space. She needs time alone and social time with girlfriends. Just like a man does, she needs secure boundaries, a sense of privacy, and her own pursuits and interests.

A man who constantly breathes down his wife's neck, scrutinizing her and hanging on her apron strings, so to speak, makes a woman feel uncomfortable and claustrophobic. If a man becomes unbalanced and overzealous in gluing himself to his wife and making her the center of his universe, he might communicate desperation. Nothing repels a woman faster than a man who appears to be desperate for her. A woman does not want a man who continually lays at her feet, scraping for her attention. She wants a man strong in his own sense of self-confidence and independent in his identity yet who dotes on her nonetheless. A man who comes across as needy and groping for her affirmation makes her uncomfortable. Such a man has nothing to offer her. He wants to take from her, not give to her. A husband should pray for wisdom in this matter. He needs to draw his essence, vitality, and sense of self-confidence directly from the LORD. Then he will have vitality and attention to give to his wife rather than sucking it from her.

Instead of smothering his wife with unwanted attention or affection, he should help her cultivate her own interests and pursuits. He should encourage her to pursue those things that inspire her, whether they be in entertainment, education, study, vocation, or avocation. He should give her the sense that it's OK to have her own space, her own interests, her own tastes and preferences, and her own hobbies, even if they are not things that draw his personal interest. A man should help his wife develop a sense of purpose and passion independent of her roles as wife and mother. By applauding her and supporting her as she pursues her own interests, he makes her feel like number one without feeling squished.

THE LITTLE THINGS

Showing your wife that she takes first place in your life consists of a lot of little things that add up to communicate love, respect, and admiration. Take the time to tell your wife all the things you love about her. Applaud her for the good things she does. Spend time with her. You can enjoy fellowship with her by helping her with tasks such as washing the dishes, doing yard work, or preparing for Sabbath. Keep her on your radar at all times. Leave her little notes expressing your affection. Call her on your lunch break just to chat. Send her a text message just to say "I love you." Surprise her with flowers for no particular reason. Remember important occasions such as anniversaries and birthdays, and plan ahead to make them special.

Most importantly, pray together. Ideally, spend some time together each day in prayer. You don't have to be a spiritual giant to lead your wife in prayer. Just a few quiet words together in the presence of the Father will open portals of blessing into your home.

THE PAYOFF

Making your wife into your top priority means making the important things in life the most important. A married woman derives her vitality from her husband because of the spiritual hierarchy: "The head of every man is Christ," and "the head of a wife is her husband" (1 Corinthians 11:3).

The real source of a married woman's unhappiness often comes from her husband's disregard for her. When he ignores her, places other things ahead of her, prioritizes his work or his fun ahead of her, he devalues her. A husband must not divide his loyalties between his wife and his family, and he must not take sides with his children against her. The godly man places his wife second only to God.

Maybe this chapter makes it sound as if a husband can have no time to himself, no time to pursue his career, no time to develop his own interests or enjoy life at all. He must be a slave to his wife, ready to leap to meet her every whim. On the contrary, once a woman realizes that she really is her husband's first priority, she will relent from constant demands and tests of character. As long as the "he doesn't really love me" switch is flipped off, she will not feel compelled to nag at him. She will feel happy and confident in her relationship, and her insecurities will no longer drive her to continually pester her husband and test his loyalties. She will respect him and grant him the freedom to invest in his own pursuits and pastimes without feeling threatened by them. When she lacks that security, however, she feels compelled to continually compete for her husband's attention.

The husband who puts sincere work into making his wife into his first priority, second to nothing and no one else, will receive the immense payoff of a low-maintenance woman who does not require constant assurances. The wise man realizes that this payoff will be worth far more than the investment of time and attention that he must make on the front end. In reality, a woman does not want her man following her around doggedly like a butler or hanging over her shoulder. Once she knows that she rates first in his life, she will prefer to give him his space because she herself needs space.

8

THE LOG AND THE SPECK

Your wife is a human being. That means she is imperfect. Not only that, she is a sinner. A husband needs to learn to deal with these basic, obvious realities.

Human beings tend to overlook, justify, and rationalize their own shortcomings while fixating upon and condemning the shortcomings of others. That's just normal, natural behavior for both men and women. But the Bible calls upon us to be abnormal and supernatural. Jesus teaches us not to look at the shortcomings of others. Instead, when we see a character flaw or some shortcoming in another person, we should take that as a reminder of our own sins and imperfections:

> Do not grumble against one another, brothers, so that you
> may not be judged; behold, the Judge is standing at the door.
> (James 5:9)

Jesus teaches that to the same extent we concentrate on the sins and imperfections of others, God will concentrate on our own: "Judge not, that you be not judged. For with the judgment you pronounce you will be judged, and with the measure you use it will be measured to you" (Matthew 7:1–2). This principle of measure for measure in matters of judgment is fundamental to both the teaching of Jesus and the teaching of Judaism. Rabbinic literature contains several parallel sentiments:

> Hillel said, "Do not judge your neighbor until you have
> reached his place." (m.*Avot* 2:5)

> The Holy One, blessed be He, said to Israel, "The same mea-
> sure which a man gives is measured out to him." (*Exodus
> Rabbah* 25:9)

> By the same measure with which a man measures out to others, they [i.e., heaven] measure it out to him. (m.*Sotah* 1.7)

> He who calls down [God's] judgment on his neighbor is punished [for his own sins]. (Talmud, b.*Rosh HaShanah* 16b)

> All the measures of the Holy One, blessed be he, are measure-for-measure. (Talmud, b.*Sanhedrin* 90a)

In simple terms, this means that if we are strict and severe in condemning others for their shortcomings, God will be strict and severe in condemning us. The inverse also holds true. A person who judges others favorably will receive the full measure of favor in return:

> Judge not, and you will not be judged; condemn not, and you will not be condemned; forgive, and you will be forgiven; give, and it will be given to you. Good measure, pressed down, shaken together, running over, will be put into your lap. For with the measure you use it will be measured back to you. (Luke 6:37–38)

Naturally, these principles also apply to the way we judge our wives.

LOOK THE OTHER WAY

The man who concentrates on his wife's failings and weaknesses invites God to concentrate on his own. When you live with someone, it's easy to see the person's failings and weaknesses, but it's low and unloving to focus on those things. Love looks the other way: "Love covers all offenses" (Proverbs 10:12); "Above all, keep loving one another earnestly, since love covers a multitude of sins" (1 Peter 4:8). A man who focuses on his wife's shortcomings is not loving her. He says to himself, "Why does she behave that way? Who does she think she is? Why does she treat me like that? Doesn't she realize that she has deep character flaws?" This man has chosen not to love his wife. Rather than covering over offenses and covering over a multitude of sins, he is dwelling upon offenses and sins, making a list and checking it twice. But love keeps no record of wrongs; "love bears all things" (1 Corinthians 13:7).

When a man pays attention to his wife's deficiencies and flaws, he cannot help but verbalize them at some point. He feels an irresistible urge to point out to his wife how she is wrong, why she is wrong, and where her weaknesses are. Perhaps the cutting words will spill out in the heat of an argument (God forbid), or perhaps he will make a sarcastic comment or criticism in an unguarded moment. Once he has launched the poison arrow, he can never take it back. It always finds its mark and buries itself deep in her heart.

His wife cannot understand why the man she depends upon to protect her, guard her, and care for her would turn against her and attack her. Why would he want to expose her weaknesses? Why would he delight in hurting her?

The godly man must learn the art of looking away from any perceived deficiencies in his wife. He should train his mind to refuse to see them. When dark, critical thoughts arise in his mind, he should drive them out. He should recognize at once, "These are the words of Satan speaking in my ear," and he should rebuke the adversary, who seeks only to destroy his marriage. He should remind himself, "I love my wife. I am on her side. Love covers offenses and sins. Love keeps no record of wrongs."

REBUKING A SINNER

But let's just suppose that your wife does have some problems and issues that you feel obligated to correct. For example, perhaps you have observed her treating someone else unfairly. You feel that you have a moral obligation to correct her. After all, the Bible says, "You shall surely rebuke your neighbor, and not bear sin because of him" (Leviticus 19:17 NKJV).[26] If you see your wife sinning, don't you have an obligation and duty to correct her?

Perhaps certain circumstances require a husband to rebuke his wife. These will be discussed in a later chapter along with the right and wrong way to rebuke. For now, let's consider how the rabbis understood this commandment. The rabbis understood the commandment "You shall surely rebuke your neighbor" to be mitigated by the words that follow immediately: "And you shall not bear sin because of him." They explained this to mean that a person must be exceedingly careful not commit a transgression himself in the process of rebuking his neighbor. For example, if a man rebukes his neighbor and causes him public shame or humiliation, then he has committed a sin.

Based on this warning, a man should never rebuke his wife. A man cannot practically rebuke his wife without sinning against her, causing her shame and humiliation and wounding her dignity. In the eyes of heaven, the sin he commits against his wife by rebuking her will weigh heavier in the scales of guilt than the sin he attempted to correct.

The Jewish sages discussed at length this unpleasant obligation of rebuking one's neighbor. They noticed that the Torah repeats the verb—"you shall *surely* rebuke"—for emphasis.[27] They proposed several explanations for the repetition. Rabbi Israel ben Eliezer (the Baal Shem Tov) explained that the double expression teaches that one should first reprove himself. This particular teaching is in line with the saying of the Master: "First take the log out of your own eye, and then you will see clearly to take the speck out of your brother's eye" (Matthew 7:5).

Judaism warns against carelessly rebuking and reproving others. Rabbi Eleazar ben Azariah said, "I wonder if there is anyone in this entire generation who knows how to properly deliver a rebuke?"[28] He lived in a generation of great sages and wise men, yet he felt that none of his colleagues were of a spiritual caliber worthy to rebuke another.

If that was true of Rabbi Eleazar and his colleagues, what makes you think you are qualified to start rebuking your wife? Remember, you are her husband. You are supposed to be on her side. God did not appoint you to be her rabbi, her pastor, or her judge. He appointed you to glue yourself to her. The moment you begin to rebuke your wife, you are no longer honoring her, and she will take it as a grievous sign of your disloyalty to her.

The Talmud wisely mitigates the impossible responsibility of continually rebuking all sinners by juxtaposing Leviticus 19:17 with Proverbs 9:8 as follows:

> Rabbi Ilea stated in the name of Rabbi Eleazar son of Rabbi Shimon, "Just as a man is obligated to rebuke a sinner who will heed him, scripture commands him not to rebuke a sinner who will not heed him." Rabbi Abba stated, "In that case, it is a duty not to rebuke a sinner who will not heed, as it says [in Proverbs 9:8], 'Do not reprove a scoffer, or he will hate you; reprove a wise man, and he will love you.'" (b. *Yevamot* 65b)

Jewish law derives from this proverb that just as one is obligated to rebuke a sinner in order to correct him, he is also obligated not to rebuke someone who will neither heed the rebuke nor correct his behavior. This prohibition certainly applies to husbands. Do you really think that rebuking your wife will correct her behavior? If men are honest, they will admit that they do not really expect any good or positive corrections to result from rebuking their wives. They just want to blow off steam and deliver some choice remarks.

Both men and women have a hard time taking a rebuke from anyone, but a rebuke from a spouse feels inappropriate. A wife finds it exceedingly difficult to receive a husband's rebuke. It only angers her; it does not correct her. Therefore, when a husband rebukes his wife, he transgresses the prohibition on rebuking a sinner who will not heed him.

THE LAW OF THE LOG AND THE SPECK

Rabbi Yeshua teaches us an important principle for dealing with other people's shortcomings. This is the law of the log and the speck. When you see a shortcoming or sin in someone else's life (the speck in your brother's eye), remember that you are overlooking your own sins and deficiencies (the log in your own eye). Rather than focusing on someone else and trying to correct the other person, we should use the opportunity to correct our own lives.

Have you ever noticed that Jesus repeats this teaching three times in three subsequent phrases?

> Why do you see the speck that is in your brother's eye, but do not notice the log that is in your own eye? (Matthew 7:3)

> Or how can you say to your brother, "Let me take the speck out of your eye," when there is the log in your own eye? (Matthew 7:4)

> You hypocrite, first take the log out of your own eye, and then you will see clearly to take the speck out of your brother's eye. (Matthew 7:5)

Our Master always spoke succinctly and directly to the point. He did not needlessly repeat himself. Each of these three statements contains a separate lesson.

First, he asks, "Why do you look at another person's shortcoming but fail to notice your own deep flaws?" With these words he correctly diagnoses the human condition. We always notice other people's faults, but we are almost completely blind to our own. This first statement implies that looking at another person's sins and shortcomings betrays spiritual blindness. A person who is honest with himself about his own sins and shortcomings feels too ashamed to be leering at those of another. If a man saw himself as God sees him—filthy with sin and selfishness—he would never even consider mentally criticizing someone else for his sins.

Second, Jesus asks, "How can you verbally criticize someone else or try to correct another person's behavior when you yourself are guilty of the same things and worse?" Whereas the first statement warned us not to criticize someone mentally, the second statement warns us not to attempt to correct another person's behavior when we need to correct our own. Only a spiritually conceited person would try to fix a problem he sees in someone else when he himself has the same problem or worse.

Third, Jesus says, "To try to correct someone else when you yourself need correction is hypocritical. Before you rebuke someone else, rebuke yourself. Before you try to correct someone else, correct your own behavior." Once you have successfully eliminated all sin and spiritual conceit from your own life, then you will be able to see clearly to actually help someone else. This does not mean that a man should work on correcting his own behavior so that he will be free to correct his wife. The point is that he needs to learn to turn his critical gaze away from her and focus it on himself.

THE MIRROR

Rabbi Menachem Mendel Schneerson (the Lubavitcher Rebbe) once said something to the effect of, "When a person criticizes someone else's character flaws, it indicates that he himself suffers from the same flaws." That teaching affirms Jesus' law of the log and the speck. The flaws and deficiencies you detect in your wife are there to teach you about your own.

Every man who wants to correct his wife should instead learn to play the log-and-speck game. The rules to the game are simple: When you see some flaw, sin, or shortcoming in your wife, turn it around and use the opportunity to search your own life for the corollary failing.

For example, suppose you notice that your wife is lax with personal devotions. Is God trying to communicate to you about your own neglect of Bible study? Suppose you notice that your wife is often irritable and complains. Is God tired of listening to your complaints and ungrateful murmuring? You feel angry that your wife is not showing you enough sexual affection (a common complaint). Is God showing you how he feels when you deny him the intimacy of focused, regular prayer? You notice your wife speaking unkindly about someone else. Is God sending you a message about your own tendency to engage in evil speech?

By playing the log-and-speck game, a man will teach himself to turn his critical apparatus away from his wife. At the same time, he will teach himself to receive the LORD's instruction and rebuke. His wife becomes a valuable part of his own spiritual discipline as she reveals to him his own weaknesses through hers.

LISTEN TO YOUR WIFE, SARAH

At this point you are probably thinking, "How is this fair? I'm not supposed to criticize my wife, correct her, or point out any deficiency in her character. I'm not even supposed to allow myself to think a negative thought about her. Meanwhile, she never stops dishing out a constant barrage of petty criticisms, negative comments, ceaseless nagging, and tireless complaints."

Maybe you are right. Maybe it's not fair. But you are a man, and she is a woman, and that's not fair either. She depends on you, but you depend upon God. She directs her unhappiness toward you just as you turn to God to express your own in fervent prayer. Moreover, as a man, you are spiritually designed to be able to take correction, rebuke, and criticism. As a woman, she does not have that same capacity.

Aside from all this, a man receives communication from God in the form of his wife's criticisms and rebukes. God uses your wife as his mouthpiece to send you important messages as he works to refine your character and conform you into the image of his Son.

The world has rarely ever known a spiritual giant like our father Abraham, but when Abraham's wife, Sarah, assaulted him with seemingly irrational complaints and capricious demands, "the thing was very displeasing to Abraham" (Genesis 21:11). He felt that Sarah was acting out of line and speaking out of turn. Then the LORD said to him, "Whatever Sarah says to you, do as she tells you" (Genesis 21:12). Even though Abraham was a great prophet who heard directly from God, he had failed to perceive God's will in the matter at hand. God had to speak to him through the complaints and demands of his wife.

The rabbis say that the deeds of the fathers are portents for the sons. This means that whatever happened to the forefathers—Abraham, Isaac, and Jacob—established a pattern for their children to follow. If Abraham needed to heed his wife, how much more do we need to heed our own wives when they chastise us or make demands upon us? Rather than shooting the messenger, we should stop and listen to the message, realizing that God might be trying to tell us something.

FINDING YOUR SOUL MATE

What if you married the wrong woman?

Sometimes married people talk nonsense about having married the wrong person. For example, Peter and Marsha asked their Messianic rabbi to conduct their wedding. The only problem was that Marsha had a friend who did not like Peter. A few days before the wedding, the young couple came to talk to the rabbi. They told him that Marsha's friend had warned her, "God showed me you should not marry this man." The rabbi told Marsha, "If God really had a message like this for you, he could deliver it to you, to Peter, or even to me. He would not speak to you through your friend who already disliked Peter." This seemed to satisfy her, but the entire incident planted a seed of doubt in Marsha's heart. She began to wonder if she should have listened to her friend. Was God trying to warn her? Did God have a different soul mate for her somewhere? As Peter and Marsha began to have the typical difficulties that any young couple experiences, the seed of doubt in Marsha's heart took root and bore bitter fruit. She openly questioned the marriage and began to speak wistfully about divorce and finding her true soul mate. Ultimately, their marriage failed.

How do you know when you have found your soul mate? And what exactly is a soul mate? People who talk about soul mates believe that God has preordained a single individual as a perfect match for each person. A person's ideal soul mate complements his personality perfectly and fulfills his physical, spiritual, and psychological needs. Soul mates are like two halves of the same soul, and if you marry the wrong person, you will never be truly happy because you missed your soul mate. This is not a biblical idea.

The search for a soul mate sounds romantic, but how do you know if the woman you are with is really your soul mate? Isn't it possible that you missed your true soul mate or might still encounter her? What if you were married previously and are now on your second marriage? Was your first spouse your soul mate, or is this one the true soul mate? The soul mate concept is a foolish idea that ultimately discourages people from getting married because they fear that their prospective match might not be their soul mate. For people already married, the soul mate concept leads to discontentment and uncertainty as it becomes clear that the current spouse could not possibly be anybody's soul mate.

The soul mate idea does exist in Judaism today but only as a misunderstanding of the original concept. Yiddish-speaking Jews speak of finding one's *bashert* (באשערט), but *bashert* does not mean "soul mate." *Bashert* means "destiny." Your spouse is your "destined one." How is this different from the romantic soul mate concept? You cannot seek your destined one because you will not know if you are destined to be together until you marry each other. Once you are married, destiny has been fulfilled and proven your soul mate. In other words, your spouse *is* your destined one. The woman to whom you are currently married is the person God has ordained for you. If she was not, you would not be married.

This rule applies even if you are remarried. Your wife—your current wife—is your soul mate. That's why you are married to her.

So don't waste time trying to find your soul mate or dreaming that she is still out there somewhere, waiting for you. She does not exist and cannot exist outside your marriage. Once you are married, you can be confident that your spouse is your true *bashert*.

THE WIFE YOU DESERVE

Men are notorious for feeling sorry for themselves. A man suffering the symptoms of a distressed marriage might say to himself, "What did I do to deserve such a woman?" He fantasizes about having a wife who understands him and meets his needs. This man is a fool. He does not realize that the wife he has is meeting his needs—the needs of his soul.

The fool forgets that God controls everything and that God is the matchmaker. He gave you the wife you have because he knew that she is exactly the wife you need. There are not accidents with God. Nothing is random. The LORD knew you before you were conceived in your mother's womb. He knows exactly what your soul needs. He knows what trials you need to endure in order to complete your mission on earth. He knows what punishments and corrections you need. "Through many tribulations we must enter the kingdom of God" (Acts 14:22). In his love and concern for you, the Almighty personally selected exactly the woman you need to spiritually balance you, polish you, and bring you safely into the kingdom. Paul reminds us, "For those who love God all things work together for good" (Romans 8:28). That includes your wife. God uses her for good in your life, to conform you into the image of his Son.

What makes you think you deserve the perfect woman? Are you perfect? What makes you think you deserve a woman who better satisfies your sexual needs? Who told you that you deserve something better? Who said that you "deserve" anything?

A man says, "But I deserve to be happy." Why? What makes a man think that he deserves to be happy? He learned that value from today's self-centered popular culture, not from the Bible. The Bible never says that every person deserves to be happy. What makes you think that God owes you something? Maybe you deserve a painful, turbulent marriage. We may be sure of this: Not only does God give us what we deserve, he gives us what we truly need.

Once three of us from the First Fruits of Zion teaching team were sitting at dinner when the conversation turned to how each of us found his spouse. One after another, each man admitted that God had spoken directly, either to him or to his wife, saying, "This person will be your spouse." Maybe you did not hear God tell you, "This woman will be your wife." Maybe your wife did not hear God speak either. Nevertheless, there is absolutely no doubt that God arranged the marriage.

He chose your wife for you because he knew that you have certain flaws and weaknesses for which her strengths would compensate. At the same time, he chose her for you because he knew that her flaws and weaknesses would cause you to embark on the type of introspection you need to correct your own.

SUFFERING UNJUSTLY

Suppose you find yourself in an unhappy marriage. We have already determined that God arranged your marriage and destined you to marry this woman. If you are unhappy with your wife, you are actually unhappy with God. Chances are good that you feel discontented with your wife because she is a discontented woman. If you had treated her in a godly manner, honoring her as a fellow partner and protecting her as the weaker vessel, she would not be unhappy and neither would you.

But just for the sake of argument, let's suppose that your wife really is a miserable, unhappy malcontent and a vicious creature through no fault of your own at all. You are a complete saint and always have been. You have never shown her any disrespect, and you have fulfilled all your biblical spiritual obligations to her flawlessly. Despite all this, you are suffering from this woman's constant assaults, complaints, and outright hatred. Why did God do this to you?

The New Testament is full of teaching about the virtue of unmerited suffering. After all, our Master did not deserve any of the suffering that befell him. He did not deserve the rejection of men, the shame of the cross, or the torment of execution. The LORD offers special blessing for those who remain unshaken despite unmerited suffering:

> Behold, we consider those blessed who remained steadfast. You have heard of the steadfastness of Job, and you have seen the purpose of the Lord, how the Lord is compassionate and merciful. (James 5:11)

The Apostle Peter teaches, "This is a gracious thing, when, mindful of God, one endures sorrows while suffering unjustly. For what credit is it if, when you sin and are beaten for it, you endure? But if when you do good and suffer for it you endure, this is a gracious thing in the sight of God" (1 Peter 2:19–20). In other words, if a person suffers unjustly, God assigns that suffering to his account as merit. If you actually do suffer unjustly from a wife's harassment, and you endure it patiently and without malice, God assigns you credit in heaven. Moreover, he promises to bestow blessing upon you. Peter says, "Do not repay evil for evil or reviling for reviling, but on the contrary, bless, for to this you were called, that you may obtain a blessing" (1 Peter 3:9). In other words, God allows his children to suffer unjustly so that they will receive a blessing: "If you should suffer for righteousness' sake, you will be blessed" (1 Peter 3:14).

This important principle will allow you to face any amount of unjust persecution and harassment—even from your wife. Peter says, "To this you have been called, because Christ also suffered for you, leaving you an example, so that you might follow in his steps" (1 Peter 2:21). God calls us to suffer. If you feel as if you are suffering from something you don't deserve, you might be right. It might be that God wants to bless you and allow you to share in the suffering of Messiah: "Husbands, love your wives, as Christ loved the church and gave himself up for her" (Ephesians 5:25).

How you react to unjust suffering, however, will determine whether or not you receive blessing and reward. If you react with bitter indictment, complaining, or retaliation, you will lose any merit you might have earned from enduring the suffering. The pains you have endured become pointless. Instead, the one who believes that he suffers unjustly must follow Messiah's example: "When he was reviled, he did not revile in return; when he suffered; he did not threaten, but continued entrusting himself to him who judges justly" (1 Peter 2:23).

FORGIVENESS

Whether or not you deserve the suffering your wife inflicts upon you makes no difference. In either case, your only job is to patiently endure it and forgive it. If you store up bitterness in your heart, you lose the merit. If you retaliate in any way, you lose the merit. Instead, a man must emulate the Messiah, who said from the cross, "Father, forgive them, for they know not what they do" (Luke 23:34).

A man who loves his wife forgives his wife for all offenses, both big and small:

> Put on then, as God's chosen ones, holy and beloved, compassionate hearts, kindness, humility, meekness, and patience, bearing with one another and, if one has a complaint against another, forgiving each other; as the Lord has forgiven you, so you also must forgive. (Colossians 3:12–13)

A man who does not forgive his wife will not have his own sins forgiven: "If you do not forgive others their trespasses, neither will your

Father forgive your trespasses" (Matthew 6:15). On the other hand, if you forgive your wife from your heart when she offends you, hurts your feelings, or commits some transgression, your Father in heaven will likewise forgive you for your sins.

With the same measure you judge others, God will judge you. With the same measure you forgive your wife, God will return forgiveness and grace to you. With the same measure you ignore her shortcomings, God will ignore yours. On the other hand, with the same measure you rebuke her, God will rebuke you. If you withhold forgiveness from your wife, God will withhold it from you.

One critical word of warning: Unless your wife asks for forgiveness, you should not be telling her "I forgive you." Do not verbally declare unsolicited forgiveness. It's a petty, selfish, and condescending thing to do, and it will only incite her resentment. Saying "I forgive you" when she has not apologized or asked you for forgiveness is the same as saying "You have offended me, but since I am such a spiritual giant and noble person, I forgive you." She won't appreciate your forgiveness.

Instead, show her that you forgive her by your actions, by your tender compassion and undiminished affection. When she sees that you refuse to retaliate, raise your voice, get angry, storm out, slam doors, or whatever it is that you ordinarily do to indicate your displeasure, she will know that she is forgiven, and she will be in awe of your spiritual growth.

SPIRITUAL LAWS

In this chapter we have learned several basic spiritual laws. Just as surely as the laws of gravity produce predictable results, we can predict the results of violating these spiritual laws. God has given you the wife you need and deserve—your soul mate and God-appointed destiny. You will receive from God measure for measure according to the way you treat her. If you judge her and rebuke her, you can expect to receive the same from God. If you forgive her and show her mercy, you can expect the same from God.

If you see some flaw in her character, it means that God is trying to show you some flaw in your own character to which you are otherwise blind. If you ignore her when she corrects you, demands of you, or brings complaints against you, you will be ignoring the voice of

God. If you find yourself suffering unjustly, and you do not retaliate or become embittered, you will receive blessing from God and merit in heaven because you are sharing in the suffering of Messiah. After all, your job is to love your wife as Messiah loved us, and for him that meant suffering unjustly for us.

It doesn't sound like an easy path, and it's not, but the payoff is worth the effort. Just keep your eyes on Christ and stay optimistic, and you will find it's easier than you thought. Remember, think good, and it will be good.

9

OTHER WOMEN

Jesus taught that the secret to marital peace and happiness can be found in the garden of Eden. From the beginning God created human beings male and female—one man and one woman. The man must leave his father and mother and his world to glue himself to his wife. Then the two will become "one flesh," which is to say, one new creature: "They are no longer two but one flesh. What therefore God has joined together, let not man separate" (Matthew 19:6). Let not any woman separate what God has joined together either.

When a wife feels she needs to compete with another woman for her husband's affection, the joy immediately leaves her marriage. God did not design marriage to withstand rivalry with outsiders. He made us to be physically, sexually, and spiritually monogamous.

In this chapter we will learn how a man can protect his wife from jealousy and himself from divided loyalties, wandering eyes, and lust. We will learn the spiritual discipline of singular devotion to one woman.

OUR FATHERS AND MOTHERS

The rabbis teach that the deeds of the fathers (Abraham, Isaac, and Jacob) are portents for the sons. This means that the things that happened to the forefathers created spiritual patterns destined to impact later generations. This principle holds true in the realm of marriage.

Abraham and Sarah shared an ideal marriage of unbroken harmony, despite their unmet desire for children, until the introduction of Hagar.

Abraham's wife, Sarah, had no hope of having children. Her child-bearing years were gone. Like many women in her position, her thoughts turned to the idea of adoption. She had a handmaid named Hagar who was young and fertile. "The best solution," Sarah thought, "would be to have Hagar conceive a child for Abraham and bear it on my behalf."

In the days of the patriarchs, men practiced polygamy. Abraham was free to take a second wife at any time. In eighty-seven years, however, despite Sarah's bareness, he had chosen to remain singularly devoted to his one wife.

In desperation Sarah asked Abraham to take her maidservant Hagar as a second wife and impregnate her. She said to Abraham, "Go in to my servant; it may be that I shall obtain children by her" (Genesis 16:2). In the Hebrew she says, "Perhaps I will be built through her."

Sarah's plan to have another woman conceive on her behalf seems strange to us, but it is probably not as strange as our use of artificial insemination and in-vitro fertilization would have seemed to her.

At first the plan seemed to be working well; young and fertile Hagar conceived quickly. But Sarah did not feel any joy over the good news, because the plan quickly backfired. Instead of bearing a son for Sarah, Hagar regarded herself as a wife in equal standing. She made it clear that the child was to be hers and Abraham was to be hers. Sarah had taken a risk and lost.

Distressed and brokenhearted, Sarah went to Abraham to lodge a complaint and inquire about his intentions. She said, "May the wrong done to me be on you! I gave my servant to your embrace, and when she saw that she had conceived, she looked on me with contempt. May the LORD judge between you and me!" (Genesis 16:5).

What would you have done if you had been Abraham? He had consented to the affair only at Sarah's behest. Now she came lodging accusations at him, calling down curses on him, and blaming him for her mistake. Most husbands would have responded with a sharp rejoinder: "Hey, it was your bright idea; now it's your problem. Don't blame me." But Abraham was not like most husbands. Instead of returning Sarah's recriminations, he listened past the verbal abuse and heard the pain of her heart. She was wounded, hurting, and desperately afraid of losing her husband to her maidservant. If only spouses in troubled marriages could learn from Abraham's example.

Abraham saw that Hagar no longer considered herself to be Sarah's servant; she considered herself to be Sarah's peer. He told Sarah, "Behold, your servant is in your power; do to her as you please" (Genesis 16:6). In doing so Abraham affirmed that Hagar was still subordinate to Sarah. Sarah had not been replaced by the younger woman in Abraham's eyes. Nevertheless, the insertion of Hagar into their relationship bore consequences that divide the Middle East to this very day.

Jacob had domestic problems, too. His unfortunate marriage to two sisters spawned an intense rivalry between the women that triggered repercussions throughout Jewish history, eventually dividing the nation of Israel into two separate, competing kingdoms.

Only Isaac enjoyed the unbroken harmony of marital oneness. Isaac's love for Rebekah and her love for him provides us with a model that follows the original pattern described by the Torah: "They shall become one flesh" (Genesis 2:24).

JUST FRIENDS

A husband must understand that his wife cannot abide any real or imagined competition with other women, past, present, or future. When a man gets married, his relationship with all other women must immediately undergo a complete transformation. Other women cease to exist. Friendships with other women must be downgraded to acquaintances.

Today's liberal dating culture undermines marriage before bride and groom ever meet. Most people getting married today bring with them all the baggage of past relationships. A man cannot help but feel jealous to think of his wife with another man, even if she had just a high-school romance. A woman feels that jealousy even more deeply. For her love and relationships occur on a much deeper spiritual level. She cannot easily dismiss the idea that her husband once loved someone else. An old flame will always be a rival in her mind. Her husband's old girlfriends are like demons haunting her insecurities, tormenting her. He must never mention them except to dismiss them. He must never praise them or compare his wife with them. He must cut off all contact with them. They do not have anything positive to contribute to his relationship with his wife. They are strictly off limits. They cease to exist.

A rabbi was once counseling a young man a few weeks before his marriage. The groom-to-be was upset with his fiancée because she had objected to the idea of his inviting an old girlfriend to the wedding. He said, "It's not fair. Linda used to date my buddy Jim, and Jim is my best man at the wedding! It's my wedding too, and I can invite whoever I want." The rabbi explained to this luckless fellow that by inviting his old girlfriend to his wedding, he had put a black mark on what was supposed to be the biggest day in his wife's life. Not only that but he communicated to his wife that he still had feelings for the girl. He said, "That's not true at all. There is nothing between us. That was all in the past." The rabbi said, "Of course that's true from your perspective, but from your bride's perspective, if there was nothing at all between you anymore, you would not be inviting her to your wedding."

Both men and women entertain the ridiculous illusion that a man and a woman can be "just friends." This is not true. In any relationship in which a man and a woman both claim to be just friends, one of them is lying. God has hardwired human beings with a sexual-spiritual attraction to the opposite sex. A married man has no business harboring a friendship with another woman. Friendship with another woman constitutes a spiritual infidelity. His wife deserves his undivided loyalty. His friendship with another woman feels like adultery to her. This goes both ways. Wives have no business having a male friend on the side of their marriage. Most men would not be comfortable with their wives spending time with some other man. A man who is comfortable with the idea of his wife having another man for a friend should prepare for the almost inevitable affair that will result.

According to Jewish law, a man has grounds for divorcing his wife if she merely spends time secluded and alone with another man, even if nothing sexual transpired between them. Traditional Jewish standards of marriage do not allow either husband or wife to have any "just friends" of the opposite gender. The popular culture objects to these standards as prudish and even sexist. On the contrary, these fences are designed to protect the most important thing in life: marital harmony.

In many churches today it's common for men and women to form religious relationships with members of the opposite sex. It's also common for these religious relationships to blossom into adultery. Despite the frequent occurrence of adultery among clergy and church people, churches continue to sanction friendships and relationships between members of the opposite sex under the banner of spiritual fellowship.

Do yourself and your marriage a favor: Don't develop a friendship with a woman. A man should always be polite and courteous to other women but never close and personal. Again, there is no such thing as "just friends" in a relationship between a man and a woman. One of the so-called friends, if not both, secretly harbors a physical, emotional, or psychological attraction to the other.

NO TOUCH

Jewish law teaches the principle of *shomer nagia* (שומר נגיע) between unmarried men and women. *Shomer nagia* means "guarding contact." The standard of *shomer nagia* prohibits a man from physically touching a woman other than his wife (or close family member). In Orthodox Jewish communities, even the casual handshake across genders does not occur.

People sometimes misconstrue the rule against physical contact as part of the Bible's ritual purity laws. They suppose that an Orthodox Jewish man refuses to touch a woman because she might make him ritually unclean. That's not the case at all. He refuses to touch a woman other than his wife because he reserves all physical contact for his wife. He never wants to give a woman the wrong impression that he feels attracted to her or has special affection for her.

Every adulterous affair begins with one simple touch. A handshake that lasts just a moment too long communicates a message. A "platonic" hug crosses a spiritual barrier and brings a host of suggestions to the mind. A sympathetic back rub is asking for sex. God has physically created us to escalate sexually through physical contact. It's completely natural and normal, and one thing leads to another. Men who disagree with that basic principle of human biology are living in denial in order to justify their flirtatious adventures.

Whenever we teach about the standards of *shomer nagia*, people get upset. Anti-traditionalists object, "Who do you think you are foisting man-made rabbinic standards on us?" Let's take a look at the biblical perspective.

In the days of the apostles, Jewish people had similar rules governing physical contact between men and women, and we never see Jesus or the apostles violating those rules. Notice that Jesus never touches a woman in the gospel stories unless he does so to heal her. Several women, on the other hand, want to touch him, but they never dare transgress the boundaries of physical contact beyond his feet. They anoint his feet, wash his feet, dry his feet, clasp his feet, and even cry on his feet, but they never touch him above the feet. In those days conventional Jewish standards apparently considered a man's feet to be within the bounds of acceptable cross-gender contact. Any further contact between a man and woman outside of marriage did not happen.

Funny as it may sound to modern ears, Jewish culture in the days of the apostles considered contact with the feet to be permissible on the basis of two Bible stories: In the story of Elisha and the Shunammite woman, the distraught mother fell at Elisha's feet and took hold of his feet with her hands. Elisha's servant tried to push her away, but the prophet rebuked him, saying, "Leave her alone, for she is in bitter distress" (2 Kings 4:27). Likewise, in the story of Ruth and Boaz, Ruth clandestinely "lay at his feet until the morning" (Ruth 3:14). These stories provided biblical precedent for women making platonic contact with a man's feet.

Jesus felt compassion for people, and he mingled with sinners, tax collectors, and even so-called prostitutes (that is, women who had sexual relations outside of wedlock). Despite that, he never felt compelled to offer women consoling or encouraging hugs such as are commonly practiced in some church circles today. He did not touch women except to heal them of disease or disability.

The Apostle Paul says, "It is good for a man not to touch a woman, nevertheless, to avoid fornication, let every man have his own wife and each woman her own husband" (1 Corinthians 7:1–2). This is a literal translation. Some translators take the words "It is good for a man not to touch a woman" idiomatically as "It is good for a man not have sex with a woman." In the Jewish culture from which Paul wrote, the difference between "touching a woman" and "having sex with a woman" was simply a matter of degree. In this passage Paul recommends marriage instead of a life of abstinence lest a man or woman fall into temptation and commit a sexual act outside of marriage. But notice that he contrasts marriage with "touching a woman." In the sexual ethics of the Jewish world from which Paul taught, unmarried men did not "touch" women. From Paul's perspective, a man had two alternatives: refrain from touching a woman, or get married. Obviously marriage frees the man to touch his wife, but it does not sanction him to touch other women.

Those ethical standards ruled the relationships between genders in the Apostolic Era, but what about today? Is it reasonable to impose first-century standards on people in today's world? Not only is it reasonable, we would argue that it is more necessary than ever.

Although most modern people chafe at the suggestion, traditional Jewish standards tell young couples who are dating or courting to implement the rule of no touch with one another until marriage: no hand holding, no walking arm in arm, no cuddling on the couch. Telling a romantically involved couple to go ahead and enjoy physical intimacy but to stop short of sexual intercourse has predictable results. Healthy heterosexual human behavior is completely predictable when it comes to sexuality. It's preprogrammed.

In Messianic Judaism we see many happy marriages in which the young man and woman have never been physically intimate with another person, or even with each other, until their wedding night. These standards make for strong healthy marriages with a solid foundation in sexual purity.

Once a couple is married, we advise them to implement the rule of no touch with members of the opposite sex for the rest of their married lives. Anything more than a polite handshake is probably inappropriate. Of course, there might be several exceptions to such a rule. For example, helping a woman who has fallen or catching a woman before she falls. Elders called to lay hands upon a sick woman to pray for healing will obviously need to touch her just as a medical doctor must treat a patient. A little common sense needs to mitigate the standard, but the general rule should be observed. Hugs, pats on the back, playful jabs, back rubs, and the like are all forms of flirtatious foreplay and inappropriate between unmarried people.

THE DANCE FLOOR

Traditional Christianity and Judaism both prohibit mixed-gender dancing. It's strictly taboo. Nevertheless, today's lower standards see mixed-gender dancing happening routinely. Ironically, it often happens at weddings, where we should be celebrating the singular, monogamous fidelity of marriage, not compromising it on the dance floor.

Dancing with a woman is a form of sexual communication and flirtatious behavior. Dance is sensual. Ask a professional dancer whether or not he or she considers dance to express sensuality. That's not to say that dance serves no other purpose. Dance can express joy, hope, sorrow, anger, and the whole range of human emotions. Most often, however, when a man and woman dance with one another, their dance becomes a form of sexual communication and suggestion. Again, old-fashioned traditional Judaism and traditional Christianity both prohibited mixed-gender dancing. What makes us think we are so much smarter today?

Should a married man dance with a woman other than his own wife? Of course not. Mixed-partner dancing is one of the ways of the world, a social rehearsal for adultery, and a recipe for unhappiness. How do you feel about the idea of your wife dancing with another man? Hopefully it bothers you to think of your wife shaking it on the dance floor with another man. These things should go without saying, but they no longer do.

OTHER WOMEN

To the married man, other women do not exist. He must never place his wife in the position of feeling threatened by another woman. It happens more often than you might think. For example, your wife observes you enjoying a conversation with so-and-so's wife. She sees you laugh at her jokes, exchange witty remarks, and discuss ideas. She thinks to herself, "He never pays attention to me like that. He does not laugh with me like that. He does not find me intellectually stimulating." In reality, the man might only have been doing his part to engage in polite conversation with Mrs. So-and-so, but his wife's insecurities set off alarms. Her "he does not love me" switch flips back to the "on" position. On the car ride home that night, he observes that a frosty silence has settled over her. He has no idea why.

The reason why is because a woman feels that she is in competition for her husband, especially if he has not done a good job of making her first place in his life. Simple innocent remarks like "Mrs. So-and-so looked nice in that blue dress" are absolutely prohibited. A remark of that nature is neither simple nor innocent, and it sends your wife into an emotional tailspin and crash. A man should never, ever comment on another woman's appearance. Neither should he allow himself to offer any comparisons. A comment such as "Mrs. So-and-so does such a fine job with hosting" says to your wife, "Why can't you be more like Mrs. So-and-so?" A remark like "That Mrs. So-and-so really knows what she is talking about" says to your wife, "You do not know what you are talking about. Why can't you be smarter like Mrs. So-and-so?"

Given the power of the insecurity filters through which all your words pass as they enter your wife's ears, it is better not to make any remarks whatsoever about other women that could possibly be construed as a comparison or a veiled criticism.

YOUR BEAUTIFUL WIFE

A man should regard all other women as primates when compared to his wife. He should condition himself to visualize them as monkeys rather than allow himself to enjoy their allure. Just as he feels no attraction to chimpanzees or monkeys, he should feel no attraction to other women.

The Talmud says that every man's wife is beautiful to her husband, even if she appears ugly to everyone else. God has programmed the male to find his wife attractive. He sees her as no other man can see her. He sees her inner beauty shining through, and he finds her desirable even after she has put on a few pounds and is not as young as she used to be. The man who stays singularly focused on his wife as the object of his affection and sexual attention will find that she grows increasingly more beautiful in his eyes with each passing year.

Not so the man with a wandering eye. If a married man lets his gaze rest on the pretty faces and shapely bodies of other women, feasting his eyes on women other than his wife, he will find that his wife becomes less and less attractive to him. He will continually hunger for something outside his marriage, and he will find himself less and less content with his own wife.

The Proverbs say, "Drink water from your own cistern, flowing water from your own well ... Rejoice in the wife of your youth, a lovely deer, a graceful doe. Let her breasts fill you at all times with delight, be intoxicated always in her love" (Proverbs 5:15–19). If a man resolves to fix his gaze and sexual attention only on his wife, she will blossom ever more beautiful in his eyes. On the other hand, a man who enjoys "eye candy" in movies, magazines, on the Internet, or while out and about will find that his wife does not measure up to his expectations. Candy rots the teeth, but eye candy rots the soul.

ADULTERY IN THE HEART

Feasting your eyes on other women not only damages your marriage, it is a sin. As you know, Jesus teaches, "I say to you that everyone who looks at a woman with lustful intent has already committed adultery with her in his heart" (Matthew 5:28). What does that mean?

The Bible uses the word "heart" the way English speakers use the word "mind." English speakers use the word "heart" to mean the seat of emotions. In biblical idioms, however, emotions take place in a person's liver and kidneys, not in his heart. The biblical "heart" refers to the seat of will, where a person does his decision making, thinks his thoughts, imagines and fantasizes, and performs other cognitive functions. In view of this, adultery in the heart means "mental adultery." Jesus says that when a man looks at a woman lustfully, he commits mental adultery.

The art of guarding one's eyes and rooting out mental adultery needs to be treated in another book dedicated to that subject. Every heterosexual man knows that this is the battlefield for his soul. For our purposes we will summarize the main issues.

The eyes are the primary gateway to the brain. If a man's eyes linger on a woman's body, his brain immediately begins to process the image, firing the appropriate neurological and chemical responses. Mental adultery follows quickly. That's how God made men. Women's bodies are supposed to be attractive to men, and they are supposed to "turn men on." The problem is that God also made men to be monogamous and devoted to only one woman. Just as it would be inappropriate and unnatural for a man to sleep with every woman he saw, so it is not healthy for him to do so mentally. A spiritually healthy mind does not consider women as just so many sexual targets. The spiritually healthy man keeps his sexual impulse under control and his natural attraction to females focused on his relationship with his spouse.

Our eyes feed our brains, and our brains commit the sin. This is why the Bible warns you "not to follow after your own heart and your own eyes, which you are inclined to whore after" (Numbers 15:39). According to this verse, a man is naturally inclined to go astray sexually if he follows his eyes and his heart. Many men are faithful to their wives on the surface, but in their minds they are mental adulterers. Their eyes are always wandering, catching a sexual charge from every attractive woman.

If your wife sees your eyes wandering after another woman or feasting on another woman's body, you are doomed. No point in trying to deny it, but neither will you gain anything by admitting to it. To your wife your mental adultery feels like real adultery. She feels devalued and disrespected. Her insecurities blaze up and make her feel ugly, unwanted, unloved, and pathetic. This translates into pure angry bitterness toward you. She might not say anything. Perhaps you think she does not notice your roving eyes. But she certainly does.

> Let your eyes look directly forward, and your gaze be straight before you. Ponder the path of your feet; then all your ways will be sure. Do not swerve to the right or to the left; turn your foot away from evil. (Proverbs 4:25–27)

Even if your wife is not aware of your lust habit, it is still a sin, and it is still wrong. Most men say, "God does not really expect us to control our eyes. No man can help himself." That's not true at all. You certainly can help yourself, and with God's help you can control your eyes and your mind. The eyes do not have a mind of their own, and you can train them to bounce away from alluring images.

If you are like most men, you have trained your eyes over many years to scan for and focus on attractive women and sexually alluring images. You don't even have to think about it. Your eyes go automatically to whatever they should not be looking. This is good news because it means that you can also train your eyes to do the opposite. It's simpler than you think. Just train your eyes to bounce away from women's bodies, from sexually alluring images, and from your so-called eye candy. Be like the righteous Job, and make a covenant with your eyes not to look on a young girl.[29]

If you prayerfully work at it, you can train your eyes to reflexively look away. It will take some practice, but it can be done. You don't need to make every attractive roadside jogger into a road hazard. In fact, you don't need to give her a second look at all.

In addition to bouncing your eyes away from women's bodies and sexual images, you need to take charge of your thoughts. As sexual thoughts suggest themselves to your brain, shove them away. Visualize yourself shooting them down the way you would shoot skeet. Mentally quarantine them, and force them out. At first you might find this difficult to do, and it will require mental vigilance. But with God's help and with lots of prayer, as time goes on, and as you keep your eyes pure, you will find it easier and easier to control your thoughts and put an end to the mental adultery.

SINGULAR DEVOTION

As explained above, a man needs to beware of committing mental adultery. Men tend to laugh it off, saying, "Hey, I'm just a human being. I can't help being a guy." Jesus said that if your eye is causing you to commit mental adultery, better to gouge it out and throw it away than go into the fire of Gehenna with both eyes. He said that if your hand is causing you to sin (meaning masturbation), better to cut it off and throw it away than go into the fire of Gehenna with both hands. Of course he does not expect his disciples to literally cut off their hands or gouge out their eyes, but this only underscores the seriousness of the situation. A man simply cannot afford to neglect this aspect of his spiritual well-being. He must take it on with all seriousness and fight for his own life.

Mental adultery is not the same as actually committing adultery, but it is still damaging to your soul and to your relationship with your wife. It creates spiritual damage in your marriage, which will result in all sorts of sexual unhappiness. Your wife will smell the sin on you, and she will eventually start to recoil from your touch. Even if she never suspects that you are lusting after other women, she will intuitively sense it in her spirit. Besides, she knows you better than anyone in the world—and even a hint of indiscretion on your part makes her shudder.

Do yourself a favor, and do your wife a favor, and clean up your act. You don't need to tell her about it. In fact, it's a bad idea to say, "Honey, I used to lust after other women and fantasize about them, but now I quit. Aren't you happy?" Too much information. Don't dump your sins on your wife. Show a little discretion. Find a brother in the LORD to talk with, but don't turn your repentance into yet another opportunity to wound your wife.

As a married man, you committed to a life of singular devotion to one woman. You agreed to marriage under our Master's teaching of monogamous fidelity. Time to be a real man and live up to your vows.

PORNOGRAPHY

In this book we are only briefly mentioning the issues with which men struggle in their battle for sexual purity. As mentioned above, the topic merits a whole book dedicated to the subject of attaining sexual purity in light of Messianic Jewish teaching. Such a book would need to contain a few chapters on the problem of pornography in the modern world. In this book a few short sentences will have to suffice.

Since the dawn of modern media, pornography has become an inescapable problem with which men of faith must deal. With only a few clicks of a button, a man can access anything he desires. Many men think of viewing pornography as an innocent indulgence—not a big deal. That's not true. It is a big deal. Not only does it severely damage your spiritual health, it is a portal that allows unclean spirits and satanic influence into your life and into your home. The spirit of pornography is to the modern world what idolatry once was to the ancient world. It comes with evil spirits. A man who indulges in a little pornographic entertainment does not realize that he is inviting Satan to take up residence in his mind and in his home.

Psychologists report that pornography is physiologically and psychologically addictive. In other words, it works like a drug in your mind. This explains why men get dragged into it deeper and deeper, like cocaine addicts, and find it almost impossible to break the habit.

If you admitted to your best friend that you viewed Internet pornography last week, he might chastise you and tell you to shape up and be a godlier man, but he would probably understand. You slipped up. You had a moment of weakness. You're ashamed. You are repenting. He's a guy. He gets it. He understands that a momentary lapse or a stumble like that does not necessarily indicate that you are a demented pervert capable of committing horrible sex crimes.

Your godly wife, on the other hand, is not a guy. She cannot empathize with you because, as a woman, she does not suffer from the same sexual drive or respond to visual stimulation in the same way you do. She has no frame of reference for understanding why a man, especially a married man, especially a married man who claims to be a disciple, would view pornography. When women find out that their husbands have been viewing pornography, they feel cheated on. The wife feels as angry and hurt as if she had caught her husband having an affair with a real woman. She loses sexual interest in her husband. The thought of sleeping with him makes her feel sick. It repels her godly soul.

This may sound strange, but most rabbis would advise a husband not to confide in his wife about his sexual sins. Grant her some dignity by sparing her that information. Confess your sin by seeking your pastor, your rabbi, or a brother in the Master, and do the hard work of serious repentance, but don't drag your wife into the sewage with you.

Guys have no clue about how devastating pornography is to their wives. A man attending a First Fruits of Zion seminar privately told a tragic story about how pornography had destroyed both his marriage and his ministry. He and his wife were missionaries. They had served together for more than two decades. That whole time he'd had a secret problem—an addiction to pornography. His wife never knew. He felt tormented by the guilt. After much prayer and repentance, he found help at a Christian men's conference. He finally felt set free from decades of addiction. In great joy he went home and told his wife about how God had set him free from years of addiction to pornography. She did not share his joy and enthusiasm. The news that her husband had even once viewed pornography struck her like an unseen oncoming truck. The idea that he had been indulging in it behind her back for years while at the same time sleeping with her and serving the kingdom—the betrayal was more than she could handle. She left him immediately, ending their marriage and their ministry for the kingdom.

Many men complain that their wives do not sexually satisfy them. Since their wives are not sexually available enough, they feel justified by compensating with a little pornography on the side. It does not work that way. You have no more right to indulge in pornography and masturbation than you have the right to visit a prostitute. Imagine explaining before the throne of glory, "My wife did not have sex with me often enough, so I had to masturbate while watching videos of prostitutes having sex." Is that excuse going to justify you before the Almighty? If not, why would you use it justify your behavior now?

The truth is that the more you pollute yourself with pornography, the more repugnant you will be to your wife. She will smell it on your soul and retreat from you sexually. Pornography invites Satan to take up residence in your bedroom, and he will do his best to frustrate your sex life even further as he herds you along toward the brink of destruction.

THE ONLINE RELATIONSHIP

The Internet has brought a whole new world of marital problems to us. Social networks and online services allow men and women to hook up over the Internet and engage in private conversations that would have been impossible two decades ago. Old girlfriends and new prospects are lurking in cyberspace, looking for opportunities to chat. Don't kid yourself. A man has no business whatsoever exchanging e-mails or text messages or chatting with another woman online or on a smartphone. Just because an affair does not involve sexual contact does not mean it's kosher. According to the *New York Daily News*, in 2011 Facebook was named in two thirds of all divorce proceedings.

Online relationships with members of the opposite sex are real affairs. Infidelity can happen through e-mail far more easily than in real life. It's discreet, easy, and easy to hide.

As a rule, a married man should not engage in any regular correspondence with a woman without including his wife on the correspondence. Of course, this goes both ways. Husbands and wives need to understand that a virtual relationship is actually very real.

A woman came to her Messianic rabbi for urgent counseling. She felt guilty because she had been texting back and forth with an old boyfriend. The rabbi told her she needed to cut it off at once. He offered to contact the old friend on her behalf, and he warned her that if she did not cut it off, he would need to speak to her husband. She assured the rabbi that she would end the relationship immediately, but when he followed up with her, she was evasive about the matter. A week later she called him in tears. Her husband had found her phone messages, and their marriage now teetered on the brink of divorce. She felt terribly ashamed, full of regret, and she hated herself for not heeding his advice.

In a similar story, a woman came to her congregational leader with stack of e-mails she had printed off from her husband's computer. He had found a "friend" in whom he felt he could confide. This so-called friend was a woman he had met in a church. They had begun by exchanging e-mails about spiritual matters, Bible questions, and so forth. The correspondence quickly escalated into inappropriate levels of intimacy. Naturally the poor wife felt devastated as she read her husband's descriptions of his disappointments with her and his praise of his new online friend.

Both these stories have something in common. They both involved otherwise godly people who had good marriages and solid homes. In both cases the person involved excused the behavior on the basis that since it was all just electronic correspondence and involved no real sexual contact, it was not actually adultery. Their spouses did not see it that way.

Guard yourself. Make sure your wife has access to your computers and devices, your accounts and your correspondence. Stay far away from private conversations with other women.

THE PROFESSIONAL RELATIONSHIP

In today's work world, a man often finds himself working closely with a female colleague. This creates a serious problem. Even if he has no wrong intentions and keeps the relationship completely professional, it still plants a seed of doubt with his wife. When a man and a woman work closely together, the natural human physiological and psychological attractions begin to work. One of them, if not both, begins to flirt. It might be innocent banter. He feels flattered. She feels flattered.

Meanwhile, the spouse at home observes this professional relationship flowering while her own wilts. If you are required to work closely with a woman, go the extra mile to keep it completely professional. Keep every conversation as short as possible and connected only to business. Do not take calls from her or exchange correspondence outside of work. Mention your wife frequently. Make the borders very clear. Do not become her friend. Men and women are never "just good friends."

SINGULAR DEVOTION

This chapter calls upon husbands to exercise singular devotion to their wives, governing their eyes and their thoughts and keeping all other women at arm's length. It's not difficult. It just takes a little bit of conscious effort.

A happy wife knows that she need not compete with any other woman for her man's attention or admiration. A man needs to communicate clearly to his wife, both in words and deeds, that he has no interest in any woman other than her. As far as he is concerned, other women are like primates. He needs to work hard to insure that he is not looking at other women or indulging in sexual sins. He must never compare his wife to other women or praise other women in her presence. His wife should feel confident that her husband would never cross the boundaries of their marriage to look at another woman or engage in even a private social relationship with another woman.

In so doing a man will insure that he enjoys the peace of Isaac and Rebekah rather than the discord between Sarah and Hagar.

10

IF YOU WIN, YOU LOSE

When two people live together, they inevitably have disagreements. There is nothing wrong with disagreeing with your wife, and in some cases, you might even engage in argument. But it's the argument that creates the problem, not the disagreement. Arguing with a woman creates a no-win scenario for a man. If you lose the argument, you lose. If you win the argument, you lose.

In this chapter we will try to understand the differences between men and women in the field of argumentation and establish some ground rules for successfully surviving arguments.

ARGUING WITH YOUR WIFE

Guys sometimes think that it's normal to argue with their wives. If you watch enough television, you realize that it's completely normal for husbands and wives to have terrific arguments in which they exchange all sorts of witty, sarcastic verbal assaults. By the end of the typical half-hour situation-comedy television episode, the husband and wife have resolved their differences and returned to a happy status quo. That's how marriage works on television.

We are in big trouble if we believe that real life follows the same pattern. You might think it's completely normal to have the occasional heated argument with your wife. Maybe you are bewildered when the immediate reconciliation does not come at the end of the episode as it does on television, but you probably blame that on your wife.

Men love to argue. We enjoy arguing a point to its conclusion, especially when that conclusion proves we are right and the other person is wrong. A man will argue with his wife over just about anything. Whenever he feels she is wrong, it feels to him as though he has a sacred duty to show her where she is wrong and why she is wrong. He will use logic and analysis to systematically work through the points being discussed, falsifying or verifying each one in order to arrive at the correct conclusion. When his wife raises seemingly irrational objections, he compensates by raising his voice and restating the obvious cogent points in a louder, more aggressive, more adamant tone of authority.

Sometimes it might seem as if these types of tactics work. The woman drops her side of the argument. The husband seems to win. In reality, the wife pulls out of the argument, not because the husband has proven his point and she has realized that he is right and she is wrong but because he has bullied her to the point where it hurts her too much to fight back.

Men love to be right, and we love to prove that we are right. We don't mind adding a little heat to an argument to give it some extra punch. A raised voice adds emphasis. We like to logically deduce our way to a conclusion, tearing down feeble objections. That might work fine when arguing with other men, but it's not at all appropriate for arguing with a woman.

A woman's mind does not work the way a man's does. His logic and deductive linear reasoning mean nothing to her. His raised voice sounds like a threat. When he gets angry, it frightens her. When he tries to prove that she is incorrect, she feels personally attacked. She does not disconnect herself from her argument. She does not say to herself, "He is not attacking me; he is simply trying to prove a point." Instead, she feels invested in her side of the argument, and she takes his attempt to dismantle it as a personal assault to her dignity.

If you do corner your wife with truth and rational conclusions and force her to admit that she is wrong, she feels like a trapped animal, ready to lunge and strike at anything and in any direction to escape the trap.

BEING WRONG

Being wrong offends men. A man hates to admit that he is wrong. It humiliates him to have to back down and concede defeat. Many men would prefer to go on the rest of their lives, belligerently defending a point they secretly know to be wrong, rather than humble themselves and admit to an error. Despite this enormous and childish male ego, a sound and persistent argument can usually convince a man that he is wrong. Then he eats humble pie, deals with it, and goes on with life. The fact that he was wrong does not scar him, nor does losing an argument leave him feeling wounded. Instead, he is probably ready to argue some other point to try to even the score.

Women are different. Their minds work differently. Since they often become personally invested in an argument, they do not have the capacity to be wrong and to be OK with that. Their insecurities, private fears, and low sense of self-worth utterly forbid them from being wrong. She would rather die than admit to having done something wrong or argued for something wrong—especially if the person challenging her is her husband, the one person who is supposed to be on her side and backing her up.

This means that if you win your side of an argument with your wife, you have actually lost. By proving that your wife is wrong, you have gained a small victory over some insignificant point of disagreement, but in the process you have run over your wife's dignity with a tank. Don't expect her to apologize: "Oh, now I see your point. How could I have been so blind? I'm sorry for being so obtuse. Thanks for clarifying that for me." She can barely breathe.

When you realize how much damage you do to your wife by winning an argument, you will be less eager to contradict her and correct her every time you perceive that she is in error about something. You will learn better ways to discuss things and navigate around points of disagreement. Most important of all, you will learn that being right is simply not worth it. Better to let the matter drop.

LETTING OUT WATER

According to the Bible, a person should avoid an argument, even if it means letting someone's wrong idea go unchallenged. The book of Proverbs says, "The beginning of strife is like letting out water, so quit before the quarrel breaks out" (Proverbs 17:14). According to this piece of biblical wisdom, an argument is like urinating. Once you start, you can't easily stop. So don't start arguing. The book of Proverbs contains numerous admonitions along similar lines. The fool must speak his mind. His argument comes bursting out of him. He cannot contain his words. The wise man, on the other hand, remains silent. He lets a matter go. He overlooks an insult and ignores a slight. He does not attempt to correct someone who will not accept correction. He avoids strife. His lips create the fruit of peace and righteousness.

Arguments usually start over small things that, in the larger scheme of things, are inconsequential. Once the argument starts, the human ego inflates the significance of the point of disagreement. Suddenly it's all-important. Emotional reactions cloud all sense of perspective. All at once nothing could be more important to a man than proving to his wife that she is wrong about this issue they are disagreeing over—suddenly it's the most important thing.

In reality, once an argument starts, neither you nor your wife are arguing about the actual point of disagreement. Instead, you have engaged in a war of egos. In such a war, there are no winners, only losers. The holy apostle and brother of our Master says, "What causes quarrels and what causes fights among you? Is it not this, that your passions are at war within you?" (James 4:1). In an argument, the point of disagreement becomes only an excuse to vent the warring passions within you.

ANGER

An argument between a husband and wife entails more than a simple disagreement between two dispassionate, rational parties. The domestic argument inevitably ignites anger in both husband and wife, and anger is a real problem. Anger short-circuits logic in the brain. Blood pressure rises, thoughts become clouded, and cutting words fly like arrows.

James, the brother of the Master, warns us, "Let every person be quick to hear, slow to speak, slow to anger; for the anger of man does not produce the righteousness of God" (James 1:19–20). A man thinks he can use his anger as a tool to accomplish some higher objective, but James says that anger can never "produce the righteousness of God." That means that whatever outcome a man does achieve through his anger, it falls short of righteousness. For this reason alone we should be eager to root all anger out of our lives, especially out of our marriages. Nothing good results from anger.

The rabbis compare anger to idolatry because an angry man denies God's providence. He becomes angry when his will and desire are challenged, thereby denying God's will and God's desire. Paul lists "fits of anger, rivalries, dissensions, divisions" as the "works of the flesh" (Galatians 5:19–20), and he warns us that "those who do such things will not inherit the kingdom of God" (Galatians 5:21). Do you still think you can justify anger toward your wife? In another passage Paul warns that anger gives "opportunity to the devil" (Ephesians 4:27). A little further on he states that "wrath and anger and clamor" all "grieve the Holy Spirit of God" (Ephesians 4:30–31).

How much is that argument worth to you? If you feel that winning the argument and convincing your wife justifies denying God's providence, engaging in the works of the flesh, giving opportunity to the devil, grieving the Holy Spirit, and forfeiting the kingdom of heaven, then have at it. Tear into her. But if you have any sense in your head at all, you will realize that your anger will never "produce the righteousness of God," and you will renounce anger completely:

> Now you must put them all away: anger, wrath, malice. (Colossians 3:8)

> Let all bitterness and wrath and anger and clamor and slander be put away from you, along with all malice. Be kind to one another, tenderhearted, forgiving one another, as God in Christ forgave you. (Ephesians 4:31–32)

A man should add to his prayer list, every day, "My God and God of my fathers, please deliver me from anger."

SAYING NO TO ANGER

The angry man raises his voice to add emphasis to his words and communicate his wrath. The godly man never raises his voice with his wife. Most men would never consider striking their wives, but no man ever strikes his wife unless anger compels him. Why would a man allow the demon of anger into any conversation with the woman he loves? Perhaps he will never strike his wife, but he does not mind letting the same spirit of anger loose in the room.

From now on, make this a hard and fast rule: Do not raise your voice. Do not slam doors. Do not knock over chairs. Do not throw objects. Do not punch walls (ouch!). Do not allow anger to take hold. When you feel anger rising up in you, let that be the signal that the time to drop the conversation has arrived.

JACOB SCOLDS RACHEL

The Torah tells a story about a husband's angry reaction. Desperate to have children and sickened with jealously over her sister Leah's success, Jacob's wife Rachel demanded of her husband, "Give me children, or else I die!" The rabbis explain that Rachel spoke in this impertinent manner in order to provoke Jacob to pray on her behalf. She knew that Isaac had prayed with Rebekah for twenty years until the LORD reversed her barren condition. Rather than praying, Jacob became angry. He responded harshly, "Am I in the place of God, who has withheld from you the fruit of the womb?" (Genesis 30:2).

The sages scolded Jacob for speaking harshly with his wife. Abraham never scolded Sarah so harshly. He prioritized peace with Sarah above putting her in her place or correcting her:

> One must always be careful to honor his wife with the dignity
> a wife deserves because blessings rest on a man's home only
> on account of his wife, for it is written [in Genesis 12:16], "He
> treated Abram well for her sake." (Talmud, b.*Bava Metzia* 59a)

Jacob threw Rachel's distress back in her face. Rather than comfort her or pray for her, he snapped at her and even implied that the LORD had cursed her with barrenness:

> The Holy One, blessed be he, said to Jacob, "Is this the way to
> answer a woman in distress? By your very life, your children
> by your other wives will be humbled before her son, suppli-
> cating before him, and he will reply [in Genesis 50:19], 'Am
> I in the place of God?'" (*Genesis Rabbah* 71:7)

Jacob spoke harshly as if he had forgotten that Rachel was a woman and not a man, much less his wife. The rabbis remind us, "A man should always be careful not to wrong his wife, for her tears are frequent and she is easily hurt."[30] Peter reminds us that when a man is harsh with his wife, his prayers are hindered, and he invites divine anger. The prayers and cries of a wounded wife, however, rise straight to heaven to accuse him. Therefore, a husband should never react harshly to his wife or criticize her. Instead, husbands must be "harmonious, sympathetic, brotherly, kindhearted, and humble in spirit" with their wives (1 Peter 3:8 NASB).

THE MALICE OF MR. SPOCK

Some men are adept at controlling their anger. We can call this man Mr. Spock, the Vulcan character from *Star Trek* who felt no human emotions. When Mr. Spock gets into an argument with his wife, he can push all her emotional buttons while he remains as cool as a cucumber. While his wife flips out, he remains calm and remorseless, feeling smugly superior to his wife while she goes through her tantrum. As she rages, he calmly interjects a well-placed zinger here and a well-placed zinger there. He can leave the argument feeling as if he is the moral superior because he did not raise his voice or lose his cool.

In reality, his so-called moral superiority amounts to nothing more than manipulative malice. He keeps his cool because he knows that in so doing he will have the upper hand in the argument, but he has no compassion for his wife. He does not contain his anger in order to be kind, tenderhearted, and forgiving toward her. He contains his anger in order to better puncture her ego.

Rather than playing malicious Mr. Spock, try being your wife's friend. Try seeing things from her perspective. Even if you disagree with her, you can at least sympathize with her and refrain from hurting her. That's the path of a real man—one worthy of a woman's love and adoration.

WHY NOT RATHER SUFFER WRONG?

Unlike the comical quarreling couple on a television situation comedy, husbands and wives do not recover well from arguments. Even when they do make up quickly, the wounds in the woman's heart remain, festering and infected, long after the intimacy of the "make up" is over. The man goes on and forgets the whole thing, but the woman never forgets how her husband turned against her and hurt her with his words.

Arguments are never a good idea. The moment a disagreement or discussion starts to turn into an argument, its time to set the topic aside. Try revisiting it some other time if it's actually important. Most often, it's not nearly as important as you think.

In his first epistle to the Corinthians, the holy Apostle Paul rebuked the believers in Corinth for taking lawsuits against one another to secular courts. He insisted that disputes within the assembly of Messiah needed to be settled by elders within the assembly, just as the larger Jewish community handled its own affairs. Then he said to the Corinthians, "To have lawsuits at all with one another is already a defeat for you. Why not rather suffer wrong? Why not rather be defrauded?" (1 Corinthians 6:7). Paul felt that a mature believer would rather suffer an injustice than bring a brother in Messiah to court over the matter.

Let's apply the same concept to marriage. To have an argument with your wife "is already a defeat for you. Why not rather suffer wrong?" Why not simply swallow your pride, let go of your contention, leaving it in the hands of God, and show your wife love and respect? What is to be gained by arguments and disputes?

The Apostle Peter teaches that a husband must strive to have "unity of mind" with his wife, "sympathy" for her position, "brotherly love" for her as a fellow heir of the grace of life, and a "tender heart." Most importantly, he must have a "humble mind" in order to set aside differences and disagreements:

> Husbands, live with your wives in an understanding way, showing honor to the woman as the weaker vessel, since they are heirs with you of the grace of life, so that your prayers may not be hindered. Finally, all of you, have unity of mind, sympathy, brotherly love, a tender heart, and a humble mind. (1 Peter 3:7–8)

The husband who insists on arguing his point and forcing his wife to see her error will not be able to fulfill any of Peter's instructions. The belligerent husband has no unity of mind with his wife. He has no sympathy for her as the weaker vessel. He shows her no brotherly love as a fellow child of God and disciple of the Master. His heart grows hard, not tender toward her. His proud mind has no room for humility.

The devout disciple of Jesus understands that the road to redemption involves voluntarily sacrifice and suffering. Our Master went to the cross when he did not deserve it, but "when he was reviled, he did not revile in return; when he suffered, he did not threaten, but continued entrusting himself to him who judges justly" (1 Peter 2:23). The true disciple turns the other cheek, goes the extra mile, does not repay evil with evil. If we fail to apply those principles first and foremost to our marriages, we fail the first test of discipleship.

Better to suffer wrong than fight your own wife.

THE IRRATIONAL WIFE

When men and women start to argue, things quickly go awry because men's and women's brains reason and process information in different ways. Contrary to popular belief, women are not irrational. They are completely rational according to the way a woman's mind works. A woman typically has a broader perspective on an issue, considering multiple implications simultaneously and prioritizing things according to their emotional weight. A man typically has narrow tunnel vision on an issue, considering only one implication at a time and prioritizing things according to some pragmatic sequence. When these two very different brains start to argue, they may be using the same language, but they are talking about completely different things. Communication breaks down quickly.

Men blame arguments on their irrational wives. She's not irrational. It's just that she reasons things the way a rational woman does, not the way a rational man does. Arguing with her will not work. The man needs to stop the arguing long enough to listen to her broader perspectives, considering the multiple implications she sees and acknowledging that she assigns a different sequence of priority to things than he does. Only when he hears and understands her perspective can a rational discussion ensue. So long as he dismisses her as simply irrational, no real discussion can ever occur. By listening to and trying to understand his wife's side of the disagreement, the husband displays "unity of mind, sympathy, brotherly love, a tender heart, and a humble mind" (1 Peter 3:8).

WHAT IF IT REALLY IS IMPORTANT?

By now you should be fairly frustrated with this book. It sounds as if we are saying that you cannot criticize your wife, correct her in any way, or argue with her at all. You just need to roll over, play dead, and let her walk over the top of you. At the same time, make sure she knows she's the most important thing in your life and that nothing is more important than her. Have you got all that? Sounds like unrealistic idealism, right? Before you arrive at that conclusion and toss this book in the trash, we encourage you to spend some serious time with Matthew 5. Pray over Jesus' teachings and explain why you haven't also tossed the New Testament in the trash. Or is it possible that you think the principles of discipleship simply don't apply to marriage?

Nevertheless, a man will complain, "What if my wife seriously needs to be corrected on some matter? How can I just remain silent?"

For the most part, the things we consider so serious and urgent are actually not. Most of them are just the male ego talking. But let's consider a hypothetical example where a wife, perhaps, overspends the monthly budget. The husband has repeatedly, respectfully reminded her about the budget, but she seems to deliberately ignore his gentle reminders. Her spending is plunging the family deeper into debt every month.

The man thinks, "I need to tell her off and put her in her place for the good of the family." Go ahead and try. Then write to us six months later and tell us if it worked. Maybe it did work for the short term. For one month or maybe two months, the wife, feeling shamed and humiliated, tried to watch her spending habits more carefully. Within a few months, however, her old pattern resumed. The entire confrontation accomplished no lasting good, but it did damage the marriage.

Great men of prayer such as George Müller and Hudson Taylor practiced a principle they called "moving men through prayer alone." By this they meant that when they had a need, they elected not to publish it or try to engage in active fundraising. Instead, they spent serious time on their knees, beseeching God, and they left the matter with him. Anyone who knows the stories of Müller and Taylor knows that their method worked.

Apply the same principle to your marriage. Rather than arguing with your wife or trying to correct her, try moving your wife through prayer alone. Spend an hour in prayer over the matter. You will come out way ahead. A typical argument involves at least twenty minutes of the initial exchange, a few hours of sulking, a second exchange, more sulking, a day of the silent treatment, and then the long apologizing and appeasement efforts. How much better to have simply spent an hour in prayer, pouring out your heart like water before the Almighty:

> O what peace we often forfeit,
> O what needless pain we bear,
> All because we do not carry
> Everything to God in prayer.

POWER OF PRAYER

Men underestimate the value of intensive personal prayer. The typical Christian man offers a few half-breathed prayers throughout the day. He may never have actually spent a day in real prayer. In Messianic Judaism the typical man knocks out his obligatory, liturgical prayers (morning, afternoon, and evening) like a man punching in and out of a shift at work. But men of real prayer do not hesitate to set aside an entire afternoon, an entire day, an entire weekend to pray over a single matter.

Three hours of heartfelt, devout personal prayer can move a mountain of problems. Instead of praying, however, a man feels as though he can handle the situation himself with a few well-placed cutting words. This man is a fool.

The immense power of prayer can make miracles happen. Does a man really think he will accomplish more by arguing with his wife than by pouring out the situation before his Father in heaven? If so, why does he even call himself a believer?

THE DEAL BREAKERS

But let's suppose that your wife has fallen into serious transgression (God forbid) such as one of the three cardinal sins: murder, idolatry, immorality. The rabbis taught that a person must willingly accept martyrdom rather than transgress one of these prohibitions.[31] Suppose that a husband notices that his wife (God forbid) has committed a homicide, bowed down to an idol of Pan, or engaged in an adulterous affair. Should a husband just remain silent, pray about it, and hope that things improve? Of course not. A little common sense goes a long way. So does a little biblical literacy.

God's Law makes it clear that anyone committing one of these sins has forfeited his or her own life. The Bible forbids leaving murder unpunished.[32] It forbids showing mercy to a family member who entices to worship idols.[33] The Torah says that an adulterer must be put to death.[34] In modern times, outside the land of Israel, outside the jurisdiction of the civil law of the Torah, and without the existence of a Sanhedrin to try such cases and execute such punishments, we do not stone people to death. Nevertheless, the sentence still applies to the marriage, so to speak. The marriage is over.

According to biblical principles, at the point when a wife strays outside her marriage, the marriage is over. Modern Christian counselors will disagree, but Jewish Law is pretty clear on the matter. In the days of the Sanhedrin and the Temple, the sin of adultery ended with a stoning at the hands of the court, so long as two witnesses could provide corroborating testimony. Of course, this does not sanction violence. There is no Sanhedrin today, and all corporal and capital punishments are suspended. A man cannot stone his wayward wife without being guilty of the sin of murder. At the same time, he cannot remain in the marriage. After adultery is proven, the marriage is officially over. This is why Joseph sought to divorce his betrothed fiancée, Mary, when he suspected her of infidelity. Even Jesus himself does not ask a husband or a wife to forgive the sin of adultery. Jesus sanctions divorce in cases in which sexual immorality has occurred.[35]

God forbid that any disciple of our holy Master besmirches his name with the sin of infidelity. If it were to happen, however, the Bible releases the offended spouse from the marriage. Many spiritual leaders encourage marriages to reconcile after adultery. They look to the story of the woman caught in adultery in John 8 (despite the fact that there is no indication whatsoever that Jesus sent the woman back to her husband). Reconciliation after infidelity might be a worthy goal in keeping with the principles of forgiveness and restoration taught by our Master, but it may be too much to ask of a human being. God will surely reward those brave men and women who do sacrifice themselves in order to forgive and take back an adulterous spouse. Surely they have done a noble thing, but once again, this is not something that the Bible requires of us.

On the flipside of this coin, however, if a man has ever been unfaithful to his wife, he is in no position to end the marriage if his wife commits an unchaste act. He should give her a chance to repent and reconcile with him on the basis of Jesus' words, "If you do not forgive others their trespasses, neither will your Father forgive your trespasses" (Matthew 6:15). Our Master says, "Let him who is without sin among you be the first to throw a stone at her" (John 8:7).

A WOMAN HEADED TOWARD ADULTERY

Let's suppose that things have not gotten that far yet. Suppose that a woman has not yet committed the sins of murder, idolatry, or adultery, but her husband sees that she is clearly and unambiguously on the path in that direction. Suppose that she has definitely begun a flirtatious and sensual relationship with a man outside the marriage. Is the husband to remain silent, trusting only in prayer, while she strays toward sexual immorality?

Of course not. A husband is completely justified to say to his wife, "My love, I see that you are drawn to such-and-such a fellow. Know that I love you and will be faithful to you so long as you are faithful to me, but no further." He need not belabor the point beyond that. He should leave it with the Almighty. If she goes astray (God forbid), the LORD releases him from the marriage.

Notice, however, that this entire exchange requires no anger, no irrational jealous rage, and no heated argument. The husband could make the statement simply and in a straightforward manner without malice or anger.

Short of the three deal breakers (murder, idolatry, adultery), there are few situations that warrant a husband criticizing his wife or raising objections to her behavior. Instead, let him bring his concerns to the Almighty God who made heaven and earth and man and woman.

Obviously there are a great many other things that merit considerable concern, but the Bible does not list any of those things as grounds for divorce. The teaching of Jesus offers only sexual immorality as a legitimate reason for divorce. In that case, the disciple of Jesus should not throw down the gauntlet for anything of lower caliber because once an argument has started, who can say where it will end? "The beginning of strife is like letting out water, so quit before the quarrel breaks out" (Proverbs 17:14).

BEFORE THE QUARREL BREAKS OUT

A genuine disciple of Jesus would rather suffer wrong than engage in arguments and disputes with his wife. Arguing with our wives is never a good idea. Most of the things we argue about are simply not worth the damage the argument incurs.

Since arguing with your wife damages her emotionally, even if you win the argument, you still lose. Unlike the couples who argue on television, you and your wife will not find a happy resolution at the end of the episode. Because of the differences between the way a man's mind works and the way a woman's mind works, arguments with your wife are pointless.

Women are not irrational; their minds simply reason through things on a different path than a man's mind does. A husband should never let anger enter into an argument with his wife. Angry feelings indicate that the time has come to drop the discussion.

Remember that anger is the real enemy, not your wife. Rather than argue with your wife, commit every matter to prayer. Take it up with the LORD, and ask him to put his Son, Jesus, into the middle of the matter to make peace between you and the woman you love. With God all things are possible.

11

THE OBLIGATION OF LOVE

The Bible commands husbands to love their wives, and the apostles provide two standards by which we are to measure our love for our wives. The husband must love his wife as he loves himself, and the husband must love his wife as Christ loves the church, that is, his assembly.

LOVE AND MARRIAGE

Marriages in our culture are fragile because they are based upon a lie. The lie is this: "If you fall in love with a woman, and she falls in love with you, you should get married." A moment of logical reflection exposes the stupidity behind this idea. It's possible to fall in love with lots of women. Should you marry them all? It's just as easy to fall out of love with them. What then? Should you get divorced because you are no longer in love?

Love, as we understand it in our culture, is a terrible reason to get married. Romantic love is fickle and quickly fading. If either you or your wife are operating under the assumption that when love dies, the marriage should end, you might as well get a divorce right now. Better yet, rethink the reason for marriage, and build yours on a new foundation. Biblical love, as modeled by our Master and taught by his apostles, provides a strong foundation for a marriage.

YOUR MINIMUM DUTY

What if you don't love your wife? What should you do? What would God expect from you?

God's instructions in the Torah spell out a man's duties to his wife in a passage discussing polygamy. Exodus 21:10 specifies a husband's duties to his first wife in the event that he marries a second woman and no longer feels that he loves the first. The Torah warns that if a man takes a second wife, he still remains obligated to meet his first wife's needs. Needless to say, polygamy is not an option for disciples of Jesus. The teachings of Jesus forbid multiple wives. Nevertheless, the passage teaches us about what God considers to be the three minimum obligations that a husband must fulfill for his wife. Even if he no longer loves her, "he shall not diminish her food, her clothing, or her marital rights" (Exodus 21:10).

Food refers to more than just keeping the refrigerator filled; it refers to the standard of living to which your wife has become accustomed. The Bible requires a husband who "falls out of love" with his wife to continue to financially support her at the same standard to which she is accustomed. The Bible does not allow him to reduce the amount he spends on her just because he no longer has feelings for her.

Clothing refers to more than just the things in the closet. A wife's "clothing" is her personal belongings. The husband must not reduce her personal belongings or keep her from maintaining her things. This means buying her new clothes when necessary, but it also infers buying her a new car when necessary. The Talmud advises a man to actually spend more on his wife than he can afford because, while she depends upon him, he depends upon God.

Marital rights refer specifically to affection and sexual intimacy. Even if a man no longer feels affectionate or physically inspired by his wife, the LORD forbids him from diminishing her "marital rights." He must continue to treat her with the same level of compassion, and he must not refuse to sleep with her or grant her sexual gratification.

Remember, these are the obligations that the Torah places upon a man who does not love his wife any longer—a man who has taken a second wife. If this is what God expects of a man who no longer has feelings for his wife, how much more does he expect of a man who does love his wife?

TWO GOLDEN RULES

Actually, disciples of Jesus do not have the option of "falling out of love" with their wives. We have a direct and often-repeated commandment to love our wives. A true disciple loves his wife because he loves God, not because his wife inspires his love or even because she deserves to be loved. Maybe she does not naturally inspire his affection. Perhaps he does not find her lovable. It does not matter. He loves his wife not on her merit but in obedience to God.

Biblical love is not the same as *eros* and romantic love. The Torah says, "You shall love your neighbor as yourself" (Leviticus 19:18). This standard applies to everyone, not just your wife. But if it applies to everyone, how much more so does it apply to your wife, your closest neighbor? Paul applied the commandment directly to marriage when he said, "Let each one of you love his wife as himself" (Ephesians 5:33).

The sage Hillel paraphrased the great commandment of love for neighbor in the words, "Do not do to another that which is hateful to you." Jesus paraphrased the same commandment in the positive form of the golden rule: "Whatever you wish that others would do to you, do also to them" (Matthew 7:12). These two golden rules apply to your relationship with your wife as follows:

1. Don't do anything to your wife that you do not want her to do to you.

2. Treat your wife the way you want her to treat you.

A husband should not do anything to his wife that he himself would dislike if she did it to him. For example, a husband does not like it when his wife pushes his irritation buttons, gives him a tongue lashing, acts offended, sulks around the house, or carries a grudge. Since he does not like it when she does those things to him, the rule of love says that he must not do any of those things to her. You see how simple the rule is? A husband hates it when his wife blames him for things. He should therefore apply the rule and never make her the object of his blame. He hates it when she berates him; he should never berate her. He hates it when she breaks her promise to him; he should never break his promises to her. He hates it when she keeps secrets from him; he should be transparent with her. He hates it when she gives him the cold shoulder; he should have only warm shoulders for her. He dislikes it immensely when she sexually rejects him; he should never "get her back" by rejecting her.

On the other hand, a husband should treat his wife the way he wants her to treat him. He wants her to speak to him respectfully with love and admiration. He wants her to affirm him. He wants her to make him feel smart, attractive, and important. He wants her to sympathize with him when he is upset, and he wants her to mother him when he is not feeling well. He wants her to be sexually available to him. He wants her to attend to her duties diligently. He wants her to get up in the night with the baby. He wants her to change the diapers so he doesn't have to. Do you see how easy this is? The golden rule simply states that however a husband would like his wife to treat him, that's how he should treat her.

The two golden rules are not ploys for getting results. In other words, the golden rules do not say, "Treat your wife the way you want her to treat you *so that she will start treating you the way you want.*" They do not say, "Don't do anything to your wife that you do not want her to do to you *so that she will quit doing stuff that you hate.*" The motivation behind the golden rules must be nothing other than love. It's not about what you can get from her. If you are being kind to your wife in order to manipulate her into meeting your needs, you are not loving her at all. You are only pretending to love her. As soon as you realize that the manipulation is not working, you will drop the pretense. When she fails to meet your expectations, the golden rules go out the window. The pouting husband says to himself, "I did all that nice stuff for her, and this is how she treats me? Forget about those golden rules. They don't work." That's not the type of love the Bible has in mind; in fact, that's not love at all. That's just a selfish man hypocritically playing the part of a loving husband in order to get his needs better met.

The golden rules are extremely simple to learn, but they are difficult to implement. They challenge the selfish core of our being. A husband needs to ask God for help to internalize the golden rules and make them reflexive in his behavior. They require a keen sense of empathy and selfless resolve. They involve serious introspection, and they take constant practice.

To get started, try sitting down and writing out two lists: things you dislike and things you like. Look at the items on the lists, and make a plan for implementing them in your relationship with your wife according to the law of love. For example, "I like it when she smiles at me and greets me cheerfully. I don't like it when she scowls at me or ignores me." Now you know what to do. Always make sure that you smile at your wife and greet her cheerfully. Never scowl at her or ignore her. (Of course, a man should not keep a list of things he dislikes about his wife or leave such a damning document lying about the house. Do yourself a favor and immediately destroy it.)

By learning to practice the golden rules of love on his wife, a man spiritually disciplines himself for the service of the kingdom. He will become adept at empathizing with others and loving his neighbor because he has had so much practice at home.

FAKING IT

Husbands have a biblical mandate to love their wives. Even if you no longer feel the love you once had for your wife, you will feel it again once you start acting loving toward her. The heart follows the head, so to speak. Once you decide to act loving, the heart feels the love. The inverse is also true. As you act unkindly and cruelly toward someone, the heart follows up by generating unkind and cruel emotions for that person. If necessary, fake it at first. Your heart will follow your actions. It won't be long before it will become real.

For most husbands there is no need to fake it at all. We truly do love our wives. Loving our wives is the most natural thing in the world. We can't fathom not loving our wives. But we often fail to translate that love into loving behaviors.

On the other hand, some husbands genuinely do struggle to feel any love for their wives. A Messianic rabbi counseling a man in a failing marriage urged him to start treating his wife lovingly. The rabbi told him that he had a biblical obligation to love her. He explained that regardless of how he felt about her, it was his duty to God to love his wife. The man took the rabbi's advice. He went home and started treating his wife with love and respect. She noticed the change immediately, and she liked it. She asked him, "Why are you treating me so nicely?"

He replied, "Because I have a biblical obligation to love you, not because I have any feelings for you." Wrong answer! Things did not go well after that. The correct answer would have been, "Because you are my wife, and that means you are the most special person in the entire world to me."

LOVE YOURSELF

Paul further explained the concept of loving your wife as yourself. He said, "Husbands should love their wives as their own bodies ... For no one ever hated his own flesh, but nourishes and cherishes it" (Ephesians 5:28–29).

According to this standard, the Bible defines love as acts of kindness, compassion, and cherishing. The apostles said nothing about warm feelings of affection or the yearnings of physical attraction. They defined love to mean primarily caretaking.

Paul told the husband to love his wife as he loved his own body. You might think, "I don't love my own body." Perhaps you don't like the way you look, but you certainly do love and care for your own body. You feed yourself several times a day; you take yourself to the bathroom; you wash yourself and dress yourself; when you are sick, you care for yourself. And it goes beyond that. Whenever you are in an argument, you take your own side. You always laugh at your own jokes. You sympathize with yourself when your feelings are hurt. You work hard for your success. In other words, you do everything for yourself.

This is how Paul understood the commandment to love your wife as you love yourself. Paul wanted husbands to think of themselves as one flesh with their wives—a single creature. Whatever a man would do for himself, he should be willing to do for his wife. Provide for her, take care of her, keep her physically and emotionally healthy, take her side in arguments, laugh at her jokes, sympathize with her feelings, work hard for her success, and so forth.

ONE SELF

Paul explained that a man who truly loves his wife as he loves himself actually is loving himself because he is one flesh with his wife: "He who loves his wife loves himself" (Ephesians 5:28). From this perspective, the man should not consider himself independent of his wife, nor should he think of her as outside himself. When it comes to loving, cherishing, caring, and providing, she is him, and he is her. The husband and wife are like one being.

Naturally, this is not true on every level. Your wife is still her own person, just as you are still an individual. You both still need your space and firm boundaries. To some extent you both need to cultivate your own interests and keep your own privacy. You do not want to be one flesh with your wife to the point of smothering her. She cannot respect a man who seems to need her too much, as if he has no independent identity and self-confidence of his own.

Aside from that, a husband and wife really are spiritually and psychologically united. That's why divorce is so traumatic and painful. When a man and woman get married, their sense of self-identity changes to include the other. The man is no longer just himself. The woman is no longer just herself.

For example, try this little thought experiment. Imagine that you and your wife go through a divorce (God forbid). You say good-bye and go your separate ways. Now try to imagine her happy with another man. Imagine her smiling and laughing with him and enjoying all the delights and pleasures of a married couple. No man is comfortable with this idea. Neither are women comfortable with the idea of their husbands finding fulfillment with other women.

The discomfort we feel at the idea of our spouses with someone else comes from something deeper than simple jealousy. It offends our sense of self-identity. Since our spiritual sense of identity has changed to incorporate the other, we cannot release the spouse to be an independent person again. A wife will always be part of her husband on a spiritual and psychological level, and he will always be part of her. That's what marriage is. Therefore, a man should love his wife as he loves himself—because she actually is.

A HUSBAND'S NEEDS

The sober biblical definitions of love presented above are not the type of things that men usually think about when they talk about falling in love. When a man says he is in love, he usually means that he feels a flurry of romantic feelings for a woman that have intoxicated him like too much whiskey. Beneath the euphoric buzz, however, the man is in love on the basis of what he gets out of the relationship: affection, companionship, affirmation, and most important of all, sexual satisfaction. In other words, most men think of love primarily in terms of what they will get from a relationship. When those things are not consistently forthcoming, the husband starts to suspect that somehow love has failed him.

A biblical definition of love has a lot less adrenaline connected with it, but it is a lot more stable. Under the biblical definition of love, the man should not be anticipating what he will get from his spouse but what he can give to her.

As long as a man believes that his wife can meet his needs—emotionally, physically, psychologically, spiritually—she can only disappoint him. Only God can meet our needs, and only God can make us happy. If we expect our wives to do for us what only God can do for us, we make them into idols in our lives.

Many men keep a list of expectations in their heads. When the wife does not meet her husband's invisible list of expectations, he punishes her by withdrawing his love. He acts coldly toward her. So long as a man expects his wife to give something to him in return, he will never be able to selflessly love her. His love will always come with a contingency.

A man should pray, "Father in heaven, help me to receive from you and give to her. May I depend only upon you for everything I need. Help me not to need anything from her at all. Instead, help me to rely upon you only and give to her from your bounty."

A man thinks he needs his wife, but that's not how God designed the relationship. If a man insists on needing love, affection, and affirmation from his wife, he may find himself in a home torn asunder by two women—one of whom is him.

The wife needs the husband, and the husband needs God. The husband needs to emotionally nourish his wife, spiritually nurture her, and physically guard her and protect her. At the same time, he must look to the LORD for his own emotional nourishment, spiritual nurture, and physical protection. He does not need his wife's love; he needs God's love. Then he can take from that ample supply and shower it abundantly upon his wife.

A man should pray, "Father, give me your own love to pour out upon my wife. Help me see her as your beloved daughter. Plant your love for her within me, and help me not to need anything from her in return."

FORGIVENESS

The most powerful way to show your wife that you love her is to forgive her unreservedly for any wrongs or failings. As you know, the Bible requires us to forgive others when they sin against us. How much more so must we forgive our wives?

What does it really mean to forgive someone? It's more than just saying, "I forgive you." Real forgiveness consists of a resolution not to prosecute. In other words, the one who forgives another relinquishes his right to collect on the debt. For example, suppose you owed your father one thousand dollars. Then he sent you a note releasing the debt and forgiving the entire loan. Naturally, you are relieved, that is, until he brings the matter up a few weeks later, and every so often after that, saying, "Don't forget about that thousand dollars you still owe me."

Essentially, that's what we do every time we bring up an old offense or wound. It's not uncommon for a married couple's arguments to continually circle around the same set of wounds and offenses. If you keep a litany of your wife's sins and shortcomings handy, then you have not forgiven her.

Right now you might be thinking, "Why should I forgive her? She has never forgiven me in my life." That's exactly why you should forgive her. If she's not capable of forgiveness, then you need to be the forgiving one—or your marriage is doomed.

Of course, women are capable of forgiveness. If not for a woman's large capacity for forgiveness, she would have probably left her husband in the first year of marriage. But you should know that forgiveness comes easier for men than it does for women. Not because men are more righteous. It's just one of the differences between male and female psychologies.

God has given men a larger capacity to forgive and forget than he has given to women. Just as God has given men more upper-body strength in order to better compete in the world and provide for his family, he has likewise given men a more natural capacity for offering forgiveness. Since God designed men as warriors and competitors, he needed to also make us quick to forgive. Otherwise we would quickly kill each other off. Perhaps God made women less forgiving than their husbands because God implanted a mother-lion instinct in them to protect the children and guard the den. In any case, a man who refuses to forgive, who holds on to his list of offenses and continues to nurture bitterness against someone, is not acting like a man at all. It's not unusual for a woman to bring up past hurts, but a man should know better.

Jesus emphasized forgiveness. He said that unless we forgive others, God will not forgive us, but if we do forgive others when they sin against us, God will forgive our sins. He told the parable of the ungrateful servant to illustrate the point (Matthew 18). In the parable a man owes several million dollars to the Roman government. He pleads for mercy, and the emperor pardons the man's debt. Then the man goes out and finds a fellow servant who owes him a few hundred dollars. He refuses to have mercy on the debtor and even has him thrown in debtor's prison until he can repay the debt. When the emperor hears about this, he says, "You wicked servant! I forgave you all that debt because you pleaded with me. And should not you have had mercy on your fellow servant, as I had mercy on you?" (Matthew 18:32–33). Then the emperor hands him over to the torturers until he can repay all the millions he owes. Jesus said, "So also my heavenly Father will do to every one of you, if you do not forgive your brother from your heart" (Matthew 18:35). Do you think it is a coincidence that Matthew placed this parable immediately before the Master's discourse on marriage (Matthew 19:1–12)?

SAYING "I FORGIVE YOU"

When it comes to forgiveness, please remember this word of warning: Forgiveness is not the same as saying "I forgive you"; forgiveness means relinquishing your right to retaliate or collect on a debt. When your wife offends you in some way, you should show her that you forgive her by your actions, not your words. Show her forgiveness by overlooking the matter and refraining from bringing it up again.

As we noted earlier, unless your wife asks for forgiveness, you should not tell her "I forgive you." Saying "I forgive you" when your wife has not apologized or asked for forgiveness is the same as telling her "You have offended me, but since I am such a spiritual giant and noble person, I forgive you." She won't appreciate your offer.

THE LOVE GOGGLES

The Bible teaches that love "bears all things" and "endures all things" (1 Corinthians 13:7). "Love covers all offenses" (Proverbs 10:12). "Love covers a multitude of sins" (1 Peter 4:8). This means that a man who loves his wife deliberately decides not to notice her shortcomings and character flaws. He is not naïve. He knows his wife is not perfect; he just refuses to dwell on her imperfections. He brushes them aside; he looks the other direction.

If you bring up your wife's shortcomings in conversations with others, you are betraying her confidence in you. If you bring up her shortcomings in conversation with her, you will hurt her and alienate her. If you mull over them in your mind, you will alienate yourself from her and embitter your own heart. A man who loves his wife intentionally "covers" for her failings: "Whoever covers an offense seeks love, but he who repeats a matter separates close friends" (Proverbs 17:9).

This principle can be illustrated with a story from the Torah. Noah was a godly, righteous man. But even godly, righteous men make mistakes. Using alcohol is a sure way to make serious blunders. Noah had a few too many drinks and made a fool of himself. He did so in view of his sons: "He drank of the wine and became drunk and lay uncovered in his tent" (Genesis 9:21).

How do we react when someone we love behaves foolishly or reveals some character flaw? The Torah shows us two alternatives. Noah's son Ham "saw the nakedness of his father and told his two brothers outside" (Genesis 9:22). The other two sons, Shem and Japheth, took a blanket, "laid it on both their shoulders, and walked backward and covered the nakedness of their father. Their faces were turned backward, and they did not see their father's nakedness" (Genesis 9:23). Ham chose to focus on his father's folly and shame; the other two sons chose to look the other direction. More than that, they covered their father, as the Bible says, "Love covers a multitude of sins."

We can apply this same story to marriage. In marriage a man has a choice. He can focus on his wife's shortcomings, or he can look the other way. He can expose her sins and weaknesses, or he can cover her: "Above all, keep loving one another earnestly, since love covers a multitude of sins" (1 Peter 4:8).

When you look at your wife, or when you think of her, you should do so only through the lenses of love. Put on your love goggles, and filter everything undesirable, irritating, or offensive completely out of the picture. Train your mind to defend her and delight in her. Choose to see only the good and never the bad. If you do see anything bad, cover it with love.

THE CAR ACCIDENT

One husband told his Messianic rabbi, "I've tried to love her, but she just throws it back in my face. We've grown too far apart. I acknowledge that it's partly my fault, but she's not even interested in trying to work on the marriage anymore."

The rabbi said to him, "Imagine there was a man who fell in love with a beautiful young woman, and she loved him too. They got married and began their life together. One day, however, a terrible accident happened: late for work, the man sped down his driveway in his automobile and peeled out onto the street, striking a jogger—his own wife. She was paralyzed (God forbid). Now what should he do? Does he leave her because she will never again be able to meet his needs or fulfill her role as his wife, or does he commit the rest of life to taking care of this invalid? I think only a reprehensible and lowly man would leave the woman, especially if he himself had run her over."

The husband said, "Of course I would take care of her."

The rabbi said, "I know you would. And I know that you would never leave your wife if she contracted some dreadful disease or suffered some physical handicap. If that's the case, then you shouldn't give up on her just because her malady is emotional. Look, maybe your wife never will be able to return your affection and love. Maybe she's emotionally damaged. Maybe someone ran her over. Maybe you did. Maybe she's an emotional invalid. How is that different from a physical invalid?"

Many husbands inadvertently run over their wives almost every day. They emotionally plow over them, crippling their capacity for receiving and returning affection, intimacy, and love. A husband with an emotionally crippled wife might become bitter against her, forgetting that he himself is the perpetrator who emotionally crippled the poor woman in the first place.

A man of love would never toss his wife aside because she contracted cancer (God forbid). Instead, he would stay by her side, holding her hand through the rigors of that horrible journey, praying for her recovery, and refusing to give up hope. Maybe your wife's malady is emotional, spiritual, or psychological instead of physical, but that does not change your responsibility toward her. You still need to stay by her side, holding her hand, praying for her recovery, and refusing to give up hope. That's what it means to be one flesh and to be glued to your wife. You are one flesh with her, and you are glued to her, even if she no longer has feelings for you. Even if you no longer have feelings for her.

The good news in such situations is that our Master is accustomed to healing invalids. He made lame men walk. He healed the paralyzed. He even raised the dead. Even if your feelings toward your wife feel dead, or if her feelings toward you feel dead, Jesus of Nazareth can raise your marriage back to life. The important thing is never to give up on God or one another. Pour out your heart in prayer, and trust God.

Sometimes healing comes all at once, in a miraculous manner. More often it comes slowly, over time, little by little. Sometimes it does not come at all. Whether your marriage heals all at once, little by little, or not at all, the important thing is that you do your duty: love your wife. Leave the rest in the hands of your Father in heaven.

THE STROKE

At First Fruits of Zion, we meet a lot of people from abroad when they come to Israel to visit. One visitor to Israel told us a story that illustrates the above point well. He and his wife had shared a happy marriage for more than twenty years when she suffered a sudden catastrophic brain hemorrhage. At first it seemed that she might not recover at all. After a long hospitalization, extensive therapy, and lots of prayer from her devastated husband, however, the woman was finally able to return home to normal life. There was one problem: she was not normal. She no longer had any memories from the last twenty years. She did not recognize her husband, and she was afraid of him. She hated him.

Day after day she screamed at him, spit at him, physically struck at him, and called him horrible names. Gently he waited out the emotional storms, taking care of her as she recovered, showing her pictures of their life together, telling her about the years she had forgotten, assuring her that he loved her. Day after day he reminded her that he was her husband and that he loved her. Eventually she calmed down and accepted him as her husband, but things did not return to normal. Her hatred for the stranger in her home faded, but a strange jealous paranoia replaced it. She began to suspect him of lying to her when he said "I love you." She began to accuse him of all sorts of sinister intentions. In her paranoia and delusion, she decided that he was cheating on her. She baselessly accused him of infidelity and adultery and viciously rejected his pleas of innocence. She threw all his assurances of love and kind words back in his face.

He said, "I just had to keep telling myself, 'This isn't her. This is not my wife. This is the brain injury, but the woman I love is still in there.'" He stayed with her and continued to love her despite all the recriminations and baseless accusations. He learned to ignore her fits of rage and continued to assure her, day after day, "Honey, I love you. You have nothing to worry about."

Thanks to his gentle persistence, she leveled out and her mind has healed—somewhat. But she is not the same woman she was before the stroke, and their relationship can never be normal again. Every day he faces a new challenge, and the emotional outbursts of paranoia, delusion, or vitriolic abuse might erupt at any given moment.

When congratulated for his faithful commitment to his wife, he explained, "I love her."

The woman with the brain injury is really not so different from a woman with emotional injuries. The woman with emotional injuries deals with the same types of feelings: "Is this the man I married? Is this really my husband? Does he really love me? Is he really faithful to me? Can I trust him?" These fears manifest in a variety of unpleasantries that test a husband's patience. The godly man looks past the insecurities and emotional storms, assuring his wife, "I love you. You have nothing to worry about."

REAL LOVE

Real love is not a warm, fuzzy emotional feeling, it's an obligation. Feelings come and go, but the obligation to love our wives never changes. A husband shows his wife love by taking care of her needs, providing for her, and treating her with affection and understanding. He treats her the way he wants her to treat him. If there are things he does not like about how she treats him, those are the things he does not do to her. He knows that she is not there to meet his needs. Only God can meet his needs. He is there to meet her needs.

He shows her love by forgiving her for all offenses, never bringing them up again or reminding her of her shortcomings. Whenever he looks at her, he keeps the love goggles over his eyes because love bears all things, endures all things, covers all offenses, and covers a multitude of sins.

You do love your wife. You would not have read this far into this book if you did not. You probably wouldn't have even picked the book up in the first place. So now all you need to do is to translate that love into action. With a little bit of prayer and help from your Father in heaven, you are ready to light up your wife with your love—not fake love but the real thing.

12

SPIRITUAL AUTHORITY

The progressive modern thinkers of today criticize the Bible's family values as patriarchal, chauvinist, and even misogynist. It is true that the Bible imparts a patriarchal worldview. It vests family authority with the father of the family, and it endows spiritual and civil authority on men appointed to tasks as elders, prophets, priests, judges, and kings. Trying to impose egalitarian values on the Bible creates anachronistic interpretations. In the biblical world men took leadership positions.

The Bible presents those patriarchal values from a patriarchal worldview, but the Bible is neither chauvinist nor misogynist. Many fundamentalist Bible-believing men, however, are both. They misunderstand, misuse, and abuse the Bible's concept of male headship and authority.

In this chapter we will take a biblical look at spiritual authority in the home.

THE PIOUS CHAUVINIST

A young Bible teacher who had applied to teach full-time with First Fruits of Zion once declared, in front of his wife and in front of a Bible class, "A woman is her husband's property. Why else would the Torah list a man's wife along with his servants, his livestock, and his property?" He was referring to the prohibition on coveting a neighbor's wife "or his male servant, or his female servant, or his ox, or his donkey, or anything that is your neighbor's" (Exodus 20:17). Not a very solid interpretation of the Scripture, but it did not surprise us. That particular young man had a reputation as a bully and a bigot who continually used the Bible to justify his ugly personality. His meek and quiet wife never objected. She silently and patiently endured everything he said and did. No matter what he dished out, she obeyed as if she really was his property. She followed his selfish and capricious twists and turns without raising objections. After all, she knew her place. As the godly, submissive wife, her job was to remain silent, stay in the background, and have babies.

Most men are probably not as chauvinistic as that, but many otherwise godly men do believe that the Bible gives them a license to command their families as would a captain commanding lower-ranking men in the military. According to their interpretation of the Bible's prescription for marital bliss, the man makes all the decisions, and the wife must consent. He believes that he needs to teach his wife to submit and that he must exercise authority over her. She has no say in the affairs of the family or the decisions of her husband. If a woman does not cheerfully consent to her husband's orders, she commits the sin of rebellion and fails in her role as a biblical wife. He criticizes her for rebelling against God.

This poor woman finds herself in a terrible place. She is told that if she disagrees with her husband or fails to submit herself to his demands, she disobeys God. This puts her husband and God on the same team against her, ultimately forcing her to resent both. Meanwhile, her own dignity as an adult human being gets trampled by her pious husband as he thumps the Bible and quotes passages about a husband's headship and a wife's obligation to submit.

Before we take a closer look at those passages, take our advice, and don't ever quote those at your wife. If you do, she will perceive it as spiritual manipulation, and she will be right. Believe me, she will not think to herself, "My husband has a good point. I should be a more submissive wife so that I will be more in line with the teachings of the apostles in the New Testament." Instead, she will think, "What a bully! Every time I disagree with him he pulls out those Bible verses and uses them like a stick to hit me, and the whole time he feels completely self-righteous about it."

A HUSBAND'S AUTHORITY

From where did the apostles derive the fact of a husband's authority over his wife? They derived it from the Torah. The Apostle Paul says, "Women ... should be in submission, as the Torah also says" (1 Corinthians 14:34). The Torah makes this order of authority clear in Numbers 30 when it grants a husband the right to annul a vow made by his wife. A husband's authority to annul his wife's vow implies his authority over her. That Torah principle lies behind several often-repeated passages from the New Testament that speak about wives submitting to their husbands:

> Wives, submit to your own husbands, as to the Lord. (Ephesians 5:22)

> As the church submits to Christ, so also wives should submit in everything to their husbands. (Ephesians 5:24)

> Wives, submit to your husbands, as is fitting in the Lord. (Colossians 3:18)

> Wives, be subject to your own husbands. (1 Peter 3:1)

The Bible regards wives as subject to the authority of their husbands. This does not seem fair at all. It is not fair. Fairness, where fairness equals total equality, is not the Bible's goal for marriage. Distasteful as it may sound to us in the gender-neutralized postmodern era, the Bible has decidedly patriarchal values and prejudices. Wives do not have free agency. They are subject to their husbands.

Some teachers try to avoid the difficulty by passing it off as an Old Testament condition of fallen man that was altered in Christ. This interpretation is based on the passage that says, "There is no male and female, for you are all one in Christ Jesus" (Galatians 3:28).

If Paul had egalitarian values in mind when he made that statement, it is difficult to explain why he insists on wives being subject to their husbands in so many other places. For example, he tells the Ephesian women to "submit to your own husbands, as to the Lord. For the husband is the head of the wife even as Christ is the head of the church" (Ephesians 5:22–23). In his epistle to Titus, he encourages the young married women to be "submissive to their own husbands, that the word of God may not be reviled" (Titus 2:5).

Simon Peter had strong feelings about gender roles in the marriage, too. He instructs married women to "be subject to [their] own husbands" (1 Peter 3:1), even if their husbands are unbelievers. The biblical position on family hierarchy is unanimous.

Rather than trying to bend the plain meaning of the Bible, we should ask ourselves, why do modern people seem to have a problem with masculine headship? Is it perhaps because men have abused their authority? We know of endless examples of bad husbands and fathers who have lorded it over their wives and children. Such a man is no more biblical than a woman in open defiance to her husband. Paul enjoins married men, "Love your wives, and do not be harsh with them" (Colossians 3:19). See 1 Corinthians 13 for Paul's definition of love. The biblical principles of submission and authority within the home also call for a godly man who conducts himself according to the highest standards of discipleship. A home ruled by the iron fist of a harsh authoritarian is not worthy of the name of Christ.

The Bible models a husband who loves his wife. Paul tells us that men are to emulate the Messiah in their love for their wives. He says, "Husbands, love your wives, as Christ loved the church and gave himself up for her" (Ephesians 5:25). This is a sacrificial love. It allows no bullying; it does not force submission. Instead, the biblical husband nourishes and cherishes his wife. One cannot cherish a person and at the same time disregard her wishes, opinions, preferences, and dignity. Christlike headship calls for servanthood. The Master considers heavy-handed authority and lording it over others as something one might expect of idolaters but unworthy of his disciples:

> You know that the rulers of the Gentiles lord it over them, and their great ones exercise authority over them. It shall not be so among you. But whoever would be great among you must be your servant, and whoever would be first among you must be your slave, even as the Son of Man came not to be served but to serve, and to give his life as a ransom for many. (Matthew 20:25–28)

HER MITZVAH

Notice that the apostolic writers never command husbands, "Make your wives submit to you." The commandment (mitzvah) of submitting to one's husband belongs solely to the wife. It is her obligation and duty before God, not her husband's. A husband need not fret that his wife is not submissive to him. That is her business, not his. That is between her and God. He need not concern himself with it.

The Bible does not tell men to subjugate their wives or compel them to obey. The commandment of submission belongs entirely to the wife.

Just as the Bible tells wives to submit to their husbands, it tells all believers to submit "to one another out of reverence for Christ" (Ephesians 5:21). Now imagine that another fellow in your community of faith tried to force you into obedience to his will on the basis of this passage. Imagine he said, "The Bible commands you to submit to me, therefore you need to do what I tell you." You would reply, "The Bible commands us to submit to one another, but that act of submission is our own prerogative. You cannot force me to submit to you, and I cannot force you to submit to me."

Another example. The Bible tells us to give charity to the poor. This commandment does not permit the poor to demand charity. Suppose a poor man came to you and demanded five thousand dollars. To back up his demand, he quoted a couple of Bible verses:

> You shall not harden your heart or shut your hand against your poor brother. (Deuteronomy 15:7)

> Give to the one who begs from you, and do not refuse the one who would borrow from you. (Matthew 5:42)

These Bible verses do not entitle a poor person to demand your money. Instead, they are directives for you to observe under your own volition, not under any external compulsion. You have the prerogative to give to the poor. You determine when to give, how much to give, and to whom you give. Is your wife's commandment to submit to you really so different?

The Bible does not give husbands permission to discipline their wives in any fashion. If a husband had that type of power over his wife, then he would be in a position to demand her submission. If she failed to properly obey him, he could unleash disciplinary measures on her. He could demand obedience from her as a slave owner can demand obedience from his slaves. Since the Bible does not grant him the right to discipline his wife, however, this implies that his authority over her extends only so far as she is willing to comply with the biblical mandate incumbent upon her. Again, it is her obligation and duty, not her husband's. The prerogative remains with her, and if she submits to him, she does so of her own free will—not under any compulsion.

Again, the Bible never gives a man license to force his wife to obey him. Instead, it says that he must love her and treat her as "a fellow heir of the grace of life." She is his partner, not his servant:

> Husbands, live with your wives in an understanding way, showing honor to the woman as the weaker vessel, since they are heirs with you of the grace of life, so that your prayers may not be hindered. (1 Peter 3:7)

A brutish man or harsh authoritarian man who does not live with his wife "in an understanding way" is not worthy of even having his prayers answered. He does not listen to his wife's entreaties; why should God listen to his?

KING AHASUERUS

Believe it or not, some men appeal to the story of Esther for biblical evidence that he had the right to demand obedience from his wife. In the story of Esther, King Ahasuerus, the king of Persia, orders his beautiful wife, Vashti, to appear before his men at a drinking party so they can all leer at her beauty. She refuses to gratify the king's demand. The king's advisors warn him that if he lets her disobedience go unpunished, it will create a bad example for all the women of Persia. They say, "The noble women of Persia and Media who have heard of the queen's behavior will say the same to all the king's officials, and there will be contempt and wrath in plenty" (Esther 1:18). They advise the king to divorce his wife as a proper punishment for her insolence. At least one Bible-reading husband understood this to mean that wives who do not obey the orders and commands of their husbands should be punished.

It should go without saying that we do not emulate the ungodly, even if they are characters in the Bible. King Ahasuerus and his officials were idolatrous pagans—wicked men, not models for godly homes. If there is a hero worthy of emulation in the story, it is Queen Vashti, who refused to comply to an immoral demand from her drunken husband—even if he was the king.

JACOB AND HIS WIVES

The self-righteous, chauvinistic, Bible-thumping husband makes all the decisions. His word is final. He snaps his fingers, and his wife jumps to attention. She has no say and certainly no control over the decision-making process in the family.

This is not the biblical model. To see the biblical model in action, consider the story of Jacob and his wives, Rachel and Leah. In Genesis 31:3 the LORD commanded Jacob to leave Aram and return to the land of Canaan. This seems like a fairly clear mandate. God directly told Jacob to take his family back to Canaan. As a biblical man with biblical authority over his family, Jacob should have been able to tell his wives to start packing immediately.

Instead, the Bible says, "Jacob sent and called Rachel and Leah into the field where his flock was" (Genesis 31:4). He wanted a private conversation with them. He began to gently reason with them, laying out a persuasive argument for why the family should relocate to Canaan.

He noted that their father, Laban, and their brothers were no longer friendly toward him, despite his having served Laban with all his strength. He reminded them that their father had tried to cheat him by changing the terms of their agreement ten times. He told them about his prophetic dream and the message he had received from God. He made his case for leaving their father's household and returning to Canaan. He asked their permission to return.

Why did Jacob need their permission? The LORD had already given him the command "Return to the land of your fathers." Why put the decision in the hands of his wives?

The Jewish sages derived from this story that a man cannot compel his wife to move someplace against her will or live someplace she does not want to live. The Bible demonstrates a type of patriarchal and masculine headship over a family unlike the chauvinistic authority models touted by some ultra-conservative religious people. Jacob dealt with his wives as partners in managing family affairs, not his subjects.

What if they had refused to leave, thereby thwarting God's commandment to Jacob? Jacob had faith. Surely he could trust God to bring about his will through his wives and with his wives. When Abraham feared that his wife was acting contrary to the will of God, the LORD said to Abraham, "Whatever Sarah says to you, do as she tells you" (Genesis 21:12). Jacob applied the same rule. His wives listened to him, agreed with him, and gave him their permission to take the family back to Canaan. They bitterly remarked that their father had sold them for profit like foreign slave girls at market, and he had long since spent the profit. They said, "All the wealth that God has taken away from our father belongs to us and to our children. Now then, whatever God has said to you, do" (Genesis 31:16).

The godly man shows his wife the same dignity that Jacob showed his wives. He recognizes that she is an intelligent, thinking human being with her own desires and decision-making capacity. Mr. Chauvinist treats his wife the way Laban treated his daughters—like foreign slave girls purchased at the market. He assumes that she has nothing to contribute to the decision-making process. He assumes that she finds fulfillment and spiritual satisfaction in bending her will to his. By refusing to grant her any say in their affairs, he robs her of dignity and crushes her self-esteem. His actions communicate a clear message to her: "You are worthless." Perhaps she complies with her husband externally, but on the inside her heart turns dark toward him.

SPIRITUAL AUTHORITY

The godly husband treats his wife as an equal. Even though he has spiritual authority over her, he never uses that authority to subjugate her or make demands on her. Instead, he uses that authority to elevate her by granting her equal partnership with him in a shared life. He does this because he loves her and because this is what God has done for him. He knows that just as his wife is subject to him, he is subject to God, but God has not taken away his free will or forced him into submission. Instead, the LORD has granted him the dignity of making his own choices and decisions in life, whether for good or for evil.

The biblical husband understands the order of headship. A husband is the head of his wife, even as Christ is the head of him (1 Corinthians 11:3). He is more concerned with his own submission to the head (Messiah) than his wife's submission to him. If his wife does not submit to him, he uses that as an opportunity to apply the log-and-speck rule. He searches his own life to see in what areas he is failing to submit to Jesus. He knows that so long as he has a log in his own eye (failure to submit to Messiah), he is in no position to remove the speck from his wife's eye (her failure to submit to him).

The biblical husband understands that his headship over his wife is governed by the Master's principles of godly leadership. Jesus told his disciples, "If anyone would be first, he must be last of all and servant of all" (Mark 9:35); "The greatest among you shall be your servant" (Matthew 23:11). These principles leave no room for bullying one's wife, laying down the law, forcing her to comply, or demanding her submission.

The biblical husband knows that his headship over his wife is of a spiritual nature, and so he exerts his authority over her in the spiritual world. Even the angels recognize his authority over her (1 Corinthians 11:10). Therefore he leads her and directs her primarily through his own private prayers, submitting his concerns to God and trusting God to direct the outcome. He practices the art of moving her through prayer alone. Rather than trying to apply pressure on her in order to manipulate the outcome, he applies pressure to God in prayer and then waits for him to manipulate the outcome for his glory.

This is the proper way to lead and direct your wife. If you are concerned about a decision or some direction that must be taken, rather than trying to force her to submit to your will in that area, pour out your heart to God and then trust him with the outcome. Wield your spiritual authority over your wife by encircling her with your earnest prayers. Then be prepared to surrender to his headship in the matter.

CONTROLLING HUSBANDS

The controlling husband keeps his wife like a bird in a cage. He smothers her with his self-important and self-righteous authority. He limits her relationships, dictating her friendships and interfering in every aspect of her life. He does not have a wife as much as he keeps a pet.

Some husbands go so far as telling their wives exactly how to dress. One husband chastises his wife for dressing too modestly ("Wear something that looks hotter"), and another husband chastises his wife for dressing provocatively ("Wear something more modest, less revealing"). Both husbands treat their wives the way King Ahasuerus treated Vashti by making her a spectacle. What could be more humiliating to a woman than being told what to wear? She is a grown woman with her own tastes and preferences. She is not a child.

A wise husband does not attempt to control his wife's wardrobe choices. He knows that telling her how to dress is a sure way to inflame her insecurities and crush her spirit. He knows that the Torah spells out his minimum duty: "He shall not diminish her food, her clothing, or her marital rights" (Exodus 21:10). As her husband, he has a biblical responsibility to provide her with money for clothing of her own choosing that she can proudly wear. By demanding that she wear something that is not to her taste, he diminishes her clothing, so to speak, and transgresses that commandment. The wise husband who allows his wife to make her own wardrobe choices encourages her to blossom in her own unique self-expression.

Women take clothing seriously, much more so than the typical male might imagine. A woman's clothing becomes for her an extension of who she is. As we learned in the previous chapter, the Talmud advises a man to actually spend more on his wife's food and clothing than he can afford because, while she depends upon him, he depends upon God.

Some husbands control their wives through money, scrutinizing her every purchase and regulating her with a tight budget. (Finances will be the subject of the next chapter.) By scrutinizing her financial choices, he treats her as if she were a child rather than an adult. When the Torah says, "He shall not diminish her food," this implies providing her with ample resources to spend for her needs. The husband who tries to manipulate his wife by holding the purse strings transgresses that commandment. He diminishes her food, so to speak, doling out a meager allowance to continually remind her that she depends upon him.

PROVERBS 31 GAL

Some men seem to believe that God wants women to remain uneducated and unemployed behind-the-scenes baby-making machines. While it might be ideal for the children if their mother can stay home with them while they are young, the Bible does not discourage married women from obtaining an education, developing marketable skills, or engaging in the work force. Consider, for example, the Bible's picture of the perfect wife in Proverbs 31: the *Eishet Chayil* (Woman of Valor). This woman is engaged in several industries and vocations. She is at work in fabric manufacturing and the garment industry. She is responsible for purchasing for the whole household and for managing the servants. She is involved in real-estate transactions, making major purchases and sales, and she is personally engaged in agricultural development of land. When demand for her products is high, she works overtime hours late into the night to meet the need. She personally handles the household's charitable contributions. She is in charge of preparing adequate supplies and stores for the winter months. She sells her products wholesale to merchants. In addition to all this, she manages the household. No wonder she does not eat the bread of laziness. She doesn't have time.

This woman does not sound like the type of stay-at-home behind-the-scenes wife idealized by the ultra-conservative Christian fundamentalist. Instead, the Proverbs 31 woman operates freely with complete autonomy in the business world, managing several employees and competently executing decisions for her household. She does not need to ask her husband for permission to make purchases or other decisions, and he does not seem to feel threatened by her engagement in the work world. On the contrary, he praises her for her competence.

PARTNERS IN LIFE

The biblical woman of Proverbs 31 had complete charge over household, business, and family affairs, yet her husband was still the spiritual authority over her in life. Spiritual authority over a wife doesn't look like control, manipulation, or subjection. Spiritual authority begins with a spirit of servanthood, just as Jesus "came not to be served but to serve, and to give his life" (Matthew 20:28). Spiritual headship involves protecting and providing for a wife, just as one's head protects and provides for the rest of his body.

Likewise, the commandment for a wife to submit to her husband is incumbent only upon her, not upon the husband. A man's wife is not his property, nor is she a child. She should never be treated as if she does not have the right to make her own decisions or as if she has no role to play in the decision making for the family. Just as Jacob consulted his wives before making a major move, a man should include his wife in the decision-making process. She is "a fellow heir of the grace of life," an equal and opposite partner with him before the LORD.

This realization should be a big relief for you. The spiritual authority you wield over your wife does not make you responsible for monitoring her behavior or overseeing her spiritual development. Instead, you are on the same team with her, an equal peer with her, spiritually growing alongside her. So go enjoy life with her. Have fun with her. Stay optimistic, choose to see the good, and it will be good.

13

MARRIAGE AND MONEY

Marriages can encounter extra turbulence when husband and wife attempt to discuss household finances and financial decisions. Men and women often have different priorities when it comes to allocating the money. Simply balancing the checkbook or setting a monthly budget can ignite major confrontations. Trying to make ends meet and pay the bills is stressful enough. Our money problems become even more stressful when we add marital problems to the discussion.

In a previous chapter we learned that the Bible places three minimum obligations upon a husband: He must not diminish his wife's "food, her clothing, or her marital rights" (Exodus 21:10). In this chapter we will discuss the obligation of providing a wife with food and clothing, that is, her rights to material provision. In the subsequent chapter we will discuss a wife's marital rights—her rights to sexual intimacy.

STRIFE COMES KNOCKING

A husband and wife are partners. They work together to meet life's challenges. They are on the same team in the game of life, and they have one another's best interests in mind. But sometimes the teamwork gets twisted up around the issue of money. When it comes to money, a marriage is not supposed to be an equal partnership. Instead, the responsibility for providing falls to the husband.

The Torah says a man must not diminish his wife's food and clothing. Her "food" refers to all the money necessary to sustain her—all of life's expenses. Her "clothing" refers to her material goods. When it comes to providing for his wife's sustenance and material goods, a man should not skimp. God provides a man with what he needs so that he can provide his wife with all she needs. The more he skimps on his wife, the less God will bestow on him. The more generous he is with his wife, the more generous God will be with him.

As mentioned earlier, talmudic wisdom teaches that a man should spend less than he can afford on himself but more than he can afford on his wife and children. Why? Because his wife and children rely upon him in much the same way he relies upon God.[36] A man can make no greater investment than spending his means on the upkeep of his wife and children.

A person should always be thrifty with his money. It's a matter of good stewardship. We don't want to waste the money with which our Father in heaven entrusts us. Spending money on our wives, however, is not a waste. That's what the money is there for. It's not for us. God did not give it to us to spend on our toys and amusements, nor did he give it to us so that we could lay up treasures here on earth where moth and rust destroy. He gives us money so that we will allocate it to others: to those who depend upon us and to those in need. God gives us money to give to our wives and children.

A man who attempts to impose austerity measures on his family invites strife into his home:

> Rav Yehudah said, "A man should always make sure that there is plenty of food in his house; for strife comes to a house primarily because of food, as it is written [in Psalm 147:14], "He makes peace in your borders; he fills you with the finest of the wheat." Rav Papap said, "This explains the proverb, 'When the barley is gone from the pitcher, strife comes knocking at the door.'" (Talmud, b.*Bava Metzia* 59a)

If you want to keep strife from knocking at the door, do your best to make sure you are adequately providing for your family to the best of your ability. By abundantly providing for our families, we emulate God who feeds the birds of the air, clothes the grass of the field, and provides food for every living creature, opening his hand and satisfying the desire of every living thing. Remember how costly the price Messiah paid for his bride was. If we want to love our wives the way Messiah loves his assembly, we need to be willing to sacrifice for them.

You can keep strife away from your home by showing your wife open-handed generosity. But if your wife suspects that you are deliberately withholding money from her, especially money for something she feels to be a legitimate need, she will resent you. She will wonder how she could have been so blind to marry a man so selfish. It will not occur to her that you might be saving funds for her best interest and that of the family. She will more likely interpret your fiscal prudence as a petty attempt to control her.

Peace in the home is a treasure worth far more than money. It's not worth a conflict just to save a few dollars. The Bible warns us not to diminish the amount we spend on our wives.

Some men today act like children in the sandbox. They want all the toys for themselves, and they resent having to share. They find plenty of money in their budget to spend on cars, personal luxuries, games, sporting equipment, and indulgences for themselves, but they are tight fisted with their wives and children. A man who behaves that way is not gluing himself to his wife, nor is he making her his first priority. She will resent him for his selfishness because she knows that he should be putting his wife and children ahead of his own desires.

WORTH MORE THAN JEWELS

The book of Proverbs says that a wife is "more precious than jewels" (Proverbs 31:10). If that's the case, we should not hesitate to spend lavishly on our wives when it is possible to do so. Let a man skimp on everything else but not on his wife. A story from the Torah illustrates this point.

When Abraham's beloved wife, Sarah, died, he went to purchase a tomb for her from the Canaanites. Abraham left his tents and went to the Canaanite city of Hebron. Seated in the gates he found Ephron the Hittite, a local landowner. Abraham asked Ephron to sell him the cave of Machpelah and the field around it. He wanted to use the cave as a burial tomb for Sarah. Abraham offered Ephron full price. In a seemingly magnanimous gesture, Ephron refused the offer and instead presented the land to Abraham free of charge. What a bargain! Abraham, however, was unwilling to accept the gift. He knew that without a legal sale, his title to the property would be tenuous. He did not want to return some years later and learn that his wife's tomb was also being used by the Canaanites. He gently insisted on purchasing the tomb for full price. Ephron asked for an exorbitant amount: four hundred silver pieces. He expected Abraham to make a counteroffer and for the dickering to last for some time. Instead, to his surprise Abraham accepted the price and counted out the money. Abraham was not willing to negotiate or bargain over the dignity of his wife.

It is good to be thrifty and conservative whenever possible but not at the expense of the honor we should show for our wives. Abraham did not hesitate to pay far more than full price for his wife's burial. If that was the case after she died, he was certainly willing to spend adequate money to provide her with whatever she needed while she was still alive. A husband should endeavor to provide his wife with all that she needs because she depends upon him. He must not diminish either her food or her clothing.

A woman derives much of her personal dignity and self-esteem from her personal appearance. She wants to look pretty and smartly dressed. Men often make the mistake of telling their wives how to dress—a grievous insult to the female ego. Here's a better idea. Give her ample means to dress herself the way she wants to dress. Encourage her to buy the nice things that make her feel pretty and confident.

A woman does not need a fortune in material goods to be happy. She needs only enough to meet the same standards as her neighbors. If she is forced to live beneath the standards of those in her community, she will feel insecure and miserable. If she enjoys the same general quality of life and affluence as other women in her community and social circles, she will feel content.

This explains why the rabbis say that a man should never marry a girl from a higher economic status than his own. If he marries a woman from a higher economic status, he will never be able to satisfy her because she is accustomed to a higher standard of living. She will always feel that her husband does not adequately supply her needs, and he will always feel that she spends recklessly and beyond his means. On the other hand, if he marries a woman from a lower economic status, he will always be able to satisfy her because she is accustomed to a lower standard. She will feel that her husband treats her as a princess, lavishly treating her to things her family could not afford while she was growing up. He will be pleased to have such a thrifty and economically modest wife.

That's good advice for someone before marriage, but what if you are already married to a woman who expects more than you can afford to provide? In that case, you will have to spend more than you can afford. Don't expect her to change her expectations of life just because she married you.

SECURITY OR RELATIONSHIP

Women need financial security, especially when children are involved. A man works hard to provide financial security for his wife. But there is also a danger of letting the quest for financial security destroy marital stability. This happens when we put our jobs and quest for money ahead of our wives. Too many hours spent at work can lead to a wife feeling neglected. Too much time at the office leaves the children like orphans.

According to research conducted by Shaunti and Jeff Feldhahn (*For Men Only*), most wives say that if given a choice between financial stability and a quality marriage relationship, they will choose the relationship. A woman would rather suffer through poverty with her husband at her side than enjoy financial stability with her husband absent from her life. Don't let the quest for financial security leave your wife feeling emotionally and relationally insecure. It's better to downsize. If you feel you might be working too many hours to provide, talk it over with your wife and ask her if she would prefer more money or more quality time spent with you. Her answer might surprise you.

WHO IS IN CHARGE OF THE MONEY?

The biblical model of marriage assumes an economy in which men provide for their wives and children. That does not mean that women and children do not play important roles as contributors. In the primarily agricultural economy of the Bible, the whole family was involved in working the land and caring for livestock. Ultimately, however, the biblical worldview made men responsible for their family's material needs.

Does this mean that the Bible gives the husband authority to call all the shots? Is he in charge of the checkbook? The Bible refers to the husband as the head of the wife and the head of the family. Does that mean that he has the authority to make executive decisions regarding money? Not at all. The husband is the head of the wife in the same sense that Christ is the head of the man. Jesus teaches us about how to handle our money, but he does not take over our accounts. He leaves them in our hands and teaches us to exercise careful stewardship over the resources with which God entrusts us. In the previous chapter we saw that the ideal wife described in Proverbs 31 was very much involved in the financial decisions of the household. She conducted business transactions on behalf of the family and contributed to the family income. She felt free to make property investments and purchases for household needs. She knew that her husband had confidence in her, and he did not require her to ask his permission for every transaction.

Successful couples work out a financial system that capitalizes on the respective strengths of both husband and wife. Not everyone is great with a budget. Not everyone can balance a checkbook. Sometimes a husband handles paperwork, account balancing, and budgeting better than a wife, but in many cases, the wife has a better grasp on basic household economics. It does not matter which member of the marriage handles the finances so long as both parties agree to the arrangement. If your wife is better than you at keeping the books straight, the receipts in order, and the bills paid, then she is the better candidate for handling the money. Thank God that he has bestowed such a gift upon you, and ask her if she wants to take over the finances. If she does, your job will be much easier. You simply need to provide the money. Let her worry about how to allocate it. If she is unable to manage the accounts, or if she prefers to let you manage the accounts, then you will need to work out some sort of amicable system that avoids arguments over money.

A certain Messianic Jew, living in Israel, had a large family and many mouths to feed. He struggled to make ends meet but never seemed bothered by it. When asked how he managed to make the dollar stretch to cover his debts and expenses, he replied that his wife managed all those affairs. He told me that for years his wife had complained about the lack of money and the way he handled the family's finances, and he grew so tired of her complaints that he offered to let her take control of the finances. He said to himself, "Let's see if she can do a better job of making the dollar stretch." She gladly agreed, but she did not do a better job. In fact, she was less skilled in budget balancing than he. Despite the fact that she occasionally bounced a check and routinely overspent the budget, he preferred to let her manage the accounts because he found that, so long as she had control of the money, the complaints stopped. It was a small price to pay for peace in the home.

Hopefully that's not your situation. It's far better if either the husband or the wife (it does not matter which) is competent in managing household accounts and budgets. Nevertheless, the story illustrates an important principle: Peace in the home is more valuable than financial success: "Better is a dry morsel with quiet than a house full of feasting with strife" (Proverbs 17:1).

Major decisions require the consent of both husband and wife. This includes major purchases. Remember how Jacob felt he needed to consult his wives Rachel and Leah before returning to the land of Canaan. He did not feel that he had the authority to force them to move. Likewise, a husband does not have the authority to make major financial decisions that will impact the whole family without first consulting his wife. If it's a major purchase or major financial decision, don't do it unless your wife is onboard with you. Remember that God uses our wives to speak to us. Remember how the LORD directed Abraham to listen to his wife, Sarah, even when Abraham thought Sarah was making the wrong decision.

Regardless of which spouse handles the accounts, both spouses need to get on the same economic game plan. In some cases it might be a good idea for both husband and wife to attend a course on financial training together and then to work with a financial counselor to carve out a budget. Other couples might find it sufficient to simply work out a plan together across the kitchen table. A household budget that covers both short-term needs and long-term goals is essential for a successful household.

THE OVERSPENDING WIFE

A financial counselor or good course on financial planning can help a man and his wife establish a realistic budget that will allow them to live within their means and save toward the future. At the same time, husbands need to be careful not to chastise their wives if they overstep the monthly budget. A husband should not think of the money as if it belongs to him. Even if he is the only breadwinner, it's not his bread. He gave up the right to financial autonomy when he married his wife. God has given him the responsibility of providing for her needs. It's not the husband's job to force fiscal limits or austerity measures on her. If she overspends, chastising her for the mistake will not fix the problem. Chastising her will only make her feel humiliated and patronized. It feels humbling enough to her that she must rely on her husband's money without also being humiliated for mishandling it.

If your wife overspends the weekly budget or spends too much on a shopping trip, your job is to try to find a way to meet the unexpected shortfall.

Some husbands use money to manipulate the relationship. They keep their wives on a tight budget and a short financial leash, withholding money as punishment. They make their wives ask for money and ask permission before spending it. A man who treats his wife this way fails to be a husband to her. He is not treating her as an equal partner. Instead, he treats her more like a prostitute. She gets paid so long as he is happy with her. You don't want to be that kind of husband.

A man feels responsible for his family's financial security. Therefore, he gets upset with his wife when she spends too much or when she wants to spend money on things that do not fit in the family budget. He feels the pressure and financial pinch created by her spending, so he becomes angry and chastises her. The reason he becomes angry is that he has forgotten how he derives provision in the first place. He has forgotten that God provides for him.

When a man thinks of himself as the source of provision, he naturally feels compelled to carefully control the family finances. He knows that his earning potential has a limit and that if the family overspends that limit, he will be the one left holding the bag (and an empty bag at that). His fear compels him to control his wife's spending and ration the money carefully. He feels as though he is responsible and therefore needs to steer the family and make the decisions. He forgets that he is merely a servant of God. He forgets that he relies on God for every penny.

The man who realizes that God is the source of provision need not have such fears. He does not feel compelled to rule over the family finances or scrutinize his wife's spending habits because he knows that God will provide for all their legitimate needs. He can take a more relaxed attitude about money, relying on God rather than on himself.

The man who trusts in God does not rely upon cajoling, nagging, or persuading his wife to spend less. Instead, he commits any financial shortfall to God in prayer, and he leads his family by committing their needs to prayer. Since he knows that his provision comes from God, he knows that prayer is the best solution to all his economic problems.

THE BUCK STOPS HERE

You might find yourself in a marriage in which you are the financially irresponsible party. Does your wife have to nag you about overspending? Does she have to plead with you to stay within the budget? If so, you might wonder, "Why is it all right for her to nag me about overspending, but I'm not supposed to nag her about it?" You already know the answer. You are the head, the giver, and the provider for her. She relies upon you, but you rely upon God. If you foolishly spend all your money before paying the bills, she has no other husband to turn to for help. If she overspends, however, you have God to turn to for help. That's the hierarchy of marriage. That's how God set up the system.

What if she has her own job and makes her own money? If she has her own job, you should let her use her income however she wants. If she wants to contribute to the family's expenses or help pay family debt, that's wonderful and extremely helpful. But ultimately it's not her responsibility to do so; it's your responsibility. If she prefers to use the money she makes for her own purposes, that should be her prerogative. Most women will use their income, or a portion of it, to help offset the family expenses, but you should not require her to do so. You are supposed to be taking care of her. If she generates some spending money of her own, that should be hers to use as she likes.

In many cases both husband and wife work to support the family. In the professional world today, women are often the principle breadwinners. There is nothing wrong with that. If that's the case in your marriage, be grateful; just don't abdicate your spiritual position as provider. Don't expect your wife to carry the load. Do as much as you can to contribute toward the household expenses, and do not expect your wife to bankroll your amusements and luxuries. You are still responsible for the upkeep of the family. Maybe the responsible thing involves letting your wife's income support or supplement the household, but remember that it's ultimately not her responsibility to do so.

ON HANDS AND KNEES

A Messianic rabbi was asked to counsel a young man whose wife had recently thrown him out of the house. It seemed puzzling. His wife was a godly woman who seemed to have a sweet spirit and kind heart. She had three children by this man, all under the age of eight years old.

He was desperate to return home. There was no affair or infidelity. What could have gone wrong? The young man explained to the rabbi that it basically came down to disagreements about money. He wanted to try starting his own business, but his wife was not interested. She wanted him to work a regular job. Essentially, he did not want to work. He had quit several jobs already, leaving his family cash strapped and desperate. Every time he quit a job, her parents had to bail them out and pay the rent. He kept quitting his jobs because he could see no point to working at "a dead-end job." He wanted to spend his time cultivating various multi-level marketing schemes and other get-rich-quick plans that he had concocted or been suckered into. After several failed ventures like this, his wife had finally had enough of his nonsense. The next time he quit his job, she threw him out.

The rabbi tried to explain to him that it did not matter if he was in a dead-end job or a job that he did not like. He said, "You are a man. Do you know what a man does? A man carries his family on his back. He carries them even if he has to crawl on his hands and knees. Even if you have to work two or three jobs, you provide for your wife and your children to the best of your ability. You do everything you can. That's what it is to be a man."

The young man shook his head, and his eyes moistened with tears. "I don't know if I can do that," he said. "I need something more from life."

"Then don't expect her to take you back," the rabbi said.

She didn't.

YOUR OWN FLESH

The apostles taught, "If anyone does not provide for his relatives, and especially for members of his household, he has denied the faith and is worse than an unbeliever" (1 Timothy 5:8). We are sometimes less willing to give charity to family members in need than we are to strangers. The Bible teaches that a man must care for those of his own family first. This is the meaning of the words, do not "hide yourself from your own flesh" (Isaiah 58:7). The commandment against hiding yourself from your own flesh refers to providing for your own family members, especially to your spouse with whom you are one flesh. Adequately providing for one's wife shows a man's commitment to the second greatest commandment: "You shall love your neighbor as yourself." A man's wife is one flesh with him; she is him.

In the days of the apostles, Rabbi Yosi the Galilean had a mean and disrespectful wife who treated him shamefully. His disciples took a donation to pay for a divorce and alimony terms, and then they prevailed upon their rabbi to divorce the woman. He consented and divorced her, sending her away with a sizable sum of money. She remarried, but her second husband went blind. After several years the money was gone, and poverty reduced the couple to wandering the streets as beggars. Dressed only in rags, Rabbi Yosi's once-proud wife led her blind husband through the streets, begging from door to door.

When Rabbi Yosi found out that his ex-wife and her husband were living as beggars in the street, he took them both into his care. He secured living arrangements for them. He provided them with clothing and provided money for their daily meals and living expenses. When his disciples asked him why he did so much for an ex-wife and her husband, he explained that he must fulfill the verse that says "not to hide yourself from your own flesh."[37] If one should go to such lengths even for his ex-wife, how much more so for the woman to whom he is married and the children he has fathered.

SUMMARY

Money doesn't need to be a problem in your marriage. As the husband, you have the responsibility of providing for your family. Whether you make a lot of money or you are just barely getting by, the important thing is that you and your wife are in it together. You are on the same team, not fighting over resources.

The husband demonstrates that he is on the same team with his wife by doing his best to provide for her, spending beyond what he can afford on her and his children and less than he can afford on himself. He never withholds money from his wife or shames her for blowing the budget. The household account manager should be the spouse with the best competence in the area of balancing the books and financial planning; it shouldn't be based on a gender bias. If a wife has a supplementary income, she might contribute to household expenses if she likes, but she should be allowed to spend the money as she sees fit. If she is the principle breadwinner in the home, the husband should do as much as he can to contribute toward the household expenses. If she does not work, the husband should be all the more generous with her because she relies solely upon him, whereas he relies upon God. That's the kind of teamwork that will make your marriage, and your budget, successful.

As the Beatles said, "I don't care too much for money, for money can't buy me love." Money can't fix your marriage either, but God can. You might be on a tight budget, but you can afford to have a better marriage. It's going to be worth every penny.

14

SEXUAL INTIMACY

Sex, or the lack of it, is often at the heart of problems between husbands and wives. Sexuality is an important and fundamental part of the marriage union, but when mishandled or allowed to define the relationship, it has enormous destructive potential.

In general, men and women understand sex differently and prioritize it differently. Women consider sexual intimacy to be an important aspect of their relationship with their husbands but not the most important aspect. Men tend to think of sex as the most important aspect of the marriage relationship and, generally speaking, the most important thing in life. This disparity in prioritization has the potential to create significant frustration for married men, and that frustration tends to manifest in negative and destructive behaviors that further damage the marriage.

God commands the husband not to diminish his wife's "food, her clothing, or her marital rights" (Exodus 21:10). In the previous chapter we discussed the obligation of providing a wife with food and clothing, that is, her rights to material provision. In this chapter we will discuss the awkward topic of sex and sexuality within the marriage. The prohibition on diminishing a wife's conjugal rights seems unnecessary. Most men are not in any danger of diminishing their wife's marital rights. On the contrary, they would prefer to increase the frequency with which they fulfill that duty. What we don't realize is that there is more than one way of diminishing a woman's marital rights. Many men routinely engage in behaviors that inadvertently discourage sexual intimacy.

GARDEN OF DELIGHT

Naturally, the story of sex and human sexuality begins in Eden with the story of Adam and Eve. Everything God made was good: "And behold, it was very good" (Genesis 1:31). The only thing in creation that could be called "not good" was Adam's lack of a suitable partner. So the LORD created a woman and presented her to Adam. Adam approved of the new innovation.

Adam named the new creation Eve (*Chavah*, חוה), a word that means "living," "because she was the mother of all living" (Genesis 3:20). The Torah says that "the man and his wife were both naked and were not ashamed" (Genesis 2:25). This is the Torah's view of sexuality. God does not see sex as something sinful, shameful, or perverse. He made it. He designed it to be a beautiful and fulfilling part of Paradise. Consider the simple innocence of our first mother and father in the midst of Eden, the garden of delight. They had no embarrassment, no insecurities, no artificial inhibitions, and no emotional baggage to weigh them down.

In that place of innocence, Adam and Eve joined together in marriage and became "one flesh," a biblical idiom that means "one body." Jesus says, "He who created them from the beginning made them male and female, and said, 'Therefore a man shall leave his father and his mother and hold fast to his wife, and the two shall become one flesh' … So they are no longer two but one flesh" (Matthew 19:4–6). Marriage physically unites husband and wife into one new body through sexuality, but it's more than a physical union. This union between husband and wife is primarily a spiritual one.

Human sexuality is more than just an animal act. It involves a spiritual union with another person that reflects the innate desire of the undying soul to cleave to God. It illustrates, in a physical metaphor, the powerful union with God for which we thirst. Our physical desire for sexual union echoes a deeper, inner spiritual desire for spiritual union with the Almighty.

A man becomes "one body" with his wife on a physical level, but on a spiritual level he becomes as one soul with her as well. God did not design human beings to enjoy multiple partners. We are physically and spiritually designed only for a committed, monogamous relationship. After marriage neither husband nor wife can feel complete without the other. Sexual relationships outside of marriage are damaging because human sexuality involves spiritual transactions. Divorce leaves deep emotional and spiritual scars because it involves the tearing asunder of two souls: "What therefore God has joined together, let not man separate" (Matthew 19:6).

Today it is common for people to go through several sexual partners before committing to marriage. It is also common for marriages to end in divorce. Things are completely out of kilter.

God wants us to experience and enjoy sexuality within a committed, monogamous marriage, just as our first father and mother did. When that happens, we experience a small portion of the joy of Eden. When we take sex out of that context, however, we twist it into something ugly and destructive.

A husband is responsible for keeping the marriage bed pure:

> Let marriage be held in honor among all, and let the marriage
> bed be undefiled, for God will judge the sexually immoral
> and adulterous. (Hebrews 13:4)

Keeping the marriage bed pure requires treating a wife with dignity and respect, not pushing her, not pressuring her. It requires us to treat sex as something pure, not something dirty or common. It requires absolute monogamous fidelity.

Don't pollute your marriage bed with foreign elements or the disgusting ways of the world. Needless to say, fornication, pornography, and sexual lewdness have no role to play in a godly marriage. Keep the demonic poison of pornography far away from your home and far from your marriage, or you will regret it. It will pollute your mind, defile your spirit, and remove the presence of the Holy Spirit from your midst, transforming your sex life into something unholy.

SEX IS HOLY

People with traditional values sometimes mistakenly associate sexuality with shame, sin, or perversity. Their embarrassment around the subject prevents them from working through relationship problems connected with sexuality. They feel too shy to talk about it with their spouses.

People with postmodern values, on the other hand, think of sexuality as a basic right and entitlement that should have no limits imposed upon it. Their desensitization to sexuality causes them to treat it as something ordinary and common—a biological act on the level of blowing one's nose. They diminish the mystery of human sexuality and treat it as an animal act and basic human right.

In the Bible sex is not shameful, nor is it ordinary. It's not sinful, and it's not a basic right to which everyone is entitled. Instead, sex is holy.

Let's think about the meaning of holiness. A "holy" thing is something set apart from the normal world and used in the service or worship of God. For example, the Bible calls Israel a holy nation because God set the children of Israel apart from the other nations to be his covenant people. Likewise, God set the sons of Aaron apart from the rest of the Jewish people in order to serve him as holy priests and worship him in the Temple. For that matter, the Temple was also holy because it was set apart from the ordinary world to be a place where God dwells. The Sabbath is a holy day. God set it apart from the other six days of the week as his day of rest. He made it holy by separating it from the other days of the week.

FIRM BOUNDARIES

For something to be holy, it needs to be separated from its original context, transformed from something ordinary into something extraordinary. It has to transcend the normal. Holiness has to have firm and clear boundaries that demarcate the difference between the holy and normal. For example, the Temple had clear boundaries and borders for its various courts. Beyond a certain point, only Jews could enter, and beyond that point, only the holy priests could enter, and beyond that point, only the high priest could enter into the holy of holies. The Sabbath also has clear boundaries that define precisely when it begins and when it concludes each week. Without clear boundaries, something cannot be considered holy because one never knows where the normal ends and the holy begins. To be holy, the sanctified thing needs firm boundaries setting it apart from the normal and dedicating everything within those boundaries to the service or worship of God.

This is how we need to view sexuality too. It's not supposed to be a pleasure toy for our own amusement. If God intended it as merely a way to please or entertain ourselves, he would not have created laws governing it. The sheer number of laws pertaining to sexuality and the

Bible's constant warnings against sexual immorality indicate the sacred nature of human sexuality. The Almighty emplaced firm boundaries around it, defining permissible expressions of sexuality and forbidding other expressions of sexuality.

The first step toward experiencing a spiritually healthy sexual relationship with your wife involves understanding the sanctity of sex itself. Jewish law states that "a wife is acquired in three ways ... through payment of a bride price, through a written document, and through sexual intercourse."[38] In the eyes of the Jewish sages, sexual intercourse is not only reserved for marriage, but it also initiates marriage. Promiscuity, premarital sex, and adultery violate the basic function of sex and marriage.

Paul forbids extramarital sexual relations on this basis, stating clearly, "He who is joined to a prostitute becomes one body with her ... For, as it is written, 'The two will become one flesh'" (1 Corinthians 6:16). Paul did not have only prostitutes in mind when he warned his readers about sexual immorality. In biblical terminology the word "prostitute" applies broadly to anyone sexually active outside of marriage. In the language of Torah, a woman who indulges in extramarital sexual relations is referred to as "playing the prostitute" (*zonah*, זנה), and a man who engages with such a woman is regarded the same.[39] God's law forbids all forms of extramarital sex and promiscuity, not just prostitution. By biblical standards all sexual activity outside of marriage constitutes harlotry.

In this way the Bible makes a firm boundary around human sexuality, thereby sanctifying it. On the one hand, it forbids engaging in sexual relations outside of marriage, but on the other hand, it commands husbands not to diminish sexual intimacy with their wives. The combination elevates sexuality within marriage to the level of a holy commandment (mitzvah). Enjoying sex with your wife becomes a holy act of obedience to God. The Bible's laws separate your sex life from the ordinary world and bring it into the service of God.

If sex is truly something holy, it should be something private, only between you and your wife. It's no one else's business. Never discuss your sex life with your friends. It's none of their business. A husband should consider it his duty to protect his wife's modesty and not expose her to the world.

Protect your wife's dignity by keeping private things private. Do you really want other guys thinking about your wife in that way? Of course not. So do her a favor, and do yourself a favor, by keeping that part of your relationship completely private. This is a basic matter of modesty, decency, and common sense.

Some Jewish couples are so circumspect about protecting their physical relationship that they refrain from all public displays of affection. It's not because they are prudish; it's because they have a high respect for the holiness of their physical relationship. They regard it as something to be cherished. Hugs, caresses, and kisses are for husband and wife to enjoy, not for others to see. Keeping expressions of physical affection within the privacy of the home helps set the relationship apart, sanctifying it with firm boundaries.

ABSTINENCE DURING MENSTRUATION

Here's another boundary that the Bible places around sex to sanctify it and make it holy. Leviticus 18:19 forbids sexual relations with a woman in menstruation. The Torah ranks sex with a menstruating woman on the same level as other matters of serious sexual immorality. According to the Bible's rule, a woman remains in a state unfit for cohabitation for seven days after the onset of her monthly period.[40] From the day the woman's period begins, a man should, at a minimum, count off seven days of complete abstinence. The Torah says, "You shall not approach a woman to uncover her nakedness while she is in her menstrual uncleanness" (Leviticus 18:19), meaning a complete prohibition on any form of sexual contact during that period of time.

During this time each month, husband and wife must undertake a period of abstinence. (Jewish tradition extends the period of abstinence for Jewish couples by numbering the seven days from the conclusion of the wife's monthly period.) The laws of separation during menstruation are complex. They require further elaboration, and this book is not the place for a long dissertation on this area of biblical law. Instead, take the Apostle Paul's advice. The Apostle Paul warns husbands and wives, "Do not deprive one another, except perhaps by agreement for a limited time, that you may devote yourselves to prayer; but then come together again, so that Satan may not tempt you because of your lack of self-control" (1 Corinthians 7:5). According to this rule, the level and duration of abstinence should be determined by mutual consent between husband and wife. We also learn that the period of separation creates an auspicious opportunity to commit to heightened prayer.

Believers in Jesus should also bear in mind that the prohibition on sexual relations during the seven days after the onset of menstruation is not at all optional. The Bible lists sexual relations during menstruation along with other big sexual sins such as incest and homosexual relations:

> For everyone who does any of these abominations, the persons who do them shall be cut off from among their people. (Leviticus 18:29)

The laws of menstruation teach us that our wives are not sex toys with which we can indulge ourselves whenever we feel like it. Instead, sex is holy, and as such, it is subject to laws of holiness.

SEXUAL CHEMISTRY AND COMMUNICATION

We already know that men and women are different, but when it comes to sex, men and women are extremely different. Men think about sex far more than women do and rate its importance in a relationship far higher than women do. Men worry about the frequency of sex, whereas, generally speaking, women are more concerned with the quality of the experience. Men are quickly aroused by visual stimulation or sexual thoughts, whereas women are aroused more slowly through physical contact and intimacy. Men can attain sexual satisfaction quickly—in minutes or even seconds—whereas women take longer to obtain sexual satisfaction. Men constantly anticipate sex; women feel "in the mood" far less frequently. Emotional turbulence, stress, or exhaustion tend to turn a woman's capacity for sexuality off for the night—not so much for men.

In light of these profound differences in sexual expectation and experience, it becomes the man's responsibility to curb his appetites and desire in order to meet his wife's sexual needs according to her desire. A woman receives no satisfaction from a sexual relationship with a husband who merely uses her body as a vessel to pleasure himself. If you want a healthy sexual relationship with your wife, remember that as the man and spiritual head, you are to act as the giver and the servant in the relationship. That's your role.

Men often want to be the receivers in the relationship. They want their wives to please them. They want to receive sexual gratification with very little thought for their wives' inclinations, preferences, or needs. This is backward. God designed men to be the givers and the servants in the relationship. A man's first and most important objective should be his wife's needs and desires, not his own. The sexual encounter needs to be primarily about a man satisfying his wife, not satisfying himself. A man finds it takes hardly any effort at all for him to reach satiation. That's why his focus and emphasis needs to be on the quality of his wife's personal experience and on her needs, not his own.

The best way to facilitate that is to work toward establishing open, honest communication in the bedroom. Ask questions, learn to listen, and be open to correction. It's natural to feel shy and awkward about initiating that type of conversation. That's part of the comedy of human sexuality. A healthy marriage gets past that shy and awkward stage as husband and wife work back toward the Edenic purity of our first father and mother: "The man and his wife were both naked and were not ashamed" (Genesis 2:25).

EMOTIONAL WOUNDS

Impediments to open, honest communication will also become obstacles to quality sexual communication. If you emotionally damage your wife during the day, don't expect her to feel turned on when the lights go out. If you treat her with disrespect or wound her dignity, don't expect her to be eager to make herself vulnerable with you. Nothing turns off a woman's libido faster than an emotional wound. A woman who experiences routine emotional abuse will be reluctant to let her guard down at all, and that's not conducive to establishing sexual intimacy. If a woman is badly damaged emotionally by verbal abuse or physical abuse, or if she has suffered the indignities of infidelity, she may well find it nearly impossible to feel intimate with her husband again.

Likewise, a woman who has experienced sexual abuse in the past may find that pain returns to haunt her, especially if she begins to see her husband in the role of abuser. A man needs to be especially careful not to emotionally wound his wife regarding the sexual relationship. Sexual intimacy entails a certain emotional and psychological vulnerability as it is. A woman's insecurities exacerbate that sense of vulnerability. Criticisms about her performance, the appearance of her body, or the quality of the experience are completely inappropriate and a sure way to damage a marriage and reduce the number of sexual encounters either spouse will enjoy.

PRESSURING HER FOR SEX

Some men pressure their wives for sex. It's not unusual for a man to do this, even when she feels disinterested, but the more he does, the more likely his chance of sleeping alone. A woman who must endure a man continually pawing at her and nagging her for sexual favors is not likely to feel inspired toward intimacy. This relationship creates a cycle of disappointment and frustration. The husband nags and pressures his wife. His nagging turns her off. He increases the nagging. She feels more repulsed.

Jewish tradition solves the problem by making it the wife's prerogative to initiate intimacy with her husband. Men are discouraged from initiating because, if it was the man's prerogative, he might do so ceaselessly. When a man makes it his wife's decision to initiate intimacy, he removes the temptation to pressure her. Moreover, he fulfills the verse that says, "The husband does not have authority over his own body, but the wife does" (1 Corinthians 7:4).

Men make their wives feel guilty about not being sexually active enough. Men are selfish by nature, and most of us desire sex more frequently than most women do. As a result, we are not above using all types of manipulation to try to coerce our wives into sexually gratifying us. Recognize this for what it is: crass, self-serving narcissism. Don't treat your wife as if she is your personal whore. Merely using a woman's body to satisfy your lust has nothing to do with sanctity and nothing to do with meeting her needs. It's only about meeting your own needs and mortal desires.

A WIFE'S DUTY

Sometimes men feel as if they have a God-given right to sexual satisfaction. They insist that their wives have a duty to sexually satisfy them in order to help them resist temptation—as if they had some sort of biological condition that forces them to sin if they do not obtain regular sexual release. That's ridiculous. Think about the logic behind that idea. If that's really what marriage is supposed to accomplish for a man, how is a single man supposed to make it through life without succumbing to sexual temptation every day? A single man doesn't have a wife to offer him the release he apparently needs so regularly.

The idea that a wife has an obligation to provide her husband with a sexual release so that he does not stumble into sin is a clever, selfish lie that a man tells himself to excuse his own depravity. That lie allows him to feel justified in pestering his wife for sex even when she does not want it, and it allows him to feel justified indulging in sin when he feels that his wife has unfairly withheld sexual attention. This line of thought gives the man the best of both worlds. Not only is he free to feel self-righteous about coercing his wife into being his personal sex toy, he also has a wonderful excuse when he indulges in fornication, pornography, masturbation, or other sexual sins (God forbid). He can blame his wife. It's her fault for not giving him enough sex!

SPIRITUAL RAPE

Men who feel entitled to sexual gratification from their wives cite Paul's words regarding marital intimacy to support their argument:

> Because of the temptation to sexual immorality, each man should have his own wife and each woman her own husband. The husband should give to his wife her conjugal rights, and likewise the wife to her husband. For the wife does not have authority over her own body, but the husband does. Likewise the husband does not have authority over his own body, but the wife does. Do not deprive one another, except perhaps by agreement for a limited time, that you may devote yourselves to prayer; but then come together again, so that Satan may not tempt you because of your lack of self-control. (1 Corinthians 7:2–5)

It's sad to think of how many godly women have been repeatedly bludgeoned with this passage. Think of the countless husbands quoting these verses as they demand their sexual rights. The horny husband flips open his Bible and points out to his wife that unless she gives him the sex he wants, she is sinning against God. How convenient! If she does not supply him with a steady diet of sexual gratification, she carries the double guilt of disobeying the Bible and causing her husband to fall into temptation. She wants to please God and obey the Bible. What can she do other than submit to the man and let him have his way with her?

What do we call it when a man forces a woman, against her will, to have sex with him? That's called rape. What do we call it when a man physically bullies his wife to force her to have sex with him? That's called spousal abuse. A man who uses the Bible to force his wife into sex is guilty of committing spiritual abuse against her. He is misusing the Bible and the authority of God's Word to take power over a weaker individual for his own personal pleasure. A man who uses the authority of God's Word to force his wife into sexually gratifying him is guilty of spiritual rape. He is using the Bible to force a woman to have sex with him against her will. Do you think Paul wrote these words to give men a tool for spiritually abusing and raping their wives?

MUTUAL SUBMISSION

Paul's words in 1 Corinthians 7 are not intended to lay a guilt trip on women. That's not how the Bible works. Take another look at the passage under discussion. It's not a free ticket to unlimited sex; it's a call for mutual submission.

The passage begins by restating the Torah's commandment not to diminish a wife's marital rights: "The husband should give to his wife her conjugal rights." Paul adds that a wife should likewise grant her husband his conjugal rights, and both husband and wife should consider their bodies to be under the authority of their partners. Husband and wife should not deprive one another.

The passage does not give the husband the right to force himself onto his wife or coerce her against her will. To do so would break the unity of mutual submission that Paul prescribes. Husband and wife are to come together "by agreement," each one freely offering his or her body to the other. Mutual submission requires mutual submission. It's not mutual submission when a wife feels forced, coerced, or guilted into performing. Neither does 1 Corinthians 7 permit a husband to demand sex. Instead, the passage gives husbands three simple instructions:

1. Give your wife her conjugal rights.
2. Give your wife authority over your body.
3. Do not deprive your wife.

Notice that these three commandments can be fulfilled only by the husband. The wife cannot fulfill them for him, nor can she force him to carry them out. All three depend completely upon him. Paul does not give the wife permission to force her husband to fulfill the three duties.

Here are three things that the passage does not say but that men commonly assume it does say:

1. Make your wife give you your conjugal rights.
2. Take authority over your wife's body, and force her to submit.
3. Don't let your wife deprive you of sex.

Of course it would be wonderful if your wife was to read 1 Corinthians 7 and happily decide that it's her spiritual duty to start keeping you sexually satisfied to the very best of her ability, but that's her prerogative, not yours. It's her obligation, not yours. If you try to force her into it, she is no longer a willing party and no longer mutually submitting as Paul instructs. Her choice will depend not only on what the Bible says but also upon what she is emotionally and psychologically capable of doing.

Never try to use the Bible to coerce your wife into sex. If you do, you will only make her bitter against both you and the Bible. In the end, you will make her bitter against God, and that is the great sin of profaning God's name.

TAKING CONTROL OF LUST

It's not a sin to feel sexually attracted to your wife, but you should not let that sexual attraction turn into lust. When you do, you surrender your will to the desires of your evil inclination. That's when the trouble starts.

Don't tell yourself that without a steady diet of sex, you will fall into temptation. That's simply not true. The Talmud points out that the more sexually active a person is, the greater the sexual appetite becomes. When a person is less sexually active, the appetite decreases:

There is a small member of a man which feels satiated when it is starved but feels starved when it is satiated. (b.*Sukkah* 52b)

So long as you obsess over your sexual needs, you will never feel satisfied. No woman on earth would be able to keep the evil inclination satisfied for long. Let go of the burden of trying to feed your sex drive. Give it over to God. Let your wife set the pace and frequency, and quit worrying about it. After all, we are more than just animals. Taking control of the sex drive and forcing it to submit to God is part of making sex holy. It's part of sanctification:

> For this is the will of God, your sanctification ... that each one of you know how to control his own body in holiness and honor, not in the passion of lust like the Gentiles who do not know God; that no one transgress and wrong his brother in this matter, because the Lord is an avenger in all these things, as we told you beforehand and solemnly warned you. For God has not called us for impurity, but in holiness. (1 Thessalonians 4:3–7)

THE CELIBATE MARRIAGE

Jesus teaches that some men are called to be "eunuchs for the sake of the kingdom of heaven" (Matthew 19:12). What does that mean? It means that in some cases a person is called to undertake the path of celibacy for the sake of serving God. Obviously, Jesus referred to an unmarried, single person, but it's not impossible that God might call a married man to the same path of service. For example, imagine that your wife was injured or contracted a crippling disease (God forbid) that made sexual intimacy impossible for her. At that point your sexual life would be over. It would not be a blank check to start indulging in sin. Instead, it would be a calling from God to start living a celibate life even as a married man.

Now imagine that the injury or disease your wife suffered was not physical but emotional and psychological. Imagine that her emotional and psychological wounds left her sexually crippled. How would that be different from actual physical maladies?

A person should be willing to take the yoke of celibacy upon himself if necessary. No one has an inalienable right to sexual gratification.

A sexless or low-sex marriage is certainly not a man's ideal, but neither should he consider it to be a deal breaker or a license for sin. Instead, he should accept it as a high calling from the hand of his Father in heaven.

GOING BACK TO EDEN

Sex is an important part of marriage, but maybe your sex life has not been so great. If so, there might be good reasons for that. If you implement the things you are learning in this book, you have a good chance of seeing your marriage improve.

When you quit making critical comments, when you glue yourself to your wife, and when you make her your top priority, healing can begin. When you start treating sex with your wife as something holy, she will notice the difference. When you quit badgering and nagging your wife for sex, treating her as though she is there only for your sexual gratification, she might start to rediscover her personal dignity and feel like a woman again. When you no longer lay heavy guilt trips on her for failing to meet your sexual expectations, she might start to meet some of those expectations.

Let her be the one to initiate intimacy. It's possible that your sex life is not going to get better. It may be that God has called you to accept the yoke of celibacy or near celibacy for the sake of the kingdom. More likely, however, as you implement the lessons you are learning in this book, you and your wife will find yourselves well on your way back to the delight and innocence of Adam and Eve within the garden of Eden.

15

CHILDREARING

B eing a good husband can be challenging. Being both a good husband and a good father can be even more challenging.

You would think that being a good parent should come naturally. Wild animals don't need to take parenting classes. God makes us fertile in our early teens, so biologically speaking, it doesn't take a lot of maturity to become a parent. Unfortunately, most parenting skills are not instinctual. There's a pretty steep learning curve involved when it comes to rearing a family, and usually by the time we get it all figured out, our kids are already grown up, already scarred from our mistakes, and ready to start making their own parenting mistakes. It's sort of a family tradition for human beings.

If you and your wife are hoping to have children, or if you already have young children or teens, the material in this chapter can spare you, her, and your children a lot of stress and heartache.

Disagreements between mom and dad over how to handle the kids produce an enormous amount of marital strife. On the list of things that create trouble between a husband and a wife, childrearing ranks up there with money and sex. In this chapter we'll try to diffuse a few of the explosives buried in the path of any man attempting to be both a dad and husband.

THE LIONESS

Mom and dad both come to the parenting game with different expectations. They themselves were raised in different homes with different standards and under different methods of parenting. From the outset mom and dad have differing ideas about what normal parenting looks like.

Partnering together as parents creates innumerable opportunities for strife and discord between a husband and wife. It's possible to argue over every decision involved in the process, from birth to the empty nest. The reason is obvious: Both mom and dad are personally invested in the child. Both mom and dad want what's best for the child, but mom and dad do not agree about what's best for the child. This dynamic creates potential for frequent and explosive confrontations between the parents. Since the subject of the disagreement involves determining what's best for the child, the argument will be exacerbated by a sense of heightened moral obligation. Each parent will feel that the other one is acting completely unreasonably and without the best interests of the child in mind.

The friction between husband and wife becomes even more abrasive than under ordinary circumstances because, when it comes to matters dealing with the children, the wife is suddenly all in. A quiet wife who might normally let things slide and let her husband have his way in order to avoid conflict suddenly becomes a lioness when the children are involved. Her maternal instincts inspire her to rise up to defend her children and her territory, even against the man she loves. When mama isn't happy, nobody's happy.

NOT A PARTNERSHIP

God has wired women to be protectors, nurturers, and caretakers for their children. That part really is instinctual. It's not universally true of all women, but most moms don't have to try to be maternal. It comes naturally. Men have some of the same instincts, but they are buried deeper in the male psyche. Of course we want to protect, nurture, and care for our children, but it's not as reflexive for us. It's more of learned behavior. We have a different role to play with our children. Mothers and fathers are not the same thing.

Problems erupt between parents when men try to be both mom and dad.

A firm rule of business says, "Never enter a partnership." In a true partnership, both business partners have equal control. Eventually—inevitably—conflict will arise. Since both partners have equal control, the only solution will be to dissolve the partnership. Statistically speaking, partnerships rarely work out for long-term success.

Likewise, conflict in parenting occurs when mom and dad attempt to function as partners in the enterprise of raising the children. Eventually—inevitably—some serious disagreement will arise, but unlike a small business, parents don't have the option of simply dissolving the partnership and going their separate ways. The partnership model is a recipe for disaster.

THE FAMILY HIERARCHY

In this book we have already learned that marriage is a divine partnership. God created Eve as an equal and opposite partner corresponding to Adam. A wife is a man's lifelong partner in the business of life. But we have also learned that marriage has a hierarchy that proceeds from God to Christ to the husband to the wife: "The head of every man is Christ, the head of a wife is her husband, and the head of Christ is God" (1 Corinthians 11:3). When it comes to parenting, the hierarchy model works much better than the partnership model.

The hierarchy model functions more like an efficient corporation where authority flows from the head down. God is the president and CEO. Jesus is the vice president and head of all operations. The husband occupies a middle-management level under Jesus and reports to directly to him. He's his boss. Under the husband's management, his wife has authority over the children and the household. That's her department.

In this hierarchy the husband allocates the spiritual and physical resources his wife needs to get her job done. He obtains those resources from his higher ups. When she needs help or assistance, he is there for her to call upon, and when she encounters problems, he is available to help troubleshoot the situation and resolve any difficulties she may experience. She is able to consult her husband whenever she needs to, and if she encounters resistance to her authority, he is there to back her up. If she presents him with a problem that goes beyond his ability to resolve, he refers it higher up the ladder.

Under the hierarchical model, parenting roles are clearly defined and separated so that mom and dad are not tripping over each other. Mom is in charge of the kids and the household. Dad doesn't need to concern himself in every little detail because he can be confident that she's got it covered. If she needs input from him, she will ask.

The hierarchy model works a lot better than the partnership model, but there is a danger of taking the idea too far. Some men might misuse the model to justify disengagement from the family. Others might abuse the system to justify authoritarian behavior. Still others might overplay their management role by micromanaging their wives and children.

THE UNINVOLVED DAD

Mom takes care of the kids. They are her problem. Dad kicks back and lets her deal with them. If she needs a little help once in a while, she can call on him. Sound too good to be true? That's because it isn't true.

The biblical hierarchy is not at all like that. In the biblical hierarchy, the man is head of the wife just as the Messiah is the head of the man. As head over the man, Jesus does not take a hands-off approach to his affairs. He is with the man every step of the way. He has his back in every situation. He does not hesitate to come down to the man's level and get his hands dirty, so to speak. In fact, he was willing to lay down his life, suffer, and die for mankind.

According to that type of headship, a husband's middle-management position requires hands-on cooperation side by side with his staff—namely his wife. He needs to be fully involved in the program and contributing his time and effort every step of the way.

Most men would prefer a model of parenting that exonerated them from responsibility and the unpleasant parts of child rearing, but that's not what we are talking about here. According to the biblical model, a man is willing to suffer for the success of those below him. That means changing diapers, washing diapers (ick!), losing sleep to hold a colicky baby, taking on household chores, spending time in the sandbox, reading storybooks, and helping with bedtime routines, discipline, bicycle lessons, school issues, homework, and so on and so forth. It's a completely hands-on position.

In every type of company, the best managers are the ones who know the job from the inside. They worked up through the ranks and have experience on the floor. They know how the work gets done on the ground. They know the job and do not hesitate to take on tasks that other managers might consider beneath their dignity. Some of the worst managers are the ones who come from outside of the company.

They have a lot of theories about how the company should work, but they do not really know the job.

DAD VADER

Some men misunderstand the Bible's hierarchical structure to imply unrealistic levels of authority. The husband reasons it this way: "If I am the authority over my wife in the same sense that Christ is the authority over me, then I am basically her king and master." He conducts himself as if that were the case, dictating his will over the household like Darth Vader commanding his storm troopers.

That's not the kind of kingship and lordship our Master modeled for us. Instead, he came saying, "The greatest among you shall be your servant"; and he said, "I came not to be served but to serve"; and he said, "Not my will but yours"; and he said, "I do nothing on my own authority but only on the authority of the Father. I say nothing of myself but only what the Father tells me."[41]

A man's headship over his wife has more to do with modeling Christ to her than it does with bossing her around. Christ's headship over his disciples is about revealing the glory of the Father to us. Likewise, a man's headship over his wife should reveal the character of Messiah to her.

A man cannot forget that despite his position of headship over his wife, she is nevertheless also his peer and his spouse. If he treats her as a subordinate, an employee, or as a child, he will insult her dignity and damage their marriage bond. His dictatorial methods will damage the spiritual adhesive with which he is supposed to be glued to her. His refusal to heed her or give her veto power will show her that she ranks low in his eyes. Marital problems ensue.

Instead, the man needs to exercise his headship in broad terms of authority. He authorizes his wife to administer the household and manage the children. He authorizes her to take the lead in all matters pertaining to childrearing. The kids and home are her department. Then he backs her up, assists her in those capacities, and allocates to her all spiritual and material resources that she needs to be successful.

Darth Vader was a terrible father and not a very good husband either.

MR. MICROMANAGEMENT

Some men might misunderstand the hierarchical model to imply that they need to be fully involved, assessing and signing off on every decision the wife makes. They might suppose that it's their job to take over when it looks as if their wives are making wrong turns. In the business world, that's called micromanaging. Few things can frustrate, discourage, and deflate a workforce as effectively as a high-level manager who continually usurps the decisions made by his staff and employees. If you have ever worked at a job in which one of your superiors constantly undermined you, second-guessed you, and needlessly meddled in your work, you know what we are talking about. You don't want to be that kind of manager, and you don't want to be that kind of husband.

A good manager gives his team the freedom to get the job done, and he gives them the authority to get it done the way they deem best. He also gives them the freedom to make mistakes from time to time because he knows that a few mistakes will be less damaging to morale than his micromanaging will.

The same is true with your wife. Once you have given her authority over the kids and the household, you can't take that away from her just because you don't like the way she handles a certain situation. You have to give her the freedom to settle things on her own terms, according to her best instincts. If she needs your input, she will ask for it.

HONOR YOUR MOTHER

As head of the wife, the man's most important job in the family hierarchy involves teaching the children to honor their mother. The children have a biblical mandate, handed down from the CEO, to honor their father and mother. The only way the child can ever learn how to honor his mother is through the authority of the father. When the father steps in, backing up the mother's place of authority in the household, the child will learn about honoring both mother and father.

If a woman scolds her children, saying, "You need to honor and respect me," it only invites them to dishonor and disrespect her. When a father scolds the same children, saying, "You need to obey your mother, honor her, and respect her," the mother's authority suddenly carries weight in the household, and the children learn about respecting mom. At the same time, father's authority becomes obvious to them. How else could he demand that they must obey their mother unless he carried a higher authority? By backing up his wife in front of the children, the father trains the children to honor both parents.

On the other hand, if a father contradicts his wife in front of the children, reverses her decisions, or undermines her authority, he teaches the children to disregard her and disrespect her. Not only that, he infuriates his wife and ignites a quarrel that will breed further disrespect for both parents. By disrespecting your wife in front of the children, you train them to disrespect her, effectively teaching them to sin. You plant seeds of rebellion in them that will blossom into full fruit in later years. "A wise son makes a glad father, but a foolish man despises his mother" (Proverbs 15:20).

For this reason, a wise husband will support his wife's authority over the children even when he believes that she is wrong. He knows that the damage incurred by a few parenting missteps on her part will be inconsequential when compared to the damage he would cause by undermining her role.

If a husband ever does encounter a situation in which he feels his wife has made a seriously wrong decision regarding the children, and he feels he must speak to her about it, he should take it up with her in private, never in front of the children. To maintain the hierarchy of the family order, he needs to resist the temptation to take the children's side in a dispute with their mother, even if he believes she is in the wrong.

This principle of backing up mom and teaching the children to respect her holds true when children are toddlers and even more so when they become teenagers. It's natural for teenagers to test the boundaries and push back against authority. That's when husbands have to step up their game to make sure that mom is not being disrespected. It might be tempting at times to side with the young adult children against their mother—especially on those occasions in which the young adults seem to be in the right and mom in the wrong. But the same rule holds true. During the children's teenage years, it's even more important for a man to stand behind his wife. He must not let the children whom she has raised turn against her.

When a man takes sides with his children against his wife, it damages the children, and it damages their relationship with their mother. Moreover, it emotionally wounds the woman. She feels deeply betrayed, and she feels a fierce smoldering anger ignite deep within her.

DISCIPLINE

Children are naughty. That's part of being a human being. When children are naughty, parents are supposed to correct them. That's how we begin to learn the difference between wrong and right. It's the first step toward godliness. Without parents to correct a child by punishing bad behavior and rewarding good behavior, a child has little hope of ever staying on a path of righteousness or obtaining the fear of the LORD in his or her life.

Disciplining children is an important part of being a parent. The Bible warns us that "folly is bound up in the heart of a child, but the rod of discipline drives it far from him" (Proverbs 22:15). Another proverb tells us that punishing a child for misbehavior will eventually "save his soul from Sheol" (Proverbs 23:14). Again, an undisciplined "child left to himself brings shame to his mother" (Proverbs 29:15), but if you "discipline your son, he will give you rest; he will give delight to your heart" (Proverbs 29:17).

The problem is that we have different ideas about how to discipline our children. Husbands and wives might have contradicting strategies and methods, leading to conflict over when to discipline, why to discipline, how to discipline. The popular culture has generated as many parenting theories about how to discipline children as it has produced new miracle diets for losing weight. Which one works the best?

In reality, every diet works. It doesn't really matter which diet you choose to follow. So long as you consistently follow the diet, you will lose weight. At the same time, most weight-loss diets fail. Why? Because we don't consistently follow them. We start off all right, and maybe shed a few pounds at first, but then we begin to drift from the diet and put the pounds back on. The problem is not the type of diet, the problem is our inconsistency.

The same principle applies to disciplining children. There is no one perfect method of discipline and correction. The important thing is firm consistency. When discipline is inconsistent, the child can perceive the punishment only as capricious and unfair, perhaps even unjustified. When the child receives a punishment for an offense one day but receives no consequences for the same offense on a later occasion, the discipline loses its meaning. The child begins to perceive punishments as a manifestation of a parent's ugly mood, not a standard for correction.

If you and your wife don't work out a solid game plan, the children will run you over, turn you against one another, and take advantage of gaps in your disciplinary programs. Work with your wife to decide what the rules are. Let her take the lead, if she wants, in developing a solid strategy using whatever method of reward and punishment she deems appropriate for the age of the children. Make sure you both spell out the terms. You both need to clearly understand and agree to the why, when, what, and how of the program. Then just keep it consistent.

Make firm and clear rules. Make sure the children know exactly where the line is and what the consequences will be for crossing the line. Make sure that every time the child crosses the line, he or she receives the same consequence.

And don't forget to reward good behavior. Positive reinforcement is always far more effective in shaping behavior than negative consequences are. Praising a child for good behavior goes a lot further than punishing bad behavior. An old Jewish adage says that we should punish with the left hand and reward with the right hand; push away the child with the left hand but draw the child near with the right hand. This means that whatever effort goes into punishing bad behavior, far more effort needs to go into rewarding good behavior. A child should experience far more positive affirmations than negative corrections.

In many homes it works best for the father to be the disciplinarian. Then mom doesn't need to get flustered. She knows that she can turn the unruly child over to her husband, and the unruly child knows it too. Usually the prospect of dad's displeasure strikes more fear into the heart of a child than the prospect of mom's displeasure. This system also has the advantage of relieving the father of the duty of playing policeman. Mom polices the kids and issues the warnings. When she decides a punishment is in order, she can turn the child over to the husband. By dividing the duties in this way, both parents present a united front to the children. It also keeps anger out of the punishment because, even if the child angers mom, she won't be the one delivering the punishment.

Regardless of how you and your wife decide to conduct your institute of corrections, just make sure you both agree to the plan and then stick with it. Remember to back her up, and remember that you are on her side.

ANGER, INSULTS, AND ABUSE

Never punish or correct a child when you are angry. If you do, you will be too severe, and the child will perceive the punishment as the result of your anger, not a deliberate correction. If you punish a child when you are angry, your wife is likely to come to the child's defense. Her maternal instinct to protect the child will kick in, and you will find yourself facing off with both an unruly child and an angry wife.

Anger never has anything to contribute to parenting. Raised voices and shouting do not help correct behavior, they only model bad behavior.

Don't feel that you need to raise your voice to emphasize a point, not unless you are hoping to raise children who do a lot of shouting themselves. If you are firm and consistent with your discipline policies, you will not need to yell at your children to get their attention or correct their behavior. Besides, you are the father. It's really beneath your dignity to start yelling at your children. The children should consider dad to be an immovable rock of Gibraltar, solid and reliable, not blown around by winds of anger.

Never strike a child. Corporal punishment, such as delivering a spanking, is one thing. Striking a child, grasping a child to inflict physical pain, or hurting a child at all is abusive. As the father and the man of the house, your job is to protect your children. Blows and physical abuse have nothing to do with discipline. Those are the fruit of anger and the work of the evil one.

Paul says, "Fathers, do not provoke your children, lest they become discouraged" (Colossians 3:21). This means that a father must never insult or deride a child. Never call a child names. Never say to a child, "Why are you so clumsy? Why are you so stupid?" This is the language of the devil, and it has no place in a godly home.

As the father of the house, your word carries authority in the child's life. Calling a child names, insulting a child, or deriding a child is the equivalent of placing a curse on the child. Your words should be only positive and affirming. You can be stern when necessary, but there is never any good reason to resort to insults, name calling, or mockery. Coming from the father, the one who carries authority in the household, those types of words will lacerate a child's sense of self-esteem and emotionally scar the child for life. Moreover, they will invite your wife to turn against you.

CORRECTING MOM

What if your wife treats the children abusively, issuing verbal abuse and inappropriate physical punishments? If real physical abuse is actually taking place, you have a legal and moral responsibility to put a stop to it and get help. But if that's not the case, and mom is just losing her cool, be careful not to undermine her or turn the children against her. It's normal for moms to lose their cool, and children quickly adjust to that. They know that she will simmer down shortly and the nurturing relationship will resume. It's a different kind of relationship than the one that a child has with a father. A child perceives mom as more prone to emotional ups and downs, but dad's rebukes and angry words carry immense weight.

If your wife loses her cool with the children, and you try correcting her in front of the children, you plant in the children seeds of doubt and mistrust of their mother, robbing her of her authority. You will also trigger a nuclear explosion of anger from the offended mom. It's not worth it. It's not going to do any good. Scolding her will not prevent her from losing her cool in the future, it will only inspire her to resent you.

If you feel it is absolutely necessary to address your wife regarding her interactions with the children, fast and pray about it first. Then seek a time when you can be alone with her, and gently discuss it within the broader terms of your disciplinary agreements without making any incriminations or criticisms of her parenting.

PAWNS AND SPECTATORS

Never argue about the children in front of the children. In fact, a man should never argue with his wife in front of the children at all. Sometimes when husband and wife are in the heat of an argument, the children become pawns in the battle.

A Messianic rabbi was shocked to see members of his synagogue, a seemingly godly couple, misuse their eight-year-old daughter in this fashion in their domestic arguments. The dad would scold the mom and then call on his daughter to support him. The mom would retaliate and ask her daughter to agree with her. Then the dad would retort, always addressing his daughter and his wife:

Dad: You started the fight when you mouthed off to me. Isn't that right, Shelly? Didn't Mommy start the fight when she said that to Daddy?

Mom: Shelly, it's not OK for your dad to be yelling at me; you know that, don't you?

Dad: She knows it's not OK for you to stay in bed half the morning too.

After the argument the rabbi had the opportunity to sit down with both parents together and warn them about the damage they were doing to their daughter. They agreed. They knew it was wrong, and they both felt ashamed. They promised not to involve her in their arguments again, but they did not keep the promise. The husband was not willing to change his behavior toward his wife, and the marriage ended in divorce. Needless to say, when Shelly became a teenager, she wanted nothing to do with their religion or their God or either of them. That horrible story illustrates the damage we do when we involve our children in our arguments.

If you want a peaceful home, you and your wife should attempt to create at least a veneer of unity and peace in front of the children. Save your disagreements and arguments for time behind closed doors, out of range of the children's hearing. Better yet, study this book from the beginning, and don't have arguments with your wife. Then you won't need to pretend in front of the children.

BIBLE EDUCATION

The Bible considers the education of a child to be one of the main duties parents have toward their children. The Proverbs are full of admonitions about imparting wisdom to our children. The Torah says, "You shall teach [God's commandments] diligently to your children, and shall talk of them when you sit in your house, and when you walk by the way, and when you lie down, and when you rise" (Deuteronomy 6:7). The Apostle Paul says that "a father with his children" exhorts them and encourages them and charges them "to walk in a manner worthy of God" (1 Thessalonians 2:11–12). Every father has the sacred duty of teaching his children the Scriptures and the commandments. One should not rely on church, synagogue, Sunday school, Shabbat school, Bible camp, or other venues outside the home. The home needs to be the principle place of learning, and the father of the house should make it a top priority to teach the Scriptures to his children. This might happen with formal Bible study hours, family devotions, bedtime reading, Shabbat table stories, or other means.

When the father does not take the initiative to make these things happen, his wife feels that she must do so. This places her in an awkward position of feeling as though she must become the spiritual leader of the household. Tension between husband and wife ensues.

In order to avoid that kind of tension, take your God-given place of leadership in the home by spending time with your children in God's Word. You have the awesome privilege of introducing your children to their Father in heaven. What could be more important than that?

SCHOOLING

Schooling for the children can become another point of contention between father and mother. It's important to have consensus with your wife about how you will educate the children. Since you have already given her authority over the household and the children, and you have already agreed to allocate the resources she needs for that job, its best to let her make the final decisions on schooling.

Whether she chooses a public school, a private school, or a homeschool is less important than the fact that you are both in agreement on the plan and fully invested in it. Whatever you choose to do, your wife will need your support. If you choose to homeschool, she will need more than just your support. She will need your active participation.

HOME IS A SAFE PLACE

The most important thing you can do to properly raise your children is to make sure that your home is full of love and peace. The best way to be a good father is to be a good husband to your wife, thereby creating a healthy environment of love and godliness where the children can be nurtured.

A home torn by discord, bitterness, and angry voices does not feel safe to children. Children raised in such an environment struggle with insecurities and fears. When they come of age, they will gladly leave the house at their first opportunity and never look back. In most cases they are also eager to shed the religion of their parents because they witnessed that it did neither of them any good. Children raised in a home of strife often grow up to create their own distressed and dysfunctional marriages, just the way they learned from mom and dad. The apple doesn't fall far from the tree.

A home characterized by love between mom and dad feels safe. It feels like home. Children raised in such an environment flourish. They have self-confidence to step out into the world and take risks because they know that they have a safe, loving home to which they can retreat. They are more apt to marry spouses who share the same values they were brought up with, and they are more apt to create safe, loving homes for their own children.

In view of all this, it should be obvious that you owe it to your children to obtain a good marriage, free from the bitterness and acrimony that can poison the home environment.

THE IDEAL FAMILY

You don't have to be the perfect dad, and your wife doesn't have to be the perfect mom. Some families toil under the notion that a godly family has it all together: The house is always clean, dinner is always served at six, the dishes are always washed before bed, the kids never fight or talk back, mom is always smiling, dad is always a fountain of wisdom and gentle humor as he leads the family devotions before breakfast and before bed, and so forth. It's the picture of the perfect family featured on the cover of *Home School Moms* magazine.

Real families don't fit that mold. The families in the Bible all suffered with some form of dysfunction. Adam and Eve lost Paradise and raised a murderer. Noah had his drinking problem and a rebellious son. Abraham had issues with Sarah, Hagar, and Ishmael. Isaac and Rebekah played favorites with their children and raised boys at odds with one another. Jacob had four wives and lots of family heartache, including a daughter who was raped and a situation involving incest in the home, not to mention the problems that developed between his son Joseph and the ten older brothers. Let's not even get started with King David and his family. Most of the families in the Bible had some type of serious dysfunction.

Trying to make your home into some perfect ideal will create unnecessary stress on everyone. Remember to laugh a lot, and cut your wife and kids plenty of slack. Disagreements and arguments about how to handle the children are damaging to both your marital relationship and to the children themselves. So long as you and your wife have an equal vote in the decision-making process, handling the kids will be a source of conflict. The wise husband delegates authority over the children and the household to his wife. Then he involves himself in raising the family by backing her up, participating fully in family duties and activities, and teaching the children to respect their mother. He avoids becoming disengaged, he doesn't let himself turn into Darth Vader, and he refuses the temptation to micromanage affairs.

When it comes to disciplining the children, work out a game plan with your wife, and stick to it. Anger, insults, and physical abuse have no useful role in correcting a child's behavior. Never take sides with your children against your wife. Teach your children the Bible and the things of the kingdom "when you sit in your house, and when you walk by the way, and when you lie down, and when you rise." Do everything you can to insure that your home is a place of safety, love, and peace.

It sounds like a lot of work, but like everything else in life, it's just taking one thing at a time, one day at a time. Keep a positive outlook, and commit everything to God in prayer. He will surely send you the help you need from heaven.

16

SLAY THE DRAGON AND SAVE THE PRINCESS

Adam lived alone in the garden. It's not good for man to be alone. So God made Eve. He brought her before Adam and presented her to him. Adam took one look at her, and he was hooked. He fell in love. He said, "This creature is just like me! She is part of me! My own flesh and bone." He took her to be his wife. The Torah says, "The man and his wife were both naked and were not ashamed" (Genesis 2:25).

Wouldn't it be nice if that's where the story ended? Wouldn't it be nice if nothing ever happened to disrupt the idyllic and innocent bond of love that Adam and Eve shared in Paradise? And wouldn't it be nice if nothing ever came between you and your beloved wife, and the two of you could enjoy the blissful, innocent, unblushing love and companionship of our first father and mother in Paradise? The story didn't end there. Something came between Adam and Eve: the serpent.

THE SNAKE IN THE GARDEN

The serpent is the devil. He is "the great dragon ... that ancient serpent, who is called the devil and Satan, the deceiver of the whole world" (Revelation 12:9). He is called "the accuser" (Revelation 12:10). That's actually what the Hebrew name "Satan" means. *Satan* (שטן) is a Hebrew word that means "accuser." A better modern-English equivalent would be "prosecuting attorney." Think of him more as a high-powered attorney than a fang-mouthed ghoul. He does not live in hell, neither does he have horns and a tail, as far as we know. His realm is the earth itself. Jewish lore says that he entered this world with the specific goal of meddling with Adam and Eve and leading them astray.

As the accuser, he spends most of his time accusing people of their sins and shortcomings. He got to work on Adam right away, teaching him the fine art of blaming his wife and pointing the finger at her. When God asked Adam about what happened with the whole fruit-of-the-tree-of-knowledge thing, Adam sold out Eve without hesitation. He blamed her for his own failings: "The woman whom you gave to be with me, she gave me fruit of the tree, and I ate" (Genesis 3:12). That's probably the point at which things first broke down between husbands and wives. Imagine the stony silence Adam must have endured on the car ride from Eden.

As a man, you should learn some important things from this story. First, you should realize that Satan wants to destroy your marriage. It's in his best interest to see your marriage crumble, and he is willing to devote significant spiritual resources toward that effort. Second, you should realize that your wife is not the enemy. Satan is the enemy. He wants to turn you against her, and he wants to turn her against you. As a professional accuser, he knows how to accomplish that objective by inspiring you to criticize your wife, point out her shortcomings, and blame her for your own. It worked the first time, and it has worked pretty well for him with every couple since Adam and Eve.

Satan wants into your marriage. He wants to be part of every con-versation you have with your wife. He wants to plant bitter thoughts about her in your mind, and he wants to sow seeds of mistrust into your relationship. Satan wants to feed you the fruit of the knowledge of good and evil so that he can point out to you every evil quality your wife might have.

Satan wants into your bedroom. He wants to introduce shame into your sexuality, shaming your wife for not meeting your expectations and making you feel shamed and rejected by her.

Satan wants into every aspect of your marriage. And he's not just a metaphor. He is a real, malevolent, spiritual being with many fell and unclean servants, all eager to do his bidding. He bids them destroy your marriage by whatever means possible.

We are not trying to scare you. We just want you to know who the real enemy is.

SPIRITUAL WARFARE

Once you recognize that the real bad guy in your marriage is Satan, you can do something about it. Now you are on to his game. He is the one who inspires you to criticize and correct your wife. He is the one pointing out all her flaws to you. He is the one who tells you to blame her for your failings and shortcomings. He is the one twisting your words and making communication virtually impossible.

Are you ready to slay the dragon and save the princess? To fight the devil, you need to fight with spiritual weapons. Put on the armor of God, and then turn to prayer. Prayer and the Word of God will be your chief weapons. It doesn't do much good at all to rebuke the devil. He's well-accustomed to fools rebuking him, and he enjoys the attention. It's far more effective to spend time in prayer talking with God. Pray through the Psalms regularly. Pray the Psalms on behalf of your wife. Ask God to defend her. Ask him to close her ears to the devil's lies. Ask God to drive the enemy out from the midst of your marriage.

Satan is a liar. "There is no truth in him. When he lies, he speaks out of his own character, for he is a liar and the father of lies" (John 8:44). When accusations against your wife form in your head, don't listen to them. Don't listen to Satan's lies, and don't give him a voice. Don't offer him your services as the accuser of your wife. Instead, defend her in prayer. Give thanks to God for your wife. Extol her virtues to the heavenly judge. List off in prayer all the good things about her. Plead on her behalf before the Almighty, and ask him to forgive all her sins and overlook all her transgressions.

Close the portals that Satan uses to enter your home. Don't engage in arguments, don't level accusations and recriminations against your wife, and don't play the blame game. Those things make the devil feel at home in your home. Don't drink alcohol and let it lower your inhibitions and loosen your tongue. The devil encourages you to have a few drinks to take the edge off because he wants you to say harmful things that you would never say when you are sober. Don't let lust, pornography, and sexual immorality open a gateway for him to enter your head and defile your bed. Do not harbor anger because anger opens opportunities for the devil: "Do not let the sun go down on your anger, and give no opportunity to the devil" (Ephesians 4:26–27). Don't let him fool you into thinking that your wounded pride needs to be defended. He wants you to think highly of yourself because "pride goes before destruction, and a haughty spirit before a fall" (Proverbs 16:18).

Now that you know what he is up to, you don't have to play his games any longer. He doesn't need to be a part of your marriage.

BATTLING SATAN IN THE COURT OF HEAVEN

Slaying the dragon and rescuing the princess will require a lot of time in prayer, pouring out your heart to God like water. Budget the time for serious prayer. An hour a day of personal prayer and petition is ideal, but even if you only set aside fifteen minutes a day to pray for your wife, your marriage, and your family, you will see amazing results.

When you pray, be careful not to complain about your wife. Remember, she is God's daughter, and generally speaking, complaints irritate God. Think of all the times he punished the children of Israel in the wilderness just for complaining. So don't complain about your wife, and don't point out her faults to him. He already knows her faults. Instead, you should give thanks for your beautiful wife and praise the Almighty for selecting the perfect spouse for you. Tell him about her good qualities and everything you love about her, and ask him to bless her, protect her, heal her, encourage her, and bring cheer to her heart.

According to Jewish teaching, Satan stands as the prosecuting attorney against you and against every person in the court of heaven. He stands before the Almighty, accusing each person of his or her sins, listing off every transgression, error, mistake, rebellious act, and personal failing in a never-ending litany of indictments.

Rabbi Levi Yitzchak of Berdichev, an eighteenth-century Chasidic rabbi, realized that the best way to fight Satan was to take up the role of defense attorney in the court of heaven. He made it his habit to overlook the sins and shortcomings of his fellow Jews. Whenever he saw some sin or shortcoming, rather than point it out and call attention to it as Satan does in the court of heaven, Rabbi Levi Yitzchak gave thanks to God for the person's good qualities and virtues. He imagined himself standing opposite Satan in the heavenly court. As Satan launched his accusations against a person, Rabbi Levi Yitzchak was there to defend the sinner by reminding the Almighty of the sinner's good deeds and redeeming merits.

In your prayers remind the Almighty of your wife's good deeds, virtues, and merits. Remind him of what a dedicated wife and mother she is. Remind him of the little kindnesses she does. Remind him that she is a disciple of Christ, redeemed and washed clean in Christ's blood. In so doing you counter the accusations lodged against her by the devil, and you become her advocate rather than her spiritual enemy. That's how you slay the dragon and save the princess.

PASSING THE TEST

In chapter 1 we learned that marriage is a test. God uses marriage as a testing ground for faith and spiritual growth. The rabbis say that God tested Abraham ten times. Half of those tests had to do with his relationship with Sarah. Marriage tests a man's character. The way you treat (or mistreat) your wife and the way you react when she mistreats you reveal your inner person.

The problem with tests is that you can fail them. It's not the trials themselves that are so bad, it's the sense of disappointment with yourself when you realize you failed the test. It's possible that up until now you've been failing at the test of marriage. Don't let that depress you. The next time you are tested on marriage, you will do a lot better because you've been doing your homework. You've studied for the test, and you are going to keep studying so that eventually, with God's help, you will be able to ace it every time.

There's really no point in beating yourself up or feeling depressed about mistakes you have made in the past. Guilt and depression will only sap your energy for doing better in the future. It's important to always keep an optimistic attitude. Think good, and it will be good. Remember Caleb and Joshua, and be a man with a different spirit.

Don't expect your marriage to suddenly blossom fresh overnight. It takes a long time to reverse emotional damage in a woman's heart. It will take her a long time to learn to trust you. At first she will probably assume your good behavior is just a new phase you are going through. The new Mr. Nice Guy routine might last a week or two, maybe three weeks. She's probably right. If you don't continue studying this book, reviewing its contents, relearning its messages, and implementing them in your life, you will quickly slip back into old habits. "Like a dog that returns to his vomit is a fool who repeats his folly" (Proverbs 26:11).

If you've been married five years already, you can anticipate at least a year or two of work, sticking to the principles in this book, before you start to see things level off. If you have been married twenty years, expect the process to take four or five years.

Regardless of how long it takes, don't gauge your success on your wife's reactions. She may or may not respond positively at first. She may have her own issues to work though. If you gauge your level of success on whether or not your wife's behavior changes, you haven't learned the message of this book yet. It's not how she behaves and conducts herself in the marriage that matters, it's about how you behave. It's not just about our relationship with our wives, it's about our relationship with God.

So don't gauge your success on her reactions. Measure your success on the basis of how closely you have reconciled yourself to Christ.

PERFECT VERSUS BETTER

Maybe you feel a little overwhelmed by the enormous weight of responsibility the Bible puts on you as a husband. Maybe you feel a little beat up by the contents of this book. Don't give up so easily. Don't throw your hands in the air, saying, "What's the use? I can't be perfect. No one could be so perfect." We aren't looking for perfection, and we aren't looking for the perfect marriage. We are only looking for "better." Maybe you can't be the perfect husband, but you certainly can be a better husband.

You can do only one thing at a time. So long as you are continually improving and working on yourself, you are headed in the right direction and on the path to a better marriage. Little by little, it will get better. Remember to stay positive, think positively, trust God, and pray a lot. Now that you have finished the book, start over. Keep working through the material, rereading a little bit every day so that you continue to improve and don't fall back into old habits. Make this book part of your daily devotional studies. Add other good books on marriage to your reading list, and continue to work on mastering the art of delighting your wife.

With God's help, and through the merit and virtue of his holy Son Yeshua, you and your wife will find your way into the kingdom, into Eden, and into a better marriage.

Remember, it's not good for a man to be alone. That's why Adam loves Eve.

ENDNOTES

1 Proverbs 31:12.

2 Proverbs 14:1.

3 Cf. Proverbs 27:15.

4 Deuteronomy 24:4.

5 Talmud, b.*Kiddushin* 29b.

6 Talmud, b.*Yevamot* 63a.

7 Joel 2:28–29.

8 *Genesis Rabbah* 8:9.

9 Talmud, b.*Sotah* 17a.

10 Luke 14:26.

11 1 John 5:3.

12 Ephesians 5:25–28; Colossians 3:19.

13 Proverbs 18:24 may allude to Genesis 2:24, "A man shall … hold fast to his wife, and they shall become one flesh," by using the same Hebrew word for "holding fast" (i.e., *davak*, דבק): "There is a friend who *holds fast* (*davak*) closer than a brother" (emphasis added).

14 1 Corinthians 7:32–34.

15 Ephesians 5:23–25.

16 Talmud, b.*Bava Metzia* 59a.

17 1 Peter 3:7.

18 b.*Bava Metzia* 59a.

19 Rabbi Yosi in Talmud, b.*Shabbat* 118a.

20 Matthew 5:31–32, 19:9; Mark 10:11–12; Luke 16:18.

21 Talmud, b.*Arachin* 15b.

22 m.*Avot* 1:6.

23 1 Corinthians 7:32–34.

24 Genesis 3:16.

25 b.*Bava Metzia* 59b.

26 In Hebrew: הוֹכֵחַ תּוֹכִיחַ אֶת־עֲמִיתֶךָ וְלֹא־תִשָּׂא עָלָיו חֵטְא.

27 *Hocheach tochiach* (הוכח תוכיח): "You shall surely rebuke" (Leviticus 19:17).

28 Talmud, b.*Arachin* 16b.

29 Job 31:1.

30 Talmud, b.*Bava Metzia* 59a.

31 Talmud, b.*Sanhedrin* 74a.

32 Genesis 9:6; Numbers 35:31–33.

33 Deuteronomy 13:6–11.

34 Leviticus 20:10.

35 Matthew 5:32, 19:9.

36 Talmud, b.*Chullin* 84b.

37 *Genesis Rabbah* 17:3.

38 m.*Kiddushin* 1:1.

39 Deuteronomy 23:17.

40 Leviticus 15:19, 24.

41 Matthew 20:28, 23:11; Luke 22:42; John 5:19, 12:48–50.

APPENDIX 1

THE TWO SHALL BECOME ONE FLESH

THE BEGINNING AND END OF MARRIAGE
RABBI RUSS RESNIK

Paper presented at Hashivenu Conference 2015

> Some Pharisees came to Yeshua, and to test him they asked, "Is it lawful for a man to divorce his wife for any cause?" He answered, "Have you not read that the one who made them at the beginning 'made them male and female,' and said, 'For this reason a man shall leave his father and mother and be joined to his wife, and the two shall become one flesh'? So they are no longer two, but one flesh. Therefore what God has joined together, let no one separate." (Matthew 19:3-6)[1]

When Messiah Yeshua is tested with a question about divorce, he doesn't immediately engage with the ethical and legal arguments already current in the Jewish world of his day[2] but instead brings his hearers back to the original male-female union that came to be known as marriage. To understand the meaning, significance, and purpose of marriage, then, we will return with the Master to the beginning, exploring the accounts in B'reisheet (Genesis 1:1–6:8) and especially the key verse, Genesis 2:24, to develop a definition of marriage. Indeed, this whole paper can be seen as an exposition of Genesis 2:24 in the context of Genesis 1–3 and the treatment of this verse within the Tanach, rabbinic literature, and Apostolic Writings.

TWO ACCOUNTS OF ORIGIN

Messiah Yeshua's reference to the beginning highlights two texts: Genesis 2:24, especially its final phrase, "the two shall become one flesh," and Genesis 1:26–28, with his statement that the Creator "made them male and female":

> God created the human in His image, in the image of God He created him; male and female He created them. (Genesis 1:27)[3]

Yeshua thereby connects us with the entire creation account of Genesis 1 and 2. The Genesis 1 account of the creation of humankind stands in tension with the account in Genesis 2. In Genesis 1 male and female appear to be created simultaneously, as equal bearers of the divine image; in Genesis 2 the woman is made from the man, who is created first. To understand the relationship between these two accounts, we note first that throughout Genesis 1 God advances the process of creation by dividing, or separating, diverse elements: light from darkness (Genesis 1:4), waters above from waters below (Genesis 1:6), dry land and the seas (Genesis 1:9–10), day and night (Genesis 1:14, cf. 1:18). This distinguishing process continues as God creates plants (Genesis 1:11–12), sea creatures and birds (Genesis 1:21), and earth-bound creatures (Genesis 1:24–25) "of each kind," that is, each with its own distinctive qualities.

Reflecting Genesis 1:27, *Midrash Rabbah* pictures an original male-female Adam, who later will be split, or divided, like other elements of creation:

> R. Samuel b. Nahman said: When the LORD created Adam He created him double-faced, then He split him and made him of two backs, one back on this side and one back on the other side. (*Genesis Rabbah* 8:1)[4]

In this reading the female is not so much "created" in Genesis 2 as separated from the male. The "splitting" of Adam to give him two backs reiterates the dividing and separating process of Genesis 1. In Genesis 2:21 "He took one of his ribs" would refer to a further separating of these two backs, or sides,[5] into two separate humans, one male and one female, out of the prototypical androgynous Adam.

Against this background it is striking that only at the first marriage is the creative process of dividing reversed, as man and woman, after being made distinct, "become one flesh" (Genesis 2:24). Here God's purpose advances not through separation into distinct kinds but through merging, joining two kinds into one. The distinct bodies of male and female now reunite to become one flesh, not as a reversal of the process of creation, but as its culmination. Adam, created at the climax of the six days of Genesis 1, is now no longer alone but united with the one who is bone of his bones and flesh of his flesh (Genesis 2:23). They are together, naked and unashamed, in a moment of equilibrium that we can fittingly describe as shalom, before the entry of the serpent and all that he brings to play in chapter 3. The consummation achieved by male and female, therefore, becomes the paradigm of the consummation toward which all creation is moving.[6]

This glimpse of marriage "in the beginning" provides an outline for our entire study, which we organize under four categories:

1. *The foundation of marriage.* The creation account of the two becoming one flesh reveals a threefold purpose of marriage: creation of a family, intimate companionship, covenant with the Creator.

2. *The order of marriage.* In marriage the inherent male-female equality as divine image bearers operates in tension with differing roles. These roles are accentuated and to some degree set against each other after Adam and Eve's sin in Gan Eden and persist into the Messianic new-covenant context in modified form. This section will also include a brief look at the significance of singleness.

3. *The boundaries of marriage.* On one level, marriage is an institution that protects the covenantal, one-flesh union of man and woman. What are the boundaries of that institution? We will consider the violations and penalties outlined in Scripture, the biblical treatment of eligible and ineligible marriage partners, and the internal boundary of marriage reflected in the family purity laws.

4. *The consummation.* The wedding appears repeatedly in Scripture as a metaphor for the consummation of God's purposes for creation. The use of this metaphor reflects back upon marriage itself to reveal and heighten its significance. This section will explore some new material and then bring together various strains already discussed concerning the purpose, or teleology, of marriage.

1. THE FOUNDATION OF MARRIAGE

Messiah Yeshua cites "one flesh" as a description not simply of sexual union but of marriage itself,[7] thus reflecting the wider context of Genesis 2:18–25. The first male and female join together as one flesh only after a third party, HaShem himself, brings the woman to the man. "The LORD God built the rib He had taken from the human into a woman and He brought her to the human" (Genesis 2:22). Nahum Sarna comments, "As noted in a midrash, the image may well be that of God playing the role of the attendant who leads the bride to the groom. Without doubt, the verse conveys the idea that the institution of marriage is established by God Himself."[8] And so we have here not only the etiology of human sexuality but of marriage itself, which serves to protect and sanctify that sexuality.

Furthermore, as Sarna notes, HaShem's involvement in the primal wedding suggests the role of community in subsequent weddings:

> R. Abbahu said: The Holy One, blessed be He, took a cup of blessing and blessed them ... R. Simlai said: We find that the Holy One, blessed be He, blesses bridegrooms, adorns brides, visits the sick, buries the dead, and recites the blessing for mourners. He blesses the bridegrooms, as it is written, And God blessed them; He adorns brides, as it is written, *And the Lord God built the rib ... into a woman* (Gen. 2:22).[9]

In this midrash God's actions at the first marriage provide a model for the community's actions in subsequent marriages, a model that is developed further in halachah.

Marriage, then, is not simply sexual union but sexual union affirmed and protected by the community. This combination comes into focus gradually in the Genesis narrative. Thus, the earliest accounts of marriage are laconic. Cain's wife simply appears without introduction: "Cain knew his wife and she conceived" (Genesis 4:17); later, "Lamech took him two wives" (Genesis 4:19). The "book of the lineage of Adam" in Genesis 5 doesn't mention wives at all; the males simply beget sons and daughters, generation after generation, until the time of Noah and his three sons.

In the patriarchal stories, however, the picture changes. When Abram leaves Haran in response to HaShem's call, he takes along Sarai his (named) wife (Genesis 12:5). It's clear in the stories of Sarai-Sarah and Hagar (Genesis 16, 21) that Sarah as wife enjoys a higher status than Hagar, with whom Abraham will also have one-flesh intimacy. Marriage is sexual intimacy plus communal sanction. Thus, when Abraham sends his servant to find a wife for his son Isaac, the beautiful account of Genesis 24 includes familial negotiations for a marriage contract along with the blessing of the bride's family upon the new marriage (Genesis 24:60). Jacob's marriages are far less orderly, but they still entail family involvement. Isaac sends Jacob off with a blessing to the household of his great-uncle, Bethuel, to find a wife (Genesis 28:1-5). Jacob contracts with Bethuel's son Laban to marry Rachel. Laban deceives Jacob into marrying his older daughter, Leah, first. In the midst of this troubling tale, we first hear of a wedding feast attended by "all the men of the place" and the formality of the father (Laban) bringing his daughter to the groom (Jacob) for the marriage to be consummated (Genesis 29:22-23). We might read Laban's act as an ironic echo of the original wedding ceremony, in which HaShem "brought her to the human" (Genesis 2:22). What's clear is that the triangular shape of marriage hinted at in Genesis 2—male, female, and an attending third party or parties—is well established in the patriarchal accounts.

The shape of marriage, then, is triangular. A close reading of Genesis 1 and 2 also reveals a triangular, or threefold, purpose of marriage, including intimate companionship, procreation, and divine covenant.

Maurice Lamm lists three "Purposes of Marriage" in his summation of Jewish tradition.[10] First, companionship. Lamm supports a translation of Genesis 2:18 as, "It is not good for the man to be *lonely*," rather than the usual "alone." He comments, "Loneliness is not felt by animals; only man can experience existential loneliness, the fragmentary and incomplete nature of this world. It is the genuine companionship of Adam and Eve that humanity requires, and which is the stated purpose for marriage in the scheme of creation."[11]

The second purpose is "creation of a family," which parallels "procreation" but provides more nuance. "Procreation" could be simply biological or material; "creation of a family" comprises procreation plus the institution that nurtures the issue of procreation. Marriage is a response to the creational mitzvah "Be fruitful and multiply and fill the earth" and also creates a new nuclear family within the extended family of Israel. Marriage, then, is not primarily instrumental, merely a means to accomplish procreation. The attraction between male and female and the blessing of no longer being alone are equally foundational.

Lamm's third purpose is "sexual relations within marriage," or *onah*.[12] This term is derived from Exodus 21:10: "If another woman he should take for himself, he must not stint from this one her meals, her wardrobe, and her conjugal rights [*onatah*]." The Talmud records a discussion of "the *onah* spoken of in the Torah," which lists the length of time men in various occupations can be absent from their wives, and thus from fulfilling their sexual commitment, without their wives' permission.[13] Sexual union, here framed as the man's obligation to his wife, has value and meaning apart from procreation. Alongside the negative commandment of Exodus 21:10, Deuteronomy 24:5 stands out as a positive mitzvah: "When a man takes a new wife, he shall not go out in the army and shall not cross over on its account for any matter. He shall be exempt in his house for a year and gladden his wife whom he has taken." Note that the goal of this mitzvah is not reproduction but happiness to the bride. *Onah* is the woman's right and the husband's obligation—but it's not against the rules for him to enjoy it too!

Departing from Lamm, however, I see *onah* not as a distinct purpose but as part of the intimate companionship for which marriage is intended. There are, of course, aspects of this companionship that are not sexual, but the sexual dimension implied within *onah* is essential to it. Instead of *onah* as a third purpose of marriage, then, we can discern a third purpose in Messiah Yeshua's comment on Genesis 2:24—"what *God* has joined together." Marriage is inherently covenantal, an institution of divine-human interaction, and one purpose of marriage is to enshrine and reflect that covenantal quality.

These realities affirm the sanctity of marriage for couples who cannot or do not have children. According to halachah, a husband who failed to fulfill the mitzvah to have children within ten years after marriage was obliged to divorce his wife and seek another marriage partner (*Yevamot* 64a). But *Pesikta de-Rab Kahana* 22:2 pictures the value of marriage beyond this legal obligation:

> In Sidon it happened that a man took a wife with whom he lived for ten years and she bore him no children. When they came to R. Simeon bar Yoḥai to be divorced, the man said to his wife: "Take any precious object I have in my house—take it and go back to your father's house." Thereupon, R. Simeon bar Yoḥai said: "Even as you were wed with food and drink, so you are not to separate save with food and drink." What did the wife do? She prepared a great feast, gave her husband too much to drink [so that he fell asleep], then beckoned to her menservants and maidservants saying, "Take him to my father's house." At midnight he woke up from his sleep and asked, "Where am I?" She replied, "Did you not say, 'Whatever precious object I have in my house—take it and go back to your father's house?' I have no object more precious than you."[14]

In addition to affirming the marriage of childless couples, this story provides an essential lesson for couples with children: even when the child as a "precious object" is gone from the house, the even more precious spouse remains. Couples sometimes become divided or triangulated by their children and need to make the marriage itself a higher priority. For the sake of the children as well as the marriage itself, they need to rebuild their husband-wife intimacy, even if that requires less attention to the children. The one-flesh union is male and female, not parent and child.

THE JEWISH WEDDING

The Jewish wedding ceremony enacts the elements that we are discussing here. Today's wedding ceremony combines two ancient ceremonies, originally taking place about a year apart: *erusin*, or *kiddushin* (betrothal), and *nissu'in* (the wedding proper).[15]

Before the ceremony takes place, two prerequisites must be met: consent of both parties and the signing of a ketubah, or marriage contract, in the presence of witnesses.[16] The requirement of consent reflects the story of Rebekah's betrothal to Isaac, in which her family asks for her consent before agreeing to the proposal conveyed by Abraham's servant and allowing her to depart with him (Genesis 24:56–58). The ketubah marks marriage as a covenant, stating that the proposal of marriage is "according to the law of Moses and of Israel," stipulating an exchange of items of value, detailing obligations and responsibilities, and requiring the presence of witnesses, all features of ancient covenant enactments.[17] Lamm makes a distinction between the ketubah as a contractual document and the covenant of marriage itself:

> The Jewish concept of marriage can be summarized as follows: *The form, the contract [ketubah], and the process are* contractual. *The content, the bond, and the resulting relationship are* covenantal.
>
> The covenant is the purpose and essence of all Jewish marriage. Malachi (2:14) speaks of "the wife of my covenant," and Ezekiel (16:8) says, "Yea, I swore unto thee and entered into a covenant with thee."
>
> The contract is an agreement to abide by certain rules, but a covenant has a metaphysical dimension. By contract we share duties; by covenant we share destinies ...

The paradigm of man's marriage covenant with woman is the be'rit, the covenant of God and His people, Israel.[18]

Sharing of food and drink is also part of ancient covenant ritual,[19] and the betrothal ceremony opens with a blessing over a cup of wine, which the bride and groom share. "Because marriage is covenantal, both components, *kiddu-shin* and *nissu'in*, are initiated with the blessing over wine."[20] The rabbi recites the betrothal blessing, ending with, "Blessed are You, LORD, who sanctifies His people Israel by the rite of the canopy [*chuppah*] and sacred covenant of marriage."[21] The groom then gives a ring, or other item of equivalent value, to the bride and recites, "Behold, you are consecrated to me by means of this ring, according to the ritual of Moses and Israel." Rabbi Jonathan Sacks notes, "The use of the word 'consecration' in the context of marriage signals the sacred nature of the bond between the partners."[22]

This ritual creates a legal bond between groom and bride, but they are not yet permitted to cohabit. The ketubah is then read, and the second ceremony, *nissu'in*, begins as bride and groom are brought together under the chuppah. The Seven Benedictions are recited over a second cup of wine, and afterward the couple is provided a few moments of privacy, or *yichud*.[23] This tradition symbolizes the physical consummation of the marriage, which is also represented by the bride's joining the groom under the chuppah. As the betrothal blessing above states, the chuppah, representing consummation—the two becoming one flesh—is essential to sanctifying the marriage. This consummation in turn anticipates the consummation of creation, which is represented in the Seven Benedictions by the redemption of Israel:

> Bring great happiness and joy to the one who was barren [Zion], as her children return to her in joy … Soon, LORD our God, may there be heard in the cities of Judah, and in the streets of Jerusalem, the sounds of joy and gladness, the sounds of the bridegroom and bride, the joyous sounds of bridegrooms from their wedding canopy and of young people at their feasts of song. Blessed are you, LORD, who makes the bridegroom rejoice with the bride.[24]

SUMMARY

The creation account of the two becoming one flesh reveals a threefold purpose of marriage as the union of male and female: procreation in the broad sense of creating a family; intimate companionship that overcomes existential aloneness on a human level; and participation in covenant with the Creator, a divine-human partnership that anticipates the consummation toward which the creation is moving.

2. THE ORDER OF MARRIAGE

In Genesis 2, the creation of woman—or the division of primordial Adam into male and female—is triggered by God's observation, "It is not good for the human to be alone [or lonely]; I shall make him a sustainer beside him [*ezer kenegdo*]" (Genesis 2:18). *Ezer kenegdo* is an essential term in our definition of marriage but one that is translated in various ways. The classic King James rendering, "help meet," has survived in some circles, along with various derivations. Robert Alter's translation, however, more effectively captures the sense of the Hebrew. Alter explains, "'Help' is too weak because it suggests a merely auxiliary function, whereas *'ezer* elsewhere connotes active intervention on behalf of someone, especially in military contexts, as often in Psalms."[25] Indeed, in Psalms, the role of *ezer* is often ascribed to God himself (e.g., Psalm 33:20; 70:6 (5); 115:9–11; 146:5), thus supporting the translation of "sustainer" over "helper."

As the Genesis narrative progresses, it reveals that the *ezer kenegdo* Adam seeks is woman. On the way to that revelation, however, God forms the animals and brings them to Adam to be named, only to show that among them no *ezer kenegdo* is found (Genesis 2:20). Adam has dominion over the animals; he is to rule over them, and his act of naming them is a function of that dominion. The woman, in contrast, is formed from him, is flesh of his flesh and bone of his bone, not subject to his dominion but a sustainer beside him. His naming her *Ishah*, woman, "for from man [*ish*] was this one taken" (Genesis 2:23), seems more an act of discovery than of domination. Furthermore, these words comprise the first recorded statement of Adam, even though he probably spoke earlier in naming the animals. Alter notes, "The first human is given reported speech for the first time only when there is another human to whom to respond."[26] And, of course, that other human is his counterpart, the first woman. Accordingly, the rabbinic literature sees man as coming into his full purpose and blessing in partnership with woman: "A man who has no wife lives without joy, without blessing, and without goodness" (b.*Yevamot* 62b). "He who marries a good woman is as if he fulfilled the whole Torah from beginning to end" (*Yalkut Shimoni*, Ruth 606).[27]

Recently as my family sat together at the Shabbat table and I read *Eshet Chayil* (Proverbs 31:10–31), I was brought up short by the second verse: "Her husband's heart trusts in her, and he has no lack of gain" (*Koren Siddur*). I'd gotten some particularly good advice from my wife, Jane, that day, and I wondered out loud if this sentence was causative: "Her husband's heart trusts in her; *therefore* he has no lack of gain." Without hesitation, the women around the table answered in the affirmative. Marriage is sustained and deepened as the husband recognizes the gifting of his wife.

All this expands on the notion of "genuine companionship," or intimacy, as one of the purposes of marriage. Ramban comments on "they shall be one flesh" that the same could be said of the sexual functioning of animals. What is unique to humankind is "cleaving":

> It is for this reason that Scripture states that because the female of man was bone of his bones and flesh of his flesh, he therefore cleaves to her and she nestles in his bosom as his own flesh, and he desires to be with her always. And just as it is with Adam, so was his nature transmitted to his offspring, the males among them should cleave to their women, leaving their fathers and their mothers, and considering their wives as if they are one flesh with them.[28]

Marital intimacy in Ramban's view, then, is a uniquely human trait, part of what distinguishes humans from animals. Or rather, since singleness, as we shall see, is also a valid status, especially in today's conditions, we should say that the *capacity* for this sort of intimacy is part of what defines our humanity, whether we're married or not.

Ramban, commenting on Genesis 2:18, balances this emphasis on cleaving with the insight that true intimacy requires distinct individuals:

> And the Holy One, blessed be He, saw that it was good that "the help" stand facing him, and that he should see or be separated from it or joined to it at his will. This is the meaning of what He said in the verse, *I will make him a helper opposite him.* (emphasis added)[29]

One-flesh union doesn't mean merger or fusion of personalities but two persons joining in intimacy yet remaining distinct. Rabbi and family therapist Edwin H. Friedman speaks of this dynamic as "differentiation ... the capacity to be an 'I' while remaining connected."[30] It's striking that Genesis 2:24 says that the *man* leaves father and mother to cleave to his wife, when in the ancient near East it is normally the *woman* who leaves to cleave to her husband, as reflected in the stories of betrothal in Genesis. In 2:24, however, it is the man who leaves, which may be the precise point. In the ancient world everyone knows that the woman leaves father and mother when she marries a man. What's less obvious but equally, or perhaps even more, important is that the man must leave as well—even if he stays put physically. This leaving is an act of differentiation that provides for true intimacy between husband and wife rather than mutual dependency or enmeshment.

Leaving the paternal household also allows the man to become "master" of a new household, as in Genesis 24. After Abraham's servant finds Rebekah, the bride for Isaac, he asks her family to let him return with her to his "master" (Genesis 24:56), meaning Abraham, as is evident in his many uses of the word "master" throughout the chapter. Later, when the servant returns to the land of Canaan with Rebekah, she sees Isaac in the field coming toward them and asks who he is. The servant replies, "He is my master" (Genesis 24:65). It's as if Isaac is transformed from "my master's son" to "my master" by the presence of his bride. The prominence given in the patriarchal narratives to this story, and to the tale of Jacob's acquisition of brides afterward, highlights the importance of marriage itself, not only in creating a new family, but also in bringing the male into his differentiated individuality. Rebekah's proactive responsiveness in Genesis 24 suggests that she, too, becomes a defined individual as she approaches marriage with Isaac.

Individual differentiation provides for mutuality between husband and wife. In the biblical world, the male generally had the dominant role, and yet he is incomplete apart from the woman. Man and woman both share in the divine image and are equally essential to the meaning of humanness so that the humanity of each is completed when they unite. Accordingly, *Midrash Rabbah* highlights the interdependency of man and woman:

> In the past Adam was created from dust and Eve was created from Adam; but henceforth it shall be *In our image, after our likeness*; neither man without woman nor woman without man, and neither of them without the Divine Spirit.[31]

Within marriage the inherent equality of male and female as divine image bearers is expressed in tension with differing roles of male and female. These differing roles are accentuated, and to some degree set against each other, as a consequence of exile from the garden. They persist into the Messianic community and are upheld in the Apostolic Writings, as we will see. Furthermore, even before exile from the garden, we can detect a hierarchy in the male-female relationship. Alter renders *ha-adam* in Genesis 2 as "the human" rather than "the man," but we're still confronted by male-female hierarchy in the human's observation:

> This one shall be called Woman [*ishah*], for from man [*ish*] was this one taken. (Genesis 2:23)[32]

The Midrash simply observes, "Adam was created from dust and Eve was created from Adam." Two passages in the Apostolic Writings agree: "Indeed, man was not made from woman, but woman from man" (1 Corinthians 11:8), and, "For Adam was formed first, then Eve" (1 Timothy 2:13). After the man and woman sin, this subtle hierarchy becomes pronounced, as the LORD God tells the woman,

> I will terribly sharpen your birth pangs, in pain shall you bear children. And for your man shall be your longing, and he shall rule over you. (Genesis 3:16)

The two apostolic passages referred to here draw upon our Genesis texts to expand on the relationship of man and woman in marriage.

In 1 Corinthians 11, Paul is discussing head coverings, or veils, which he portrays as appropriate for women and inappropriate for men:

> A man ought not to have his head veiled, since he is the image and reflection of God; but woman is the reflection of man. Indeed, man was not made from woman, but woman from man. Neither was man created for the sake of woman, but woman for the sake of man. For this reason a woman ought to have a symbol of authority on her head, because of the angels. Nevertheless, in the Lord woman is not independent of man or man independent of woman. For just as woman came from man, so man comes through woman; but all things come from God. (1 Corinthians 11:7–12)

Interpreters argue whether Paul's comment here should be understood as a universal principle or a recommendation to conform to both Jewish and Roman custom of the time. Regardless of the application of these verses, however, Paul is clearly citing the order of creation, man first and then woman, rather than mere social custom to support differing practices between men and women.

At the same time he cites the mutual dependency of man and woman and the overarching "all things are from God" to deconstruct a strictly male-dominant viewpoint. Moreover, both men and women in this context are praying and prophesying, that is, exercising significant verbal ministry, within the public meeting of the *kehilah*, or community of believers (1 Corinthians 11:4–5).

Gordon Fee provides a helpful summation of this passage:

> Paul's point, of course, is that in the creation narrative this [creation of woman from man] did not happen the other way around—man from woman and for her sake. Hence he is her "head" (her source of origin) and she is his "glory." She must not be uncovered when praying and prophesying and thereby disregard one of the (apparently) visible expressions of differentiation, because in so doing she brings shame on him by trying to dissolve the rightful male/female relationship that still obtains in the present age.[33]

Fee may be signaling his own egalitarian perspective with this final phrase "in the present age." Does the male-female relationship *still obtain* in the present age until it is overcome in the age to come, when all distinctions are dissolved in the presence of God? Or is this relationship an expression of inherent, creational distinctions that will remain even in the restoration of all things? Either way, marriage is the union of two distinct persons with distinct roles, which may vary in different cultural settings. The fact of distinction between male and female and the resultant possibility of a hierarchical ordering remain within this age. But here Paul emphasizes male-female mutuality and interdependency. Paul's emphasis on male-female mutuality is evident earlier, in 1 Corinthians 7. A close reading of that chapter reveals a unique treatment of "complete mutuality between the two sexes."[34] Verses 7:2–5, 10–16, and 32–34 in particular entail a constant oscillation between man and woman and an equal appeal both to husband and wife on each point that Paul raises, with no sense of hierarchy or distinctive roles at all.

First Timothy 2, in contrast, invokes a sharp distinction between men and women in the context of teaching:

> Let a woman learn in silence with full submission. I permit no woman to teach or to have authority over a man; she is to keep silent. For Adam was formed first, then Eve; and Adam was not deceived, but the woman was deceived and became a transgressor. Yet she will be saved through childbearing, provided

they continue in faith and love and holiness, with modesty.
(1 Timothy 2:11–15)

Unlike 1 Corinthians 11, this passage is hard to read simply as an argument for maintaining social norms. The Jewish Annotated New Testament comments, "1 Timothy grounds female subordination in creation."[35] The passage, moreover, not only cites the order of creation, as does 1 Corinthians 11, but also the account of Adam and Eve's sin in Genesis 3. This passage also differs from 1 Corinthians 11 (as well as 1 Corinthians 7) in lacking the sense of interdependency noted there. On the other hand, we should not read the reference to childbearing in 1 Timothy as heightening female subordination, as if her only or highest purpose in marriage is bearing children; rather, the reference is triggered by the mention of Eve's deception. In Genesis 3, soon after Eve is deceived and she and Adam eat of the tree, the focus shifts to childbirth. First, the LORD God tells the serpent that the seed of the woman "will boot [his] head and [he] will bite his heel" (Genesis 3:15). HaShem then says to the woman herself, "I will terribly sharpen your birth pangs, in pain shall you bear children. And for your man shall be your longing, and he shall rule over you" (Genesis 3:16). First Timothy reflects this whole context, drawing out the implications not only of an ordered creation but also of the cataclysmic sin of the garden, which continues to affect husband-wife relationships, even in Messiah. The faithful woman, however, will be brought safely through the harsh conditions of childbirth imposed after the transgression in Eden.

Our purpose here is to define marriage, not to resolve all the secondary questions of the male-female relationship within marriage. Our reading of the apostolic texts, however, does uncover an inherent tension within marriage between male-female equality as divine image bearers on the one hand and disparate male-female roles on the other.[36] But "tension" may be too negative; rather, we see a dynamic balance in which the male-female distinction inherent to marriage, and expressed in varying ways in different cultures, glorifies the Creator, who distinguishes between day and night, heaven and earth, sea and dry land, and also male and female. Indeed, one purpose of marriage may be to display a quality of ordered relationship free of the dynamics of power and status that seem inherent in every human society. The dominant party is to sacrifice self on behalf of the subordinate party. The subordinate submits, not out of coercion or inferiority, but as a free act of service that reflects the service of Messiah himself. Ephesians 5:21 captures this mutuality within hierarchy: "Be subject to one another out of reverence for Messiah." We will explore the whole passage, Ephesians 5:22–33, further in section 4.

SUMMARY

The community is responsible to address this male-female distinction in ways that honor the profound mutuality and interdependency of man and woman as well as the divine image within both. The community is to provide an alternative to both the harshness of male domination that has prevailed throughout history and the current overreaction that would deny any inherent distinction between male and female. In the Messianic community the divine image shared by men and women is revealed in fuller measure through the *Ruach*, the Holy Spirit, poured out on one's sons and daughters and "even upon ... slaves, both men and women" (Acts 2:17–18).

A NOTE ON SINGLENESS

Our discussion thus far portrays marriage as the ideal and even as the fulfillment of our humanness as designed by the Creator. Accordingly, Jewish tradition generally extols marriage (although with plenty of reality checks) and devalues singleness. The Apostolic Writings, in contrast, although in line with some Jewish sectarian and apocalyptic texts of their era,[37] define a special place and value for singleness, as in Yeshua's saying about "eunuchs for the sake of the kingdom of heaven" (Matthew 19:12) or Paul's pragmatic advocacy of singleness in 1 Corinthians 7:25–40. Paul favors singleness not because he denigrates marriage, as passages such as 1 Corinthians 11:7–12 and Ephesians 5:22–33 make clear, but because of "the present distress" (1 Corinthians 7:26 ESV) and his sense that the return of Messiah was at hand. Likewise, it may be that those who make themselves eunuchs for the sake of the kingdom are responding to the immediate demands of the kingdom that is at hand and to be taken by force (Matthew 11:12).

Today, profound changes in our culture tend to promote singleness and delay or even eliminate marriage as a possibility for many.[38] The so-called sexual revolution launched a generation ago has succeeded in breaking the link between active sexual expression and marriage. One of the main motivations for marriage, at least for men, is gone. (Of course, there was plenty of sexual activity outside wedlock in previous generations, but only recently has it been completely normalized and destigmatized.) Another force contributing to widespread singleness is easy access to divorce, which returns many once-married individuals to a status of singleness, whether these individuals have chosen it or not. Also, young people are encouraged to focus on education and career before considering marriage, and postponement can decrease the likelihood of getting married at all. The Apostolic Writings affirm singleness as a choice, but we should also support those who find themselves single without choosing it. Our community needs to be careful to view and speak of single-ness without stigma and affirm the benefits of singleness clearly articulated in 1 Corinthians 7:24–40 without minimizing its difficulties and challenges.

In addition, we can affirm singleness because male-female union, as the first human relationship to be created, provides a foundation for all other relationships as well. In response to God's creation of woman, the man first speaks (or first has his speech recorded), first recognizes the other, and first differentiates himself so he can unite with other selves. These aspects of human existence come to apply to celibate singleness as well as the married state. So, for example, David cites a love beyond that of marriage partners in his lament for Jonathan:

> I grieve for you, my brother Jonathan, you were most dear to me.
> Your love was wonderful to me more than the love of women.
> (2 Samuel 1:26)

Messiah Yeshua pictures the greatest expression of love, not within marital union, but within friendship: "No one has greater love than this, to lay down one's life for one's friends" (John 15:13). The capacity created in "the two shall become one" isn't limited to sexual intimacy, then, but can be expressed in non-sexual friendship, which also defines and fulfills our humanness. And of course, beyond this is the intimacy with God in Messiah, toward which it all points. Even within a positive discussion of marriage, we see Messiah as the true bridegroom. Marriage, then, as we'll explore in detail in our final section, is a picture and foretaste of the even greater fulfillment of union with Messiah, which is the goal of all his followers, single as well as married.

3. THE BOUNDARIES OF MARRIAGE

"It is better to marry than to burn" (1 Corinthians 7:9 KJV) is one of the most famous, or perhaps infamous, statements on marriage in the Apostolic Writings. The urge to interpret and explain this phrase—as evidenced by the embel-lishment in most translations, such as "to burn with passion" (ESV) or "to be aflame with passion" (NRSV)—can lead us to miss its most important point. Paul is saying that the only alternative to sexual immorality is marriage, the only alternative to "burning" for those not called to practice celibacy.

First Corinthians 7 opens with a "Corinthian slogan,"[39] such as Paul addresses repeatedly throughout the letter: "Now concerning the matters about which you wrote: 'It is well for a man not to touch a woman'" (1 Corinthians 7:1). Celibacy is suggested as an ideal, perhaps in response to an apocalyptic perspective, as discussed above in reference to "eunuchs for the sake of the kingdom of heaven" (Matthew 19:12), or in response to ascetic pagan influences.[40] Regardless of the statement's source, however, Paul's rejoinder is clear: "But because of cases of sexual immorality, each man should have his own wife and each woman her own husband" (1 Corinthians 7:2). Celibacy might be ideal in some circumstances, but it's generally not realistic. Sexual desire is too strong, and apart from marriage it can lead to *porneia*—sexual immorality. Hence, it is "better to marry than to burn." For the one who thinks "it is better not to marry" because of Messiah Yeshua's restrictions on divorce, the alternative is not uncommitted sexual encounters but becoming a "eunuch" (Matthew 19:10–12).

Hebrews 13:4 declares, "Let marriage be held in honor by all, and let the marriage bed be kept undefiled; for God will judge fornicators and adulterers." The alternative to the marriage bed, which obviously alludes to sexual intercourse within marriage, is fornication (*porneia*), extra-marital sexual activity in general, or adultery (*moicheia*), extramarital sexual activity that involves at least one partner married to someone else.[41] Torah defines differing legal consequences of the two different acts, as we shall see, but both are violations of the proper sphere for sexual expression, which is marriage.

This clear demarcation of marriage is rooted in our foundational verse, Genesis 2:24. The two becoming one flesh refers primarily to the sexual act, which is framed communally or covenantally as the man leaving his family of origin to cleave to his wife and God bringing the two together (Matthew 19:5–6). "One flesh," then, is not limited to sexual union but involves the broader union of two separate persons, which is most dramatically pictured in the act of marital intimacy. Sexual acts outside this framework also entail the two becoming one flesh: "Do you not know that whoever is united to a prostitute becomes one body with her? For it is said, 'The two shall be one flesh'" (1 Corinthians 6:16).

In his response to my original presentation of this paper, Dr. Stuart Dauermann notes that "body" in this verse is *soma* in the original Greek, while "flesh" is *sarka/sarx*. Dauermann cites B. Ward Powers: "While 'flesh' (*sarx*) *can* be used as a synonym for 'body' (*soma*), its normal use is with different meaning. *It refers to all that it means to be human.* To say, for example, that "the Word became flesh" (John 1:14) means more than that Jesus had a body. A 'one-flesh relationship' means that marriage is a union of all that two people are as human beings in this life."[42]

Whether or not the contrast between mere sexual union and the holy union of marriage can be established simply by contrasting *soma* and *sarx* here, the contrast remains valid. Marital union isn't limited to the physical sex act but is a union of complementary persons, even if they are non- or post-physical in their one-flesh relationship. The capacity for sexual intimacy in marriage entails a capacity for intimacy that goes beyond the physical, an intimacy that more fully characterizes marriage than does physical intimacy alone. One flesh, then, encompasses physical union but is a broader concept, describing the union of two persons, not just two bodies.

Paul concludes, "Shun fornication! Every sin that a person commits is outside the body; but the fornicator sins against the body itself" (1 Corinthians 6:18). Prostitution alone isn't the issue here but any sexual union outside of marriage, that is, fornication. Resorting to a prostitute is one form of *porneia*, and today's widespread and widely accepted premarital sex would be another.

Before we see how this understanding is rooted in Torah, we'll consider Paul's statement that "the fornicator sins against the body itself." Fee concludes that *porneia* constitutes sin "against one's own body *as viewed in terms of its place in redemptive history*,"[43] because our bodies are members of Messiah (1 Corinthians 6:15), and the body "is a temple of the Holy Spirit within" us, and we "are not [our] own" (1 Corinthians 6:19). But the holiness of the body and the wholeness of the person as body and soul or spirit are rooted not only in Messianic redemption but also in creation itself.

In contrast with this holism, notes Robert P. George, today's common morality is based on a body-soul dualism in which "the person is understood as the conscious and desiring aspect of the self":

> The person, thus understood, inhabits a body, but the body is regarded (if often only implicitly) as a sub-personal part of the human being—rather than part of the personal reality of the human being whose body it is.[44]

The alternative to this morality is the view "embodied in ... our historic law of marriage."

According to this view, human beings are not non-bodily persons (consciousnesses, minds, spirits, what have you) inhabiting and using non-personal bodies. Rather, a human person is a dynamic unity of body, mind, and spirit. The body, far from being a mere instrument of the person, is intrinsically part of the personal reality of the human being.

I quote George at some length because he arrives at a definition of marriage that reinforces our direction in this paper:

> What is unique about marriage is that it truly is a comprehensive sharing of life, a sharing founded on the bodily union made uniquely possible by the sexual complementarity of man and woman—a complementarity that makes it possible for two human beings to become, in the language of the Bible, "one flesh," and for this one-flesh union to be the foundation of a relationship in which it is intelligible for two persons to bind themselves to each other in pledges of permanence, monogamy, and fidelity.

George is responding to the idea of marriage between members of the same sex, but his argument can also be mobilized against extramarital sex, whose advocates likewise seem to understand the human person as the "conscious and desiring aspect of the self" and the body "as an instrument by which the individual [person] produces or otherwise participates in satisfactions and other desirable experiences and realizes various objectives and goals." In other words, today's widespread acceptance, and even affirmation, of extramarital and same-sex intimacy reflects a dualistic understanding of the person as a radically autonomous self that inhabits and uses a body for its own purposes. In contrast, the Torah maintains a holistic view of the person as soul and body, which undergirds belief in the sanctity of sexual expression within marriage and also its illegitimacy outside marriage. Sanctity inherently entails boundaries and standards, that is, limits on the autonomous self.

Within these standards Torah portrays adultery as distinct from fornication, and more serious. Thus, adultery is prohibited in the Ten Words (*na'af*, Exodus 20:14) and receives the death penalty in Leviticus 20:10. Deuteronomy 22:22–29 assigns the death penalty for both parties to adultery, whether the woman is "married to a husband" or "betrothed to a man." Following the proscription of adultery in the Ten Words, Exodus 22:16–17 covers the case of one who seduces a virgin who is not betrothed. Sarna notes that "seduction" here is "by persuasion or deception but not by coercion. There is a presumption of consent on the part of the girl."[45] In this case the man must pay the bride price of a virgin and marry the woman, unless her father refuses to give her to him in marriage, in which case the bride price must still be paid. The financial aspect of marriage is also evident in the last of the Ten Words: "You shall not covet your fellow man's wife, or his male slave, or his slave girl, or his ox, or his donkey, or anything that your fellow man has" (Exodus 20:17). Note that the wife is included in the things that one's "fellow man has." Against this background Paul's treatment of the mutuality of marriage in 1 Corinthians 7 and 11 is all the more striking. Our point here, however, is simply to trace the parameters of fornication and adultery in the Torah. Sexual activity entails either fornication (including adultery) or marriage; there is no third category such as "premarital sex among consenting adults." The consequence of non-adulterous fornication is that the male partner must pay the bride price and help restore the standing and value of the female, as in Exodus 22:16–17. In contrast, there is no corrective for adultery. Accordingly, Lamm summarizes,

> *Sexual relations are a* mitzvah, a religious duty, *within a properly covenanted marriage in accordance with Jewish law*. Outside of that covenant, premarital sexual relations are not condoned and extramarital relations are considered crimes.[46]

INTERMARRIAGE

Lamm's reference to Jewish law raises the issue of eligibility for marriage. Scripture sets apart marriage as the sole legitimate venue for sexual union and also sets parameters for who is eligible as a marriage partner. Who are those, in the words of the wedding service, permitted to us "through the rite of the canopy and sacred covenant of marriage"?[47] Leviticus 18 lists those who are not permitted because of close relationship. First are the "six *she'er* relatives: mother, father, son, daughter, brother, sister" of the nuclear family.[48] Verses 6 through 18, in language directed toward the male, expand this list of ineligibility to include the father's wife, even if she is not one's mother; the daughter of a son or daughter; a half-sister; an aunt, whether paternal or maternal or by marriage to an uncle; a daughter-in-law; a brother's wife, although this is exempted in the law of levirate marriage (Deuteronomy 25:5–10); a woman and her daughter or granddaughter; and two sisters.[49] A discussion of the halachah regarding these forbidden categories is beyond the scope of this paper, but the simple parameters set in Leviticus would seem to still be relevant to Messianic Jews and others seeking guidance from the Torah.

The biblical treatment of marriage between Jews and Gentiles, on the other hand, is dynamic even within the Tanach, and the Apostolic Writings suggest a radical redirection of the standards set in Torah. Thus, Deuteronomy 7:3–4 explicitly forbids intermarriage with the seven nations that inhabit the land of Canaan:

You shall not intermarry with them. You shall not give your daughter to his son, nor shall you take his daughter for your son. For he will make your son swerve from following Me, and they will worship other gods, and the LORD's wrath will flare against you and He will swiftly destroy you.

The rationale for this prohibition is not ethnic but religious. Canaanites are not permissible marriage partners because they will lead Israelites into idolatry. But earlier, in Genesis, before any prohibition against intermarriage is announced, it is already portrayed negatively. When Abraham sends his servant to find a wife for Isaac, he not only forbids him to take a wife from the "daughters of the Canaanite" in whose midst they dwell, but he limits him to finding a wife only from among his own people (Genesis 24:3–4). Likewise, Isaac gives Jacob a similar charge when he sends him back to Paddan-Aram to find a wife (Genesis 28:1–2). In contrast, Esau manifests his unworthiness by taking wives from among the Hittites (Genesis 26:34–35; 27:46).

To be sure, there are numerous exceptions to this pattern, both in Genesis and beyond, but it remains as a precedent for prohibiting intermarriage altogether. Thus, 1 Kings 11:1–2 condemns Solomon's love for "foreign women in addition to Pharaoh's daughter—Moabite, Ammonite, Edomite, Phoenician, and Hittite women, from the nations of which the LORD had said to the Israelites, 'None of them shall join you, lest they turn your heart away to follow their gods.'" The Torah bans Moabites and Ammonites from entry into the congregation of the LORD (Deuteronomy 23:3), which would imply a ban on intermarriage, although Edomite, Phoenician, and Hittite women are not explicitly banned. Already in 1 Kings, a wider prohibition of intermarriage is in view and is reflected in Ezra 9:1–2 and the discussion that follows through Ezra 10:

> The people of Israel and the priests and Levites have not separated themselves from the peoples of the land whose abhorrent practices are like those of the Canaanites, the Hittites, the Perizzites, the Jebusites, the Ammonites, the Moabites, the Egyptians, and the Amorites. They have taken their daughters as wives for themselves and for their sons, so that the holy seed has become intermingled with the peoples of the land; and it is the officers and prefects who have taken the lead in this trespass.

The Jewish Study Bible notes that Ezra makes two additions to the Deuteronomy 7 ban. First, Ezra appears to extend the ban to all non-Jews, not only

Canaanites, since all intermarriages heighten the risk of idolatry. Second, he requires that the foreign wife, and any children resulting from the marriage, must be expelled (Ezra 10:2–4). A third addition in Ezra, not mentioned in the Jewish Study Bible, is concern that the "holy seed has become intermingled with the peoples of the land" (Ezra 9:2). This terminology hints at an ethnic or even racial concern beyond the concern over idolatry. The Talmud (*Kiddushin* 68b; *Yevamot* 23a) also expands the Deuteronomy 7:3 prohibition into a ban on intermarriage with non-Jews in general, basing its argument on the risk of being led astray by any non-Jew. As in Ezra, the children of Gentile mothers are not considered Israelites and therefore not included in the concern about being turned away from worship of HaShem.

In contrast, 1 Corinthians 7 appears to reverse two of the conclusions of Ezra. It argues that a believer (parallel to an Israelite in Ezra) is not to divorce a non-believing spouse (parallel to a Gentile spouse in Ezra) and that the children of such unions are holy, regardless of which parent is the believer, and hence not to be sent away:

> To the rest I say—I and not the Lord—that if any believer[50] has a wife who is an unbeliever, and she consents to live with him, he should not divorce her. And if any woman has a husband who is an unbeliever, and he consents to live with her, she should not divorce him. For the unbelieving husband is made holy through his wife, and the unbelieving wife is made holy through her husband. Otherwise, your children would be unclean, but as it is, they are holy. (1 Corinthians 7:12–14)[51]

Several factors would explain this change from the time of Ezra. First, the ethnic factor, which seems to be highlighted by Ezra's mention of "the holy seed," is not at play here at all. The issue is belief/unbelief, not ethnicity. Second, it appears that in Messiah the dynamics of holiness within a marriage change. Here, the holy sanctifies the unholy, whereas in Ezra the unholy corrupts the holy. In this Ezra reflects the concern of Deuteronomy 7:3. Paul seems to turn this concern on its head: "Wife, for all you know, you might save your husband. Husband, for all you know, you might save your wife" (1 Corinthians 7:16). We have already considered the holiness of marriage; here we learn that this holiness is "catching." This notion, however, is not new to Paul. "It is a scriptural principle that the blessings arising from fellowship with God are not confined to the immediate recipients, but extend to others. Paul teaches that the sanctification of the believing partner extends to the unbeliever."[52] Furthermore, "The parents' 'holiness' extends to the child."[53]

But what exactly does Paul mean by "unbeliever" here? Second Corinthians 6:14–16 sheds light on that question and also may serve to balance Paul's position in 1 Corinthians 7:

> Do not be mismatched[54] with unbelievers. For what partnership is there between righteousness and lawlessness? Or what fellowship is there between light and darkness? What agreement does Messiah have with Beliar? Or what does a believer share with an unbeliever? What agreement has the temple of God with idols? For we are the temple of the living God; as God said, "I will live in them and walk among them, and I will be their God, and they shall be my people."

The prohibition here seems to be concerned primarily with idolaters. It isn't ethnic or sectarian but based on the unbridgeable gulf between worship of the God of Israel and worship of idols. Paul doesn't mention marriage specifically, but marriage would certainly fall within the broad categories of partnership, fellowship, and "yoking" that he does mention. In 1 Corinthians the married believer is not to divorce the unbeliever; in 2 Corinthians the unmarried believer is not to marry an unbeliever. Is "unbeliever" to be strictly defined in terms of faith in Yeshua as Messiah or more broadly as belief in the God of Israel? The context would suggest the latter, as in Torah narrowly interpreted, Paul is arguing against marriage with an idolater. The exact application to Jewish-Gentile intermarriage within the Messianic Jewish community remains to be worked out by the community, and Paul's treatment of the issue may serve to modify traditional halachic standards. What's clear is that marriage is a sphere in which one's relationship to God, one's participation in the covenant, is to be expressed, perhaps even with transformative power.

AN INTERNAL BOUNDARY

We have outlined the boundaries between marriage and non-marriage and must note that there are also boundaries within marriage, for example, in the laws of marital purity. This term refers primarily to the limits on sexual intimacy related to the wife's monthly cycle, as in Leviticus 18:19 and 20:18. Based on Leviticus 15:19, a woman in this state of "uncleanness," or the state itself, is termed *niddah*, which is the title of a tractate of the Mishnah that deals specifically with the laws of family purity. A woman becomes *niddah* immediately upon the onset of her monthly period and remains *niddah* for the extent of her period (a minimum of five days), plus seven full, twenty-four-hour days after the end of the period. Sexual contact is forbidden during this time so that there is thus a minimum span of twelve days every month in which the couple must practice abstinence. In traditional Jewish law, husband and wife are to have no physical contact during this time and are to sleep in separate beds. At the end of the seven "clean" days, the woman is to immerse herself in a *mikveh* before the couple resumes sexual contact.[55]

Two points stand out in the context of our broader discussion of the meaning and purpose of marriage. Rabbi Isaac Klein writes,

> Of all the laws of *tum'ah* and *tohorah* [impurity and purity], to which so much space is devoted in the Torah and Talmud, only the laws governing family purity are still relevant. This is not by accident. A prominent Jewish scholar writes: "The preservation of the menstrual laws alone, with the restrictive regulations entirely unimpaired, is … a conscious emphasis on, and an attempt at the inculcation in a particularly significant area of human interest, of that self-discipline which must be—in all aspects of life—an integral element in the Jewish ideal of cultivating 'holiness' (Kedushah)" (Loewe, *Position of Women in Judaism*, p. 48).[56]

First, the laws of family purity define the marital act as holy—set apart from the ordinary and possessing a quality of glory. They emphasize that marriage cannot be fully understood or practiced without reference to the Creator who instituted it or apart from its covenantal nature, which includes laws and stipulations. Second, these laws bring sexual expression under discipline, which our dominant culture might view with suspicion or contempt but which is integral to marriage as established in Torah. Discipline and restraint are essential to maintaining holiness, which in turn lends mystery and transcendence to the sexual act. Scripture employs the simple but powerful verb "to know" to describe this mystery. In contrast, Lamm comments, "The increasing freedom from sexual restraint in this post-Freudian era is testimony to the demystification of sex and the irretrievable loss of precious 'knowledge.'"[57]

SUMMARY

The boundaries of marriage provided in Scripture run counter to the narcissism and disorder of our age. Every successful marriage involves a story of overcoming today's dominant narrative of self-fulfillment and entitle-ment. Indeed, marriage is often the means by which the partners learn the Messiah-like traits of sacrifice and denial of self. In the marriage relationship they learn to forsake self-interest and superficial fairness for the higher value of unconditional giving.

4. THE CONSUMMATION

Ephesians 5:21–33 applies Genesis 2:24, especially the phrase "one flesh," to Messiah and the *kehila*, the body of Yeshua followers. "This is a great mystery, and I am applying it to Messiah and the *kehila*. Each of you, however, should love his wife as himself, and a wife should respect her husband" (Ephesians 5:32–33). Most of Ephesians 5:21–33 draws upon the relationship between Messiah and the *kehila* to illustrate the proper relationship between husband and wife. But toward the end of the passage, it seems to do the opposite: the one-flesh union of man and woman in the beginning illustrates a more profound union to be revealed later—that of Messiah and his people. As F.F. Bruce comments,

> In the light of [Messiah's] saving work, the hidden meaning of
> Gen. 2:24 now begins to appear: his people constitute his bride,
> united to him in "one body." The formation of Eve to be Adam's
> companion is seen to prefigure the creation of the church to be
> the bride of Christ. This seems to be the deep "mystery" con-
> tained in the text, which remains a mystery no longer to those
> who have received its interpretation.[58]

One purpose of marriage, then, is to reflect and embody the intimate union of Messiah and his people, to display, as already noted, a relationship free of the pervasive social dynamics of power and status. And conversely, as we see what Messiah did to accomplish this union and how he now nourishes and cherishes the *kehila* as his own body, we understand how marriage between man and woman was intended to be all along. Marriage between one man and one woman is a reflection of the greater intimacy between Messiah and his "body," the *kehila* (Ephesians 5:28–30). Marriage is secondary, Messiah-*kehila* is primary, and every Yeshua follower, married or single, is included in that bond.

As we've seen, the Tanach pictures marriage as reflecting the union between HaShem and Israel.[59] The Apostolic Writings reveal that this union is accomplished in and through Messiah Yeshua and that marriage is given "from the beginning" to point toward that union, which is to be fully realized only at the end of the age. Thus, Revelation 21 pictures the final consummation in terms of a wedding and brings the reader back to the beginning to portray it. The elements divided in Genesis are revisited here: there is no more sea, as distinct from dry land (Revelation 21:1); heaven is united with, or present upon, earth (Revelation 21:2, 10); the separation of light and darkness is no more (Revelation 21:23). All this is framed in the metaphor of a wedding, which echoes the original wedding of Genesis:

> Let us rejoice and exult and give him the glory, for the marriage of the Lamb has come, and his bride has made herself ready. (Revelation 19:7)

> I saw the holy city, the new Jerusalem, coming down out of heaven from God, prepared as a bride adorned for her husband. (Revelation 21:2)

Bible scholar Gregory Beale cites Isaiah 52 and 62, along with 61:10 LXX, as background for the marital imagery of these two passages:

> So also here in 21:2 the intimate union of God and his people, and possibly his vindication of them, is a prophetic decree depicted as fulfilled in the future. Preparation of the "bride adorned *for* her *husband*" conveys the thought of God's preparation of his people for himself. Throughout history God is forming his people to be his bride, so that they will reflect his glory in the ages to come (so Eph. 5:25–27).[60]

Hence, the one-flesh union of man and woman, which both anticipates and reflects this union of God and his people, is sacred. The sexual act of one-flesh union must become enshrined within the communal institution of marriage, which is sanctified and inviolable.[61] This brings us back to the original setting of our discussion—Messiah Yeshua's response to a question about divorce. Now we see that his reference to "in the beginning" reveals not just rules about marriage but the profound meaning of marriage from the beginning, which is to be fully known at the end.

CONCLUSION

From our brief view of the beginning and end of marriage, then, what can be said about the purpose of marriage?

As noted above, Rabbi Lamm comments on Genesis 2:18 that "only man can experience existential loneliness, the fragmentary and incomplete nature of this world. It is the genuine companionship of Adam and Eve that humanity requires."[62] But it puts too much weight on marriage to expect it to relieve this existential loneliness, which ultimately is to be resolved in union with Messiah Yeshua. Paradoxically, one key to successful marriage is not to expect too much of it, or (especially) of the marriage partner. Some human needs only the spirit of Messiah can meet, and only in his time. Nevertheless, and again paradoxically, another key is not to expect too little of marriage. God was present with Adam when he noted that it was not good for the man to be alone, and God didn't resolve that aloneness himself but formed woman and created marriage to do so.

Marriage from the beginning serves the calling on male and female to be fruitful and multiply and fill the earth (Genesis 1:28). Yet it is significant that this aspect of marriage isn't mentioned at all in Genesis 2:18–25, where marriage provides the solution to the problem of Genesis 2:18: "It is not good for the human to be alone." Thus, marriage has two purposes: creation of family and intimate companionship. But it is not limited to these two purposes, as it also comprises a union, a (re)uniting of what was separate and distinct, which foreshadows the consummation toward which the whole created order is heading.

The creation account of the two becoming one flesh reveals this threefold purpose of marriage as the one-flesh union of male and female: procreation in the broad sense of creating a family; intimate companionship that overcomes existential aloneness on a human level; and participation in covenant with the Creator, a divine-human partnership that anticipates the consummation toward which the creation is moving. The Apostolic Writings reveal that this consummation is accomplished in and through Messiah Yeshua so that marriage provides an earthly reflection of the relationship between Messiah and his people. This lofty purpose informs each individual marriage and hence demands self-sacrificial love and respect from both partners:

> For no one ever hates his own body, but he nourishes and tenderly cares for it, just as Messiah does for the *kehila*, because we are members of his body. "For this reason a man will leave

his father and mother and be joined to his wife, and the two will become one flesh." This is a great mystery, and I am applying it to Messiah and the *kehila*. Each of you, however, should love his wife as himself, and a wife should respect her husband. (Ephesians 5:29–33)

Marriage, understood biblically, defies the consumerism and self-aggrandizement of this (or ultimately any) era. Marriage provides a foretaste of holiness in an unholy age and thus anticipates the age to come.

APPENDIX 2

RESPONSE TO "THE TWO SHALL BECOME ONE FLESH"

BOAZ MICHAEL

Paper presented at Hashivenu Conference 2015

It was refreshing for me to read the thoughts of Russ Resnik in his paper, "The Two Shall Become One Flesh: The Beginning and End of Marriage." As I contemplated his perspectives, what was so refreshing was his treatment of the biblical texts—his drawing out from them what I would define as a fairly traditional approach. His thoughts strengthened me to stand more firmly on the foundation of Scripture, as I realized that my own views on the subject of marriage, since I haven't studied this topic for some time, have relaxed—not due to biblical maturity but rather by being negatively affected by a postmodern culture.

Postmodern views of marriage, divorce, and sexuality are pervasive and incredibly influential; thus I am grateful that issues like these discussed by Resnik, which on the surface may seem basic to Yeshua followers, are being readdressed and defined within Messianic Jewish communities as the culture around us continues to evolve (or rather devolve). Resnik states that one purpose of marriage "is to reflect and embody the intimate union of Messiah and his people." If this is true, it is vital that we as a Yeshua-devoted people biblically and correctly define marriage (and live it out) within our communities.

I greatly appreciate Russ's work, although I am sure many will be offended by his traditional approach. His views may appear to some as insensitive and his definitions to others too narrow. I, however, have found little to disagree with; thus in my response I would like to augment his work in three areas that I think need further discussion in our community:

1. The laws of *niddah*—balancing sexuality and intimacy within the marriage

2. Singleness—"It is not good" (Genesis 2:18) compared to "It is good" (1 Corinthians 7:8)

3. Messiah-*kehila*—developing the character of Messiah

Before I address these three areas, I want to say something about two notable omissions from this paper—polygamy and homosexual unions—which I would like to see discussed in the Messianic Jewish community. Polygamy has been raised in some Messianic Jewish segments, and it merits a firm response. And same-sex marriage may, if it has not already, become a critical issue in the definition of marriage within our communities in the future. I, for one, would like to hear our community's consensus on both these issues through straightforward albeit gracious discussions and, ultimately, in firmly stated positions.

1. THE LAWS OF NIDDAH

Resnik makes two points regarding the matter of *niddah*:

> First, the laws of family purity *define the marital act as holy—set apart from the ordinary and possessing a quality of glory.* They emphasize that marriage cannot be fully understood or practiced without reference to the Creator who instituted it or apart from its covenantal nature, which includes laws and stipulations. Second, these laws *bring sexual expression under discipline*, which our dominant culture might view with suspicion or contempt but which is integral to marriage as established in Torah. (emphasis added)

I will examine these two points, marriage morality and sexual equality, separately.

MARRIAGE MORALITY

Resnik correctly states that the laws of *niddah* as they pertain to sexuality within the marriage "define the marital act as holy" and possess "a quality of glory." But the Torah goes a bit further in its context and description of the law of *niddah*:

> You shall not approach a woman to uncover her nakedness while she is in her menstrual uncleanness. And you shall not lie sexually with your neighbor's wife and so make yourself unclean with her. You shall not give any of your children to offer them to Molech, and so profane the name of your God: I am the LORD. You shall not lie with a male as with a woman; it is an abomination. And you shall not lie with any animal and so make yourself unclean with it, neither shall any woman give herself to an animal to lie with it: it is perversion. (Leviticus 18:19–23)

The prohibition of sexual relations with a *niddah*, also known as "family purity" within broader Judaism, is a part of the laws of purity. However, it is not only a Temple-related subject; it is a matter of sexual morality as well. (Anthropologists find purity laws like this across different cultures. These laws seem to be nearly as universal as the impulse to sacrifice animals to unseen spirits and gods. Most ancient religions make distinctions of "clean" and "unclean" on grounds similar, though not identical, to those described by the Torah. This suggests that human beings have some innate sense of purity and impurity, shamefulness and brazenness, modesty and immodesty connected with ritual fitness before the unseen world. This may also reflect on the apostolic decree in Acts 15 forbidding Gentiles from sexual immorality.)

I appreciated this issue being raised within the "An Internal Boundary" section of Resnik's paper. I linked "internal" with "unseen and private." A married couple must strictly guard its privacy, especially in such personal matters. The couple must strictly guard on a public level the time in which the wife is in a state of *niddah*. Thus the only two people who should know about this status are the husband and wife. With it being guarded so closely, however, it is easy to forego community accountability in this area; thus our personal disciplines need to be strong. In order to maintain strong personal vigilance, clear definitions should be in place. The Messianic community has a responsibility to offer halachic direction in this area.

Since it is one of the more private mitzvot in Jewish practice, the law of separation during menstruation becomes a personal discipline of developing private marital holiness and upholding marital sexual morality. Those who practice the law of separation during *niddah* often speak of the discipline as something glorious and transforming in their marriages. It strengthens a wife, thus a marriage, when she (assuming she is devoted to Jewish life) feels honored by her husband in private.

Infrastructure and encouragement is needed within our Messianic Jewish communities to support the Torah and communal demands of the multi-faceted laws of *niddah*. Many (if not most) of our Messianic Jewish communities lack a proper mikvah, and because of our Yeshua faith, most of us are either forbidden from using or intimidated to use the mikvahs in our local Jewish communities. In the cases in which Messianic Jewish couples are far away from Jewish communities, it can be a great difficulty to travel distances.

As the Torah calls this issue a matter of sexual morality, it becomes a principal issue of a healthy marriage and should be a primary concern for our marriages. I am not suggesting that Messianic Jews who do not observe the Torah's standards regarding separation during *niddah* should be condemned. Blu Greenberg wisely notes,

> If I may be permitted a theological indiscretion: my acceptance of a scheme of reward and punishment—this world or next—not withstanding, I simply cannot drum up the feeling that those Jewish couples who fail to observe *niddah* are sinners. What is more, I feel that my life and my marriage would have been blessed even had I not observed these mitzvot, for I see many happy marriages without *niddah* and some horrid ones with; I see the blessings of healthy children from non-halachic sexual unions and the children of the pious afflicted.[63]

At the same time, the Torah does not grant us permission to take it or leave it. As a matter of sexual morality, the matter is non-negotiable.

SEXUAL EQUALITY

Resnik also states that the laws of *niddah* help us "bring sexual expression under discipline." Rabbi Shalom Arush speaks to this:

> Our Sages said, "Ten units of speech came down to the world; of these, woman took nine." The Sages are not merely teaching us that women talk more than men. There must be something deeper.[64]

Resnik further states,

> These laws bring sexual expression under discipline, which our dominant culture might view with suspicion or contempt but which is integral to marriage as established in Torah. Discipline and restraint are essential to maintaining holiness.

In addition to discipline and restraint, I think one of the unseen values of the practice of *niddah* is that it brings sexual equality into the marriage:

> Because women are the arbiters of *niddah* observance, it also functions as a locus of women's power. By, for example, refusing to go to the *mikvah*, or delaying their immersion, they command the halakhically sanctioned authority to withhold sex from their husbands. This authority is significant in that it turns on its head the general Western construction that "heterosexual sex means that men enact their social power over women."[65]

Generally speaking, men tend to be more physically and sexually dominant than women in the marriage relationship. Women tend to be more emotionally and relationally dominant in the marriage. Women have rarely been seen as the arbiters of sexuality within the marriage. However, the laws of *niddah* in many ways reverse these roles, granting the wife a certain authority to forbid and permit. That reversal of power allows both parties to take a share of responsibility and leadership in the bedroom.

This principle has further ramifications in Jewish law, forbidding a man from demanding sex from his wife. This creates emotional and relational balance within the marriage around areas of sexuality. It also represents a departure from the world's stereotype of male dominance in sexuality. The Torah places the keys to sexual authority within the grasp of the wife.

2. SINGLENESS

God declared everything he created to be good: "And behold, it was very good" (Genesis 1:31). The only thing in creation God declared "not good" was man's loneliness: "Then the LORD God said, 'It is not good for the man to be alone; I will make him a helper suitable for him'" (Genesis 2:18 NASB).

The Bible can be confusing on the subject of singleness. While "it is not good" for man to be alone, Paul writes that "it is good" for unmarried individuals to remain single (1 Corinthians 7:8). Similarly, Proverbs 18:22 says, "He who finds a wife finds a good thing and obtains favor from the LORD," while Paul seems to contradict this statement: "Those who marry will have worldly troubles" (1 Corinthians 7:28).

People often read their own ideas about singleness into such passages. Addressing this problem, Resnik states,

> The Apostolic Writings affirm singleness as a choice, but we should also support those who find themselves single without choosing it. Our community needs to be careful to view and speak of singleness without stigma and affirm the benefits of singleness clearly articulated in 1 Corinthians 7:24–40 without minimizing its difficulties and challenges.

I appreciate Paul's transparency as he opens 1 Corinthians 7:24–40: "I have no command from the Lord, but I give my judgment as one who by the Lord's mercy is trustworthy" (1 Corinthians 7:25). With these words the apostle invites us to question his authority on this subject.

In Judaism, Resnik notes, singleness is devalued. It does create a stigma and makes one who is single feel marginalized within the community. Thus I appreciate Resnik's use of 1 Corinthians to bring balance to our perspective on the matter of singleness. I have met many single people in our communities who, because they hold high Messianic Jewish values, struggle with a sense of hopelessness over their singleness. We can encourage them all day long with a higher or more holy ideal—but in today's world I would say that those who are single suffer more worldly anxiety than those who are married. I think it is easier in our day for those who are married to be focused on "the things of the Lord, how to please the Lord" than those who are single. Yet Paul says,

> I want you to be free from anxieties. The unmarried man is anxious about the things of the Lord, how to please the Lord. But the married man is anxious about worldly things, how to please his wife. (1 Corinthians 7:32–33)

As I mentioned above, Paul invites us to question his authority on the subject of remaining single for the sake of serving the Lord. It seems that much of Paul's "judgment" was based upon his eschatology: "This is what I mean, brothers: the appointed time has grown very short ... for the present form of this world is passing away" (1 Corinthians 7:29–31).

We have learned the hard lessons of the length of our exile, and with the exception of special cases, in my opinion, singleness should never be encouraged under the perception that we are in the latter days.

I think we need to, as Resnik states, "support those who find themselves single without choosing it" by prioritizing their needs and our responsibilities to help them find spouses. Messianic Judaism needs growth of strong Messianic Jewish families from within that have high ideals to sustain our movement, maintain Jewish identity, and expand our influence. In reflecting on Paul's opening statement, I would say, "I have no command from the Lord, but I give my judgment that this needs to be a top priority."

I feel strongly that we must find ways to place our Messianic Jewish singles into healthy Jewish marriages. This is an urgent matter. We must prioritize our efforts on behalf of our singles, find qualified spouses for them, and give them solid communities in which to raise godly families. I hope Resnik's statement that we should "support those who find themselves single without choosing it" has this level of emphasis.

3. MESSIAH-KEHILA

Marriage can be God's primary testing ground of faith and spiritual growth. The sages say that God tested Abraham with ten trials to prove his faith. Maimonides makes a list of ten trials that Abraham endured; five of them have to do directly with his relationship with Sarah:

> The Holy One, blessed be He, saw that it was good that "the help" stand facing him, and that he should see or be separated from it or joined to it at his will. This is the meaning of what He said in the verse, I will make him a helper opposite him.[66]

Why is a person's marriage so important? Because it is the central arena in which his or her faith will be walked out. Once married, all the commandments incumbent on an individual are altered. The married person is no longer responsible just for himself or herself. The married person's core identity is changed, and that person's relationship with God will be directly affected by the individual's relationship with the spouse God has entrusted to him or her. One cannot be a godly person and a poor spouse simultaneously.

Men need to strive to be the closest and most consistent image of the Messiah that their wives will know. As Paul states, "Husbands, love your wives, as Messiah loved the *kehila* and gave himself up for her" (Ephesians 5:25). "Marriage is sustained and deepened," Resnik writes, "as the husband recognizes the gifting of his wife."

To love his wife biblically, a husband must recognize "the gifting of his wife" and understand the character of Messiah—in order to treat his wife as Messiah treats the *kehila*. This not only produces a healthy marriage but, more importantly, enables us, according to Resnik, to "reflect and embody the intimate union of Messiah and his people."

The Prophet Isaiah describes six qualities with which the Messiah will be blessed: "The Spirit of the LORD shall rest upon him, [1] the Spirit of wisdom and [2] understanding, [3] the Spirit of counsel and [4] might, [5] the Spirit of knowledge and [6] the fear of the LORD" (Isaiah 11:2).

Reviewing a short list of qualities that we see demonstrated by the Messiah in the Gospels should help us reflect on the character traits we need to nurture in our unions:

- Compassion
- Servanthood
- Love
- Forgiveness
- Commitment
- Prayer
- Gentleness
- Patience
- Self-Control
- Humility

IN CLOSING

Rabbi Akiva, a famous second-century Torah teacher, taught that "when husband and wife are worthy, the Dwelling Presence of God abides with them, but when they are not worthy, fire consumes them" (b.*Sotah* 17a).

Many of us have heard of Rabbi Akiva's observation of the letters in the Hebrew words "man" and "woman." But for the topic at hand, a review would be beneficial.

The Hebrew word for "man" is *ish* (איש); the word for "woman" is *ishah* (אשה). Both words have common letters and unique letters. When recombining the unique letters from the two words, taking the *yod* (י) from *ish* (איש)

and the *heh* (ה) from *ishah* (אשה), the two letters spell *Yah* (יה), which is part of God's holy name.

Removing those unique letters from both words changes both words to *eish* (אש), which means "fire." Rabbi Akiva used this to illustrate that when a marriage has God and godly principles in place, the Lord is present with husband and wife; but when a marriage is godless and the marriage foundation is something other than biblical, it is a consuming fire that can ultimately destroy both husband and wife.

Man	*Ish*	איש
Woman	*Ishah*	אשה
HaShem (God)	*Yah*	יה
Fire	*Eish*	אש

I would add to this powerful word analogy only that the Messiah "is the image of the invisible God, the firstborn of all creation" (Colossians 1:15). In this regard, we as Messianic Jews must have the Messiah present and visible within our marriages. When this is so, God is present.

Through our unions we need a shared and divine sense of responsibility to God's kingdom as well as a passion for it. Resnik puts it this way: "The consummation achieved by male and female, therefore, becomes the paradigm of the consummation toward which all Creation is moving … In the Messianic community the divine image shared by men and women is revealed in fuller measure through the *Ruach*, the Holy Spirit … Indeed, marriage is often the means by which the partners learn the Messiah-like traits of sacrifice and denial of self." His concluding words powerfully cap this truth: "Marriage provides a foretaste of holiness in an unholy age and thus anticipates the age to come."

As a father, I have attempted to impart many ideas and truths to my children, all of whom are now adults. One principle stands out as the foremost warning, which I have told each one of my children many times over the years: "The most important decision you will make in life is whom you will marry." Marry wisely, and the testing ground of marriage will grow us into men and women who are faithful to and passionate for the kingdom of God.

ENDNOTES

1   Unless otherwise noted, all quotations from the Apostolic Writings are from the New Revised Standard Version (NRSV). This choice is based on both my frequent use of the NRSV-based *Jewish Annotated New Testament* (New York, NY: Oxford University Press, 2011) and the NRSV policy allowing for occasional word substitutions, such as "Yeshua" for "Jesus."

2   Craig S. Keener, *The Gospel of Matthew: A Socio-Rhetorical Commentary* (Grand Rapids, MI: Eerdmans, 2009), 463. Along with numerous modern references, Keener cites the Hillel-Shammai debate on Deuteronomy 24:1, b.*Gittin* 90a.

3   All quotations of the Torah are from Robert Alter, *The Five Books of Moses: A Translation with Commentary* (New York, NY: W. W. Norton & Co., 2004). Quotations from the rest of the Tanach are from the JPS Tanakh (Philadelphia, PA: Jewish Publication Society, 1999).

4   All references to *Midrash Rabbah* are from Rabbi Dr. H. Freedman and Maurice Simon, eds., *Midrash Rabbah* (10 vols.; London, England: Soncino, 1983).

5   The Hebrew term for "rib" here, *tsela,* can also be translated as "side." Translator Everett Fox notes that this alternative is "paralleling other ancient peoples' concept of an original being that was androgynous (*The Five Books of Moses* [vol. 1 of *The Schocken Bible*; New York, NY: Schocken, 1995], 20). See *Rabbi Abraham Ibn Ezra's Commentary on the Creation* (trans. Michael Linetsky; Northvale, NJ: Jason Aronson, 1998), 70; *Genesis Rabbah* 17:6.

6   E.g., Isaiah 61:10, 62:1–5; Hosea 2:18–22; Revelation 21:2.

7   Messiah discusses "one flesh" as the antithesis of divorce, which is the topic at hand in Matthew 19:3–6. He thereby defines this one-flesh union as the paradigm of marriage.

8   Nahum M. Sarna, *Genesis* (vol. 1 of *JPS Torah Commentary*; Philadelphia, PA: Jewish Publication Society, 1989), 23, citing *Yalkut* Genesis 24 and *Genesis Rabbah* 18:4.

9   *Genesis Rabbah* 8:13 on Genesis 1:28.

10   Maurice Lamm, *The Jewish Way in Love and Marriage* (New York, NY: Jonathan David, 1991), 122–141. I draw heavily upon Lamm because I've used his book *The Jewish Way in Death and Mourning* (New York, NY: Jonathan David, 1969) in my practice for years and find it to be consistently helpful. His marriage book reflects the same balance and depth.

11   Ibid., 123.

12   *Ayin-vav-nun-hey.* Jewish sources explain the word as meaning "time" in some sense, but it may be derived from the root *ayin-vav-nun*, meaning "dwell," as noted in R. Laird Harris, Gleason L. Archer, Jr., Bruce K. Waltke,

eds., *The Theological Wordbook of the Old Testament* (Chicago, IL: Moody, 1980), 654.

13   *Mas Kethuboth* 61b. *The Soncino Talmud*, electronic version 2.2 (Chicago, IL: Davka, 2001).

14   Cited in Judith R. Baskin, "Infertile Wife in Rabbinic Judaism," n.p. [cited 14 March 2015]. Online: http://jwa.org/encyclopedia/article/infertile-wife-in-rabbinic-judaism. *Song of Songs Rabbah* 1:4.

15   This terminology is fluid. Rabbi Isaac Klein uses *erusin* and *kiddushin* in *A Guide to Jewish Religious Practice* (New York, NY: Jewish Theological Seminary of America, 1992), 391. Klein also discusses a third, preliminary, element in talmudic times, termed *shidduchin*, or engagement. Jonathan Sacks, in *The Koren Siddur* (Jerusalem, Israel: Koren, 2009), 1038ff., refers to *erusin*, or *kiddushin*, and *nissu'in*. Lamm uses *kiddushin* and *nissu'in*, 210.

16   Klein, *Jewish Religious Practice*, 392. Lamm lists consent, legal capacity, and witnesses as the "minimum legal requirements" of the wedding ceremony, which follows the signing of the ketubah, 163–168.

17   Maurice Lamm, "The Ketubah Text," n.p. [cited 16 May 2017]. Online: http://www.myjewishlearning.com/article/the-ketubah-text/. Covenant features are listed in *Theological Wordbook*, 281–282.

18   Lamm, *The Jewish Way*, 162–163.

19   *Theological Wordbook*, 281–282. See Exodus 24, in which the covenant stipulations are read to the Israelites, they are sprinkled with "the blood of the covenant" (Exodus 24:8), and then the representative elders eat and drink in God's presence (Exodus 24:11). Cf. Fox, *Five Books of Moses*, 388. Israel's encounter with HaShem at Sinai is compared to a wedding ceremony in rabbinic literature.

20   Lamm, *The Jewish Way*, 163.

21   *Koren Siddur*, 1038.

22   Ibid.

23   Klein, *Jewish Religious Practice*, 391–392, or Lamm, *The Jewish Way*, 222–231.

24   *Koren Siddur*, 1040.

25   Alter, *Five Books of Moses*, 22, fn.

26   Ibid.

27   Cited in Klein, *Jewish Religious Practice*, 381. At the same time, as we will see in "A Note on Singleness" below, the Apostolic Writings explicitly affirm the single state.

28   Ramban, *Genesis* (trans. Rabbi Dr. Charles B. Chavel; *Commentary on the Torah*; New York, NY: Shilo, 1971), 80.

29   Ibid., 76.

30 Edwin H. Friedman, *Generation to Generation: Family Process in Church and Synagogue* (New York, NY: Guilford, 2011), 27.

31 *Genesis Rabbah* 18:9. Note the similarity here to 1 Corinthians 11:11–12, which will be discussed below.

32 Ironically, in these two lines that clearly differentiate male and female, Alter chooses to render the feminine pronoun *z'ot* as "this one" rather than simply as "she."

33 Gordon D. Fee, *First Epistle to the Corinthians* (*New International Commentary on the New Testament*; Grand Rapids, MI: Eerdmans, 1987), 517–518.

34 Ibid., 270.

35 *Jewish Annotated New Testament*, ad loc. The notes add, "The view that women are subordinate to men and that the subordination derives from Genesis appears in later Jewish circles and is native to some rabbinic understanding of womanhood (e.g., *b.Ber.*61a)."

36 *Jewish Annotated New Testament* cites Galatians 3:28 and Romans 16:1–3 as defending a more egalitarian position with 1 Corinthians 14:33–36 arguing for subordination. Other apostolic passages could be cited for both positions.

37 Keener, *Gospel of Matthew*, 472. *Jewish Annotated New Testament* on Matthew 19:12: "Some Jews in the Second Temple period valued celibacy (Philo, *Cont. Life* 8.68)."

38 It's beyond the scope of this paper to review the documentation for this claim, but see, for example, the summary by Gretchen Livingston and Andrea Caumont, "5 Facts on Love and Marriage in America," n.p. [cited 23 March 2015]. Online: http://www.pewresearch.org/fact-tank/2014/02/14/5-facts-about-love-and-marriage/. They note, "The share of Americans who are married today is at its lowest point since at least 1920," and, "Americans are waiting longer and longer to get married."

39 *Jewish Annotated New Testament* on this verse, citing also 1 Corinthians 6:1 and 10:23.

40 Ibid.

41 Colin Brown, ed., *New International Dictionary of New Testament Theology* (vol. 1; Grand Rapids, MI: Zondervan, 1982), 498–500; ibid. (vol. 2), 582–583.

42 B. Ward Powers, "Some Implications Concerning Flesh and Body in 1 Corinthians 6:16," n.p. [cited 6 May 2015]. Online: https://www.academia.edu/5553953/Body_and_Flesh_Implications_in_Pauls_Corinthian_Dialogue_1_Cor_6.

43 Fee, *First Epistle to the Corinthians*, 263. Emphasis in the original.

44 Robert P. George, "Law and Moral Purpose," *First Things*, January 2008.